The Pre-Raphaelites and Orientalism

AF386379

Edinburgh Critical Studies in Victorian Culture
Series Editor: Julian Wolfreys

Recent books in the series:

Rudyard Kipling's Fiction: Mapping Psychic Spaces
Lizzy Welby

The Decadent Image: The Poetry of Wilde, Symons and Dowson
Kostas Boyiopoulos

British India and Victorian Literary Culture
Máire ní Fhlathúin

Anthony Trollope's Late Style: Victorian Liberalism and Literary Form
Frederik Van Dam

Dark Paradise: Pacific Islands in the Nineteenth-Century British Imagination
Jenn Fuller

Twentieth-Century Victorian: Arthur Conan Doyle and the Strand Magazine, *1891–1930*
Jonathan Cranfield

The Lyric Poem and Aestheticism: Forms of Modernity
Marion Thain

Gender, Technology and the New Woman
Lena Wånggren

Self-Harm in New Woman Writing
Alexandra Gray

Suffragist Artists in Partnership: Gender, Word and Image
Lucy Ella Rose

Victorian Liberalism and Material Culture: Synergies of Thought and Place
Kevin A. Morrison

The Victorian Male Body
Joanne-Ella Parsons and Ruth Heholt

Nineteenth-Century Settler Emigration in British Literature and Art
Fariha Shaikh

The Pre-Raphaelites and Orientalism
Eleonora Sasso

The Late-Victorian Little Magazine
Koenraad Claes

Coastal Cultures of the Long Nineteenth Century
Matthew Ingleby and Matt P. M. Kerr

Dickens and Demolition: Literary Allusion and Urban Change in the Mid-Nineteenth Century
Joanna Robinson

Artful Experiments: Ways of Knowing in Victorian Literature and Science
Philipp Erchinger

Victorian Poetry, Poetics and the Literary Periodical
Caley Ehnes

Forthcoming volumes:

Her Father's Name: Gender, Theatricality and Spiritualism in Florence Marryat's Fiction
Tatiana Kontou

The Sculptural Body in Victorian Literature: Encrypted Sexualities
Patricia Pulham

Olive Schreiner and the Politics of Print Culture, 1883–1920
Clare Gill

Dickens's Clowns: Charles Dickens, Joseph Grimaldi and the Pantomime of Life
Johnathan Buckmaster

Victorian Auto/Biography: Problems in Genre and Subject
Amber Regis

Culture and Identity in Fin-de-Siècle Scotland: Romance, Decadence and the Celtic Revival
Michael Shaw

Gissing, Shakespeare and the Life of Writing
Thomas Ue

The Victorian Actress in the Novel and on the Stage
Renata Kobetts Miller

The Arabian Nights and Nineteenth Century British Culture
Melissa Dickson

The Aesthetics of Space in Nineteenth Century British Literature, 1851-1908
Giles Whiteley

For a complete list of titles published visit the Edinburgh Critical Studies in Victorian Culture web page at www.edinburghuniversitypress.com/series/ECVC

Also Available:

Victoriographies – A Journal of Nineteenth-Century Writing, 1790–1914, edited by Diane Piccitto and Patricia Pulham

ISSN: 2044-2416

www.eupjournals.com/vic

The Pre-Raphaelites and Orientalism

Language and Cognition in Remediations of the East

Eleonora Sasso

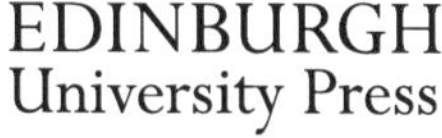

EDINBURGH
University Press

Edinburgh University Press is one of the leading university presses in the UK. We publish academic books and journals in our selected subject areas across the humanities and social sciences, combining cutting-edge scholarship with high editorial and production values to produce academic works of lasting importance. For more information visit our website: edinburghuniversitypress.com

© Eleonora Sasso, 2018, 2019

Edinburgh University Press Ltd
The Tun – Holyrood Road,
12(2f) Jackson's Entry,
Edinburgh EH8 8PJ

First published in hardback by Edinburgh University Press 2018

Typeset in 11/13 Adobe Sabon by
IDSUK (DataConnection) Ltd, and
printed and bound in Great Britain by
CPI Group (UK) Ltd, Croydon,
CR0 4YY.

A CIP record for this book is available from the British Library

ISBN 978 1 4744 0716 8 (hardback)
ISBN 978 1 4744 5486 5 (paperback)
ISBN 978 1 4744 0717 5 (webready PDF)
ISBN 978 1 4744 0718 2 (epub)

The right of Eleonora Sasso to be identified as the author of this work has been asserted in accordance with the Copyright, Designs and Patents Act 1988, and the Copyright and Related Rights Regulations 2003 (SI No. 2498).

Contents

'Victorian' is a term, at once indicative of a strongly determined concept and an often notoriously vague notion, emptied of all meaningful content by the many journalistic misconceptions that persist about the inhabitants and cultures of the British Isles and Victoria's Empire in the nineteenth century. As such, it has become a by-word for the assumption of various, often contradictory habits of thought, belief, behaviour and perceptions. Victorian studies and studies in nineteenth-century literature and culture have, from their institutional inception, questioned narrowness of presumption, pushed at the limits of the nominal definition, and have sought to question the very grounds on which the unreflective perception of the so-called Victorian has been built; and so they continue to do. Victorian and nineteenth-century studies of literature and culture maintain a breadth and diversity of interest, of focus and inquiry, in an interrogative and intellectually open-minded and challenging manner, which are equal to the exploration and inquisitiveness of its subjects. Many of the questions asked by scholars and researchers of the innumerable productions of nineteenth-century society actively put into suspension the clichés and stereotypes of 'Victorianism', whether the approach has been sustained by historical, scientific, philosophical, empirical, ideological or theoretical concerns; indeed, it would be incorrect to assume that each of these approaches to the idea of the Victorian has been, or has remained, in the main exclusive, sealed off from the interests and engagements of other approaches. A vital interdisciplinarity has been pursued and embraced, for the most part, even as there has been contest and debate amongst Victorianists, pursued with as much fervour as the affirmative exploration between different disciplines and differing epistemologies put to work in the service of reading the nineteenth century.

Edinburgh Critical Studies in Victorian Culture aims to take up both the debates and the inventive approaches and departures from convention that studies in the nineteenth century have witnessed for the last half-century at least. Aiming to maintain a 'Victorian' (in the most positive sense of that motif) spirit of inquiry, the series' purpose is to continue and augment the cross-fertilisation of interdisciplinary approaches, and to offer, in addition, a number of timely and untimely revisions of Victorian literature, culture, history and identity. At the same time, the series will ask questions concerning what has been missed or improperly received, misread, or not read at all, in order to present a multi-faceted and heterogeneous kaleidoscope of representations. Drawing on the most provocative, thoughtful and original research, the series will seek to prod at the notion of the 'Victorian', and in so doing, principally through theoretically and epistemologically sophisticated close readings of the historicity of literature and culture in the nineteenth century, to offer the reader provocative insights into a world that is at once overly familiar, and irreducibly different, other and strange. Working from original sources, primary documents and recent interdisciplinary theoretical models, Edinburgh Critical Studies in Victorian Culture seeks not simply to push at the boundaries of research in the nineteenth century, but also to inaugurate the persistent erasure and provisional, strategic redrawing of those borders.

Julian Wolfreys

Acknowledgements

I was first attracted to Orientalism when I read Edward Said's break-through study defining the latent and manifest traces of the East in Western literature and culture. I was immediately intrigued by Said's approach to investigating the interrelations between society, history and textuality, and curious to learn how the Pre-Raphaelite Brotherhood, to whom I dedicated my research for over a decade, envisioned the Eastern world. When I attended the European Society for the Study of English (ESSE) 2012 conference at Bogazici University (Istanbul), I realised how the magnificence of Byzantine architecture had deeply affected the Pre-Raphaelite artists, whose many latent forms of Orientalism were still to be investigated.

My greatest debt in writing this book is due to Francesco Marroni, who, as my PhD supervisor (2000–4) and research fellowship tutor (2008–11), stimulated my interest in the Pre-Raphaelites and Victorian literature over the years.

Thanks to another conference on *Translating East and West*, held at the University of Naples 'L'Orientale' (proceedings edited by Oriana Palusci and Katherine Russo, and published by Tangram in 2010), I had the opportunity to investigate D. G. Rossetti's translations of Oriental culture. I owe a deep gratitude to Oriana Palusci, who organised that conference and encouraged me to continue my research into Orientalism. She offered me intellectual stimulus and enthusiasm for language and translation studies.

My gratitude also goes to Andrea Mariani for his enthusiastic encouragement and useful critiques of this research work. His advice has been a great help in seeing the book through to completion.

The idea of this book then developed in discussions about the Victorians and their appropriation of the East at the joint international conference on Victorian Orientalism(s) of the Centre for the Study of Text and Print Culture at Ghent University (Belgium) and the School of

Foreign Languages and Literatures of Ragusa (University of Catania, Italy), which Sandro Jung and I organised in 2013. I am grateful to the community of scholars who attended this conference – Elisa Bizzotto, Florence Boos, Mirko Casagranda, Ben Cocking, Chris Cowell, Ann Heilmann, Fabrizio Impellizzeri, Andrew King, Gloria Lauri-Lucente, Simon Layton, Andrea Mariani, Francesco Marroni, Gigliola Nocera and Oriana Palusci – and inspired me in my research.

I am particularly grateful to Michael O'Neill, who generously supported me with his valuable expertise and knowledge of poetry. I would also like to express my very great appreciation to Roger Ebbatson and Peter Faulkner, who have commented scrupulously on draft chapters.

A special mention has to be made of Carlo Consani, Director of the Department of Modern Languages, Literatures and Cultures of Pescara (University 'G. d'Annunzio' of Chieti-Pescara) for his constant encouragement and generous interest in my studies. I have also benefited from the advice and support of my colleagues – Giovanni Brancaccio, Mariaconcetta Costantini, Nicola D'Antuono, Paola Desideri, Carlo Martinez, Julián Santano Moreno and Miriam Sette – who encouraged me to complete this project.

My grateful thanks are also extended to the Series Editor, Julian Wolfreys, for his enthusiasm for the project and for his valuable suggestions, which made the book more focused and precise. I would also like to offer my special thanks to commissioning editors Michelle Houston and Jackie Jones, as well as to assistant commissioning editors Adela Rauchova and Ersev Ersoy, who assisted in the development of this book.

I am indebted to Andrew Taylor for sponsoring my position as an academic visitor at the Edinburgh University Library, whose staff provided courteous and helpful service. Likewise, I am grateful to the staff at the Library of Trinity College (Dublin) for dealing efficiently with my numerous requests for periodicals and rare books.

Finally, I wish to thank my family for their support and encouragement throughout my studies. This book could not have been written without their boundless love.

Introduction

'[S]ince one cannot ontologically obliterate the Orient [. . .], one does have the means to capture it, treat it, describe it, improve it, radically alter it' (Said 1977: 95). In the second chapter of *Orientalism*, Edward Said suggests that we know the Orient through three different cognitive modes, which can be summarised according to David E. Rumelhart and Donald A. Norman's classification (1978) of knowledge acquisition: that is, *accretion, tuning* and *restructuring*. In Said's verbal phrases 'to capture it', 'treat it' and 'describe it', the reader may easily identify a process of accretion, which means accumulating information about Eastern culture. In order to capture, treat and describe the Orient, it is necessary to learn its history, culture and religion, which are examples of learning through accretion. Such learning about the East must occur through appropriate exposure to the concepts and classifications of Orientalism to be acquired, in order to transform information about the East into some appropriate memory representation that is added to the person's database of knowledge. Secondly, 'to improve the Orient' involves actual changes in the very categories we use for interpreting the East and what cognitive linguistics calls 'schemas'. These categories undergo continual tuning or minor modification to bring them more into congruence with the Western world. Thus, *tuning* involves the evolution of Oriental structures into new ones by adjusting the variable terms of Oriental schemas. And thirdly, 'to radically alter' the Orient means learning through restructuring, which involves the creation of new Oriental structures in order to allow for new interpretations, and therefore the acquisition of a new knowledge of the East. In this process, according to schema theory, the existing Oriental schema is restructured by substituting its variable components so that a new schema can be patterned on an old one.

Defined by Said as 'the distinction between Western superiority and Oriental inferiority [. . .] a set of constraints upon and limitations of thought' (42), Orientalism acquires new meanings for the Pre-Raphaelite Brotherhood, widely recognised as the most dynamic group of revolutionary artists ever to work in Britain. John Ruskin, Dante Gabriel and Christina Rossetti, and William Morris, as well as their friends and associates such as Algernon Swinburne, Aubrey Beardsley and Ford Madox Ford, appear to be the most eligible representatives of a profoundly innovative manifestation of the Orient, of its mystic aura, criminal underworld and feminine sensuality, or to put it into Arabic terms, of its *aja'ib* (marvels), *mutalibun* (treasure-hunters) and *hur al-ayn* (*femmes fatales*). By combining Western and Oriental schemas, the Pre-Raphaelites and their associates contributed to the task of interpreting the East in the Victorian period with original and innovative results, and, in doing so, acted as major vehicles for raising awareness of cultural diversity. The Pre-Raphaelites' acquisition of Oriental schemas, according to Said's aforementioned modes of appropriation, seems, however, to disconfirm his prophetic words about the impenetrable distinction between Western superiority and Oriental inferiority: 'we must be prepared to note how in its development and subsequent history Orientalism deepened and even hardened the distinction' (Said 1977: 42).

With their *accretion*, *tuning* and *restructuring* of the fabulous and exotic *Arabian Nights*,[1] the book defined by Marina Warner as 'a polyvocal anthology of world myths, fables and fairytales' (2011: 8) and which contributed to the popularisation of the East[2] in the Western world, the Pre-Raphaelites and their associates aimed at foregrounding the role of the East in the transformation of the socio-cultural sphere. Through cognitive linguistics and its wide range of cognitive approaches (conceptual metaphors, scripts and schemas, prominence, figure, ground, parables, prototypes, deixis and text world theory), which provide an illuminating framework for discussing the blend of East and West in Pre-Raphaelite writings, this book demonstrates how the mind styles of Ruskin, the Rossetti brothers, Morris, Swinburne, Beardsley and Ford were deeply affected by the *Arabian Nights*.

Significant insights into Victorian Orientalism have emerged from Muhsin Jassim Ali's, Peter Caracciolo's and Emily Haddad's seminal books about the reception history of the *Arabian Nights* (respectively, *Scheherazade in England: A Study of Nineteenth-century Criticism of the Arabian Nights*, 1981; *The Arabian Nights in English Literature: Studies in the Reception of 'The Thousand and One Nights' into British Culture*, 1988; *Orientalist Poetics: The Islamic Middle East in Nineteenth-century English and French Poetry*, 2002). In their overviews of the influence of Arabian stories on English and French literatures, Ali, Caracciolo and Haddad devote their attention to Romantic and Victorian authors, albeit overlooking the meaningful indebtedness of the Pre-Raphaelite Brotherhood to Oriental literature and culture. This book intends to redefine the terms of critical debate by offering a thorough and comparative investigation of the Pre-Raphaelites and their associates' fascination with the East. Apart from dispersed articles in academic journals and occasional chapters focusing on the Pre-Raphaelites and Orientalism, no book-length study exists on the topic of 'the Pre-Raphaelites and Orientalism'. For example, George P. Landow's article, 'William Holman Hunt's "Oriental Mania" and his Uffizi Self-portrait' (1982), is a most valuable artistic and biographical survey of Hunt's obsession with the East but it lacks the cognitive approach analysis that would provide detailed intertextual, stylistic and linguistic examples to understand the multifaceted Pre-Raphaelite representations of the Orient. Only through a detailed textual and visual analysis of Pre-Raphaelite works is it possible to understand the extent to which the Oriental mania pervaded the minds of such eminent Pre-Raphaelite artists and associates as Ruskin, D. G. Rossetti, Christina Rossetti, Morris, Swinburne, Beardsley and Ford.

The Pre-Raphaelite Brotherhood aimed to recover the primitive art of the fourteenth and fifteenth centuries, illustrating, borrowing and repurposing stories from medieval literary, historical and mythological sources (including Homer's *Odyssey*, the *Arabian Nights*, the *dolce stil novo* of the early Italian poets, Dante's *Vita Nuova*, Boccaccio's *Decameron* and many others). By taking property from one medium and reusing it in another remediation, the Pre-Raphaelites and their associates started a conscious interplay between media. But among all the texts to undergo a process of 'remediation', as defined by David Bolter and Richard Grusin (1996), the stories of the *Arabian Nights* seem to have seduced just about every member of the Brotherhood with their thematic vastness, parabolic power and magical appeal. The Pre-Raphaelites and their associates are, in Robert Irwin's words, 'children of the *Nights*' (2004: 236), since they all grew up reading the stories of Ali Baba, Aladdin and Sinbad. Compared by Irwin to the Bible for the power of 'shaping the mentality and temperament of a writer' (236), the stories of the *Arabian Nights* help us to make sense of the world. Endowed with an extraordinary parabolic power, the *Arabian Nights* project stories and parables that facilitate the carrying out of everyday cognitive acts. When immersed in the stories of Ali Baba, Aladdin and Sinbad, the reader must remember that there are a number of dynamic, cognitive capacities at work in his/her quest for literary meaning. Inputs are uploaded and blended across a network of ongoing meaning creation. Parabolic projection, originally developed by Mark Turner in the 1990s, is particularly useful for revealing how the Pre-Raphaelites used their everyday experience to provide an interpretation of the Arabian texts and then project that interpretation back on to their own writings. From this perspective, parables of love, low life, street entertainments and marvels seem to be haunting the Pre-Raphaelites' minds, elaborating several source domains (linguistic and pragmatic) that help to construct their interpretative mental model and facilitate the understanding of other texts that can be projected parabolically on to their central cognitive models.

The first discernible cognitive phenomenon we might identify in the *Arabian Nights* is the use of numerous conceptual metaphors that appear to be running through the stories. Conceptual metaphors, as theorised by Lakoff and Johnson (1980), offer new insights in the study of language and thought. Seen as a mapping of properties between two spaces (or domains), the process of metaphor involves restructuring the possible patterns of the figurative language. Such conceptual metaphors as EAST IS CRIME, EAST IS SEX and EAST IS MAGIC are projected in the *Arabian Nights* as ways of representing the Oriental world. More than one thousand and one conceptual metaphors arise from the reading of the *Arabian Nights*, which stirred the Pre-Raphaelites' interest in the East.

But it is blending that is central to the notion of parable, the general model for much of the Pre-Raphaelites' conceptual processing of the East. Originally investigated by Fauconnier and Turner (1994), conceptual blending consists of combining various input spaces into a blended space. This can be applied to the way Pre-Raphaelite works operate intertextual relations with the *Arabian Nights*. As this book illustrates, sometimes a Pre-Raphaelite text relies heavily on another single identifiable tale from the *Arabian Nights*, such as through direct citation as in D. G. Rossetti's play-picture *Aladdin, or The Wonderful Lamp* (1835; the title is taken from the Arabian tale 'The Story of Aladdin, or, the Wonderful Lamp'), or through the transposition of an Arabian plot into a different world, as in Ruskin's *The King of the Golden River* (1841; a loose version of 'The Story of Two Sisters Who Envied their Younger Sister') and in Christina Rossetti's 'The Dead City' (1847; the poem reproduces the plot of 'The Story of Zobeide'). Sometimes the intertextuality recreates and extends the same world (some narrative poems in Morris's *The Earthly Paradise* (1868–70) recreate the tales of the 'Forbidden Chamber' cycle in the *Arabian Nights*; Swinburne's *The Masque of Queen Bersabe* (1866), inspired by the sensuous and unfaithful women described in the frame story of the *Arabian Nights*, represents Bersabe as a Scheherazade-like figure), or restructures old Arabian schemas into new ones by undermining the ideology of the original world (Aubrey Beardsley's *Under the Hill* (1896) is an Orientalised version of the legend of Tannhäuser that reproduces *hammam* (Muslim public bath) scenes by perverting and eroticising the Islamic world; Ford Madox Ford's *The Queen Who Flew* (1894) blends together elements from 'Sinbad the Sailor' and 'The Adventures of Hasan of Basrah' by subverting gender roles). From this perspective, Ruskin, the Rossetti brothers, Morris, Swinburne, Beardsley and Ford lift characters, plots, settings and themes out of their original Arabian environments and place them into new blended spaces. This is the mechanism by which, through parable, the Pre-Raphaelites and their associates alter our perspective on, knowledge of and way of thinking about the East.

Chapter 1 ('"[S]elling old lamps for new ones": D. G. Rossetti's Restructuring of Oriental Schemas') outlines Rossetti's fascination with the East, as exemplified by his illustrations and paintings remediating the stories of the *Arabian Nights*. As a 'child of the *Nights*', Rossetti illustrated the stories of Aladdin, Sinbad, Amine and Princess Parisad by employing the magical lamp of translation, fostering cultural diversity and Oriental pluralisms. By conceiving the East as a blended space, he produced Oriental 'double works of art' that blend together poetry and painting, East and West, and experiment with forms of Turkish and biblical Orientalism. Such conceptual metaphors as EAST IS VIOLENCE and LOVE IS DESTRUCTION are projected on to *Cassandra* (1861) and *Helen of Troy* (1863), examples of Turkish Orientalism that remediate Oriental schemas by applying a tuning approach. Other Oriental double works of art, such as *The Girlhood of Mary Virgin* (1849), *Ecce Ancilla Domini!* (1849–50), *The Beloved, or The Bride* (1865), *Astarte Syriaca* (1876) and *Mnemosyne* (1881), represent Rossetti's mental picture of biblical Orientalism. By restructuring a few variables of the Oriental biblical schema, and by blending Western female beauty with Eastern symbology, Rossetti creates an entirely new vision of the East. Deeply concerned by the acquisitions of the British Museum throughout the imperial period, Rossetti wrote poems that denounce colonial crimes against art.

In Chapter 2 ('Toward a Corporeal Orientalism: Foregrounding Arabian Erotic Figures in Algernon Swinburne and Aubrey Beardsley') I investigate the corporeal Orientalism envisioned by Swinburne and Beardsley, two Pre-Raphaelite sympathisers who envisioned the East as a sexual dimension inhabited by Oriental female figures such as Scheherazade, Dunyazad, Salome and Bersabe – namely, *hur al-ayn* – evoking the sensual and pornographic content of the *Arabian Nights*. Both Swinburne and Beardsley exalted Sir Richard F. Burton and his uncensored translation of the *Arabian Nights*, which aimed to reveal the erotic customs of the Muslims. On the one hand, Swinburne's cognitive grammar reveals the use of binary world-builders (West and East) attesting to the superiority of the East, as exemplified by his poems dedicated to Burton and *The Masque of Queen Bersabe*. The latter, characterised by conceptual metaphors, cognitive prominence and foregrounding, seems to reproduce the scenario of the *hammam* in which Scheherazade/Bersabe's beauty is entirely externalised. On the other hand, Beardsley's conceptual metaphor EAST IS SEXUAL FREEDOM is projected on to his grotesque pen-and-ink illustrations of Salome and Ali Baba and on to his Oriental poems ('The Ballad of a Barber' (1896) and *Under the Hill*) by blending together the sacred and the profane, the Middle East and the Far East. His radical mode of repatterning old Oriental schemas into new ones is aimed at desacralising the Orient and, in a way, at (de-)Orientalising Western and Eastern schemas. Mapping from Middle East frames on to Far East frames, Beardsley over-Orientalises a biblical topic such as the Annunciation of the Virgin Mary in *The Mysterious Rose Garden* (1895), which is imbued with Japanese visual reminders. On the contrary, in a lithograph entitled *Ex-Libris by John Lumsden Propert* (1894), which restructures the legend of the African King Cophetua and the beggar maid, Beardsley de-Orientalises the scene by replacing Oriental figures with Western ones and by subverting Oriental gender roles. Furthermore, in Beardsley's text worlds of grotesque erotic sensuality, Scheherazade's *hammam* ritual is replaced with Salome's, Helen's and Fanfreluche's, and with the barber's toilet scenes. As illustrated by *Under the Hill*, Oriental variable components are replaced with Western obscene and parodic ones, and Oriental world-builders are mapped on to blended and perverted ones.

Chapter 3 ('The Cognitive Process of Parable: John Ruskin, William Morris and the Oriental Lure of the Forbidden') examines the pervasive influence of Arabian marvel tales on Ruskin's *The King of the Golden River* and *Sesame and Lilies* (1865), as well as on Morris's

The Earthly Paradise. More similarly to Marx's ideological Orientalism, Ruskin and Morris sympathise with people's misery, with their material life and the Arab townsfolk, and thereby with the criminal underworld. Ruskin's ideological Orientalism is particularly evident in his lectures and autobiography (*The Ethics of the Dust* (1908), *Sesame and Lilies* and *Praeterita* (1907)), whose rhetorical language may be analysed through possible world theory, Fauconnier's mental space analysis and Oatley and Johnson-Laird's cognitive theory of emotions (1987). By projecting such Oriental conceptual metaphors as EAST IS POVERTY and EAST IS CORRUPTION, Ruskin aims at sensitising his readers to the perils of imperialism. Likewise, *The King of the Golden River*, a fairy tale for children, develops the Oriental schema of 'The Story of Two Sisters Who Envied their Younger Sister' by modifying certain variables (protagonist, location and ending). The reader's textual understanding of *The King of the Golden River* may be explained in cognitive terms with *memory organisation packets* (MOPs) and *thematic organisation packets* (TOPs) in relation to what the reader already knows about the *Arabian Nights*. Such an Oriental image schema as GOLDEN WATER provides the basis for abstract thoughts by serving as source domain in metaphoric mapping. If the Arabic tale projects the conceptual metaphor VANITY IS GOLDEN WATER, then Ruskin's fairy tale uses the metaphor CHARITY IS GOLDEN WATER. The GOLDEN WATER schema, in Johnson's words, is 'a recurring dynamic pattern of our perceptual interactions [. . .] that gives coherence and structure to our experience' (1987: xiv).

Morris's fascination with the East is first and foremost connected with the Byzantine decorative arts and carpet-making. As founder of the Society for the Protection of Ancient Buildings (SPAB), he promoted a campaign against the restoration of St Mark's Basilica in Venice, the paramount example of Arab influence on Venetian architecture. His connection with the East can be better understood, however, by investigating the Oriental love scenarios in *The Earthly Paradise*, whose narrative poems ('The Writing on the Image', 'The Land East of the Sun and West of the Moon' and 'The Man Who Never Laughed Again') seem to restructure the Arabian tales of the 'Forbidden Chamber' cycle. By creating new Oriental schemas based on old templates, Morris's narrative poems contain Oriental variable terms that he further specifies. The figures of Aladdin's African magician, Hasan's bird-woman and Baharam are the focus of the narrative and carry along specific psychological and personal traits that Morris modifies according to his own schemas. A cognitive analysis of the sequence of action concepts in Morris's Oriental love scenarios, as well as of the world-builders and function-advancing propositions in *The Earthly Paradise*, demonstrates how Morris's metaphors of love are mapped on to the *Arabian Nights*' language of emotion.

In Chapter 4 ('Consumers of Intoxicating Fruits and Elixirs: The Cognitive Grammar of Christina Rossetti's and Ford Madox Ford's Oriental Fairy Tales') I provide a cognitive grammar analysis of Christina Rossetti's and Ford's Oriental fairy poetry and narrative fictionalising scenes of drug consumption. Like consumers of *banj* (hashish) and opium, Rossetti's and Ford's characters (the petrified banqueters, Laura, the princess wearing poppies, Queen Eldrida, Princess Ismara and the blind ploughman) experience moments of hallucination caused by intoxicating fruits, elixirs of life and infusions of wind-flowers. Probably written in reaction to the Opium War, which facilitated the diffusion of opium-based laudanum, used for recreational purposes and health remedies, Rossetti's 'The Dead City', 'Goblin Market' and 'The Prince's Progress', as well as Ford's *The Brown Owl* (1892), *The Feather* (1892) and *The Queen Who Flew*, blend together parts of Oriental narratives in order to visualise the temptations of the East. In particular, Rossetti's iconic language can be analysed through *foregrounding*, since her stylistically deviant features (enumeration, adjectives preceding and following nouns, as well as alliterative patterns) profile the same participants in the action chains of 'The Story of Zobeide', 'Sinbad the Sailor', 'The Story of Anime' and 'The Adventures of Hasan of Basrah'. Through Fillmore's 'buying and selling' frame (1982, 1985) and idealised cognitive models, it is possible to offer a new reading of 'Goblin Market', in whose phrasal verbs we profile Oriental violence against women. Likewise, 'The Prince's Progress' seems to be repatterning the buying and selling frame of 'The Story of Anime' and the action chains of 'The Adventures of Hasan of Basrah'. Rossetti's shifts in relational and spatial deixis reveal the proximity of her poems to the originator: that is, to the stories of the *Arabian Nights*. By balancing the use of what cognitive linguistics call 'pops and pushes' (shifting up to the narrative voice and pushing down to a deictic centre), Rossetti projects the conceptual metaphor OPIUM IS DEATH.

Likewise, Ford, commonly known as 'the last Pre-Raphaelite' (Goldring 1948), develops a cognitive grammar of Oriental ambience in his fairy tales, which are rich in tonal effects and ambient features evoking the stories of Aladdin, Sinbad and Hasan. If the role archetypes of the figures of *The Brown Owl* (King Intafernes, Princess Ismara and Merrymineral) appear to be mapped from several source domains, then the Oriental prototypical figures in *The Feather* and *The Queen Who Flew* are visually and linguistically associated with Sinbad the Sailor. *The Feather*, projecting the metaphor FOOD IS DEATH, refreshes and expands the schemas and slots[3] of Sinbad through instrumental and locale headers that instantiate the script. Likewise, *The Queen Who Flew* is characterised by such anomalies as the elixir of life and the infusion of wind-flowers resulting from the process called *patterned schema generation*, according to which new schemas are patterned on old ones. By encouraging a subjective construal of the foregrounded scenes, Ford offers his own personal version of the East, whose image schemas (magical flight, market place, treasure and elixir) are aimed at Orientalising his writings in order to make sense of imperialist issues.

Pre-Raphaelite modes of art (narrative, poetic and visual) position themselves as instruments of knowledge of the Orient, which is not only a place of romance, exotic beings, haunting memories, landscapes and remarkable experiences but also, as Said maintains, 'a marvellous instance of the interrelations between society, history, and textuality' (1977: 24). Orientalism is, after all, a 'system for citing works and authors' (23) that allows me to bring this work to the attention of researchers and students in different areas – those interested in both Pre-Raphaelitism itself and the contextual socio-cultural problems of Orientalism.

The particular contribution of the Pre-Raphaelites and their associates to the issue of Orientalism has been either ignored by Victorian Studies, or given limited treatment by specialised scholars. Because the topic of Pre-Raphaelite Orientalism has figured mainly in the work of art historians, the Brotherhood's personal and imaginative appropriations of the Orient have yet to be examined in a way that brings together cognitive, literary and socio-cultural investigations of the Orient. The aim of this book is to fill this void by looking at how selected examples of Pre-Raphaelite writings contributed to the task of interpreting the East in the Victorian period, and, in doing so, acted as major vehicles for raising awareness of cultural diversity.

Notes

1. All quotations from the *Arabian Nights*, unless otherwise indicated, are taken from the Oxford World's Classics version (*Arabian Nights' Entertainments*), edited by Robert L. Mack (Oxford University Press, 1995). This edition reproduces in its entirety the earliest English translation

of Galland's *Mille et une nuits*, which were rendered into English by an anonymous 'Grub Street' translator in the earliest decades of the eighteenth century.

2. On the Orientalism of the *Arabian Nights* see Yamanaka and Nishio (2006), as well as McMichael Nurse (2010). For new readings of the *Arabian Nights* see Wen-chin Ouyang and van Gelder (2005).

3. A script consists of slots. The term slot was taken from the sphere of research on artificial intelligence. Information units are stored in cells: that is, slots.

Chapter 1

'[S]elling old lamps for new ones': D. G. Rossetti's Restructuring of Oriental Schemas

The Lamp of Translation: Rossetti's Eastern Conceptual Metaphors

Of all the Pre-Raphaelite artists who were deeply affected by the *Arabian Nights*, Dante Gabriel Rossetti appears to be the most eligible representative of what Said terms 'latent Orientalism' (Said 1977: 223), a profoundly conservative manifestation of the Orient dedicated to its self-preservation. Though showing an overt Oriental interest in his formal and personal representations of the East, Rossetti keeps intact the separateness of the Orient, its mystic aura, its criminal underworld and its feminine sensuality, as isolated from mainstream European progress in the sciences, arts and commerce.

Unlike William Holman Hunt, the Pre-Raphaelite artist who visited the Middle East and promised himself 'to return in spirit to the Land of good Haroun Alrachid' (letter to William Bell Scott, February 1860), Rossetti did not directly experience the alien, simple and beautiful world of the Middle East but nevertheless shared Hunt's fascination with the 'unsophisticated and simple grace' (Hunt 1905: 377) of the Orient. As George P. Landow maintains, 'exotic places [were] a logical extension of Pre-Raphaelitism' (Landow 1982: 650) because, by promoting a simple and archaic form of art, the Pre-Raphaelites identified themselves with the kind of mystical primitivism embodied by the Middle East.

From the pages of Edward William Lane's (1853) highly criticised translation of *Alf Layla wa-Layla*, literally 'One Thousand Nights and a Night', Rossetti undertook the material appropriation of Oriental tropes, creating a personal Oriental mythology in the Nervallian imaginative sense of the word: that is to say, 'to *consume* the Orient, to appropriate it, to represent and speak for it, not in history but beyond history, in the timeless dimension of a completely healed world, where men and lands, God and men, are as one' (Said 1977: 175). Far from a scientific and impersonal vision of the East, Rossetti elaborates an original Oriental aesthetics by projecting such conceptual metaphors[1] as East is crime,[2] East is sex and East is magic.

To him the East as envisioned in the *Arabian Nights* is a blended space, a 'labyrinth of labyrinths' (Borges 1970: 48), a maze of marvels and tortures, of archetypal and individual figures, of sorcerers and virtuous sages. By shedding light on the Islamic underworld and medieval private life, he maps stories on to other stories, stories of sexual fiction, marvels and low life, whose prototypical figures are Scheherazade, Aladdin, Sinbad and Ali Baba.

In the preface to *The Early Italian Poets* (1861), Rossetti describes the task of the translator in Oriental terms: '[the translator's] path is like that of Aladdin through the enchanted vaults: many are the precious fruits and flowers which he must pass by unheeded in search for the lamp alone' (Rossetti 1861: ix). Behind these lines lies Rossetti's vision of translation as a process of temptation, which is enacted by what Dinda Gorlée calls 'improvised desire and free will' (Gorlée 2012: 52).

Like Aladdin, Rossetti the translator, assaulted by an improvised desire, is tempted to choose a variety of treasure options but, thanks to his free will, he is able to adhere to his path in search of the magic lamp of cultural translation. It is highly significant that Rossetti – Pre-Raphaelite Japonist *par excellence* and collector of blue china and exotic animals,[3] as well as devoted reader of the *Arabian Nights* – compares himself to Aladdin, one of the most fantasised figures of Oriental culture.

The model of the Aladdin-like translator is a constituent principle in Rossetti's double work of art: that is, a combination of poetry and painting in a unique work, a kind of intersemiotic translation able to promote the conceptual aspects of the image and the iconographical powers of the text by eliciting a blissful response from the audiences for whom it is intended.

This chapter intends to redefine the terms of critical debate by offering a thorough and comparative investigation of Rossetti's fascination with the East. I will investigate Rossetti's response to Oriental culture through his double works of art, which appear to be characterised by a blending of the traditional Western European canon of beauty and the Eastern notion of Oriental eroticism. For Rossetti, leader of 'The Fleshly School of Poetry', the East is a conceptual metaphor, a correspondence between sensual concepts across conceptual domains, which projects an alternative world of beauty wherein the material and the spiritual are successfully integrated. Rossetti's personal vision of the East, as depicted in such Oriental double works of art as *Helen of Troy* (1863), *The Beloved, or The Bride* (1865) and *Astarte Syriaca* (1876), may be ascribed to his fascination with cultural diversity, with African, Syrian, Turkish, Chinese and Japanese female beauties. Almost a precursor of cultural studies, a powerful agent for cultural change, Rossetti aims at avoiding ethnocentric violence and resisting the British practice of domestication. For this Anglo-Italian artist who looked at the East for inspiration, literary creation takes place in a continuum, never in a void, following 'a movement of fragmentation, a wandering of errance, a kind of permanent exile' (Bhabha 1994: 228).

Fiercely criticised by Dickens for founding the Pre-Raphaelite Brotherhood, which he calls 'an old lamp market [. . .] selling old lamps for new ones' (Dickens 1850: 265) because of its 'retrogressive techniques' (266), Rossetti had been fascinated by the *Arabian Nights*, and in particular by 'The Story of Aladdin, or, the Wonderful Lamp', since he was seven years old. As a 'child of the *Nights*', in Irwin's words (2004: 237), Rossetti composed a brief dramatic skit entitled *Aladdin, or The Wonderful Lamp* in 1835. Rossetti, the *pasticheur*, who defined himself as 'a painter of play-pictures' (D.G. Rossetti 2008: 24), projects in words and paints the prototypical marvel story of the one fated child from Baghdad who can lead the African magician to the treasure. Though considered 'totally uninteresting' (W. M. Rossetti 1895: 66), D. G. Rossetti's prose, consisting of only a few lines, is mapped on to the target domains of Oriental abstractions such as quest, mystery and dream since they focus on the conceptual metaphor THE ORIENT IS A BEAUTIFUL GARDEN. The following excerpt exemplifies the fascination exerted by Arabian marvels on the young Rossetti:

Act 1. Scene 1[st].
Enter African Magician & Aladdin.
Al. Where will you lead me?
Mag. Into a bea[u]tiful garden, where all sorts of fruits grow.
Al. Is't this?
Mag. Nay, it is not.
Al. What is't then?
Mag. A much more beautiful garden than this. (D.G. Rossetti 2008: 26)

Rossetti's Oriental rewriting of the most significant dialogue in 'The Story of Aladdin' appears on the page with sketch drawings of a smiling face (probably the genius's face) and an inked triangular shape (which may represent the wonderful lamp). Similar to William Morris's 'The Writing on the Image' (1870), a satirical rewriting of 'The Story of Aladdin, or, the Wonderful Lamp', Rossetti's juvenile work centres on the chronotope of the garden, the materialisation of medieval time in the Oriental space, on what Lakoff cognitively calls an 'imaginative container' (Lakoff and Johnson 1999: 117) of marvels. Unlike Coleridge and Thomas De Quincey, who envisioned the story of Aladdin as a form of dark Orientalism since, as children of the *Arabian Nights*, they were literally terrorised by the magician of Africa seeking and captivating Aladdin, Rossetti emphasises the pleasurable dimension of the Oriental garden, suggesting that unexpected things may happen in this mysterious place.

Usually found in royal palaces and harems, Oriental gardens are the domain of love, intrigue, fabulous creatures and mysterious happenings. These gardens of 'unearthly delights', in Harold Bloom's words (2012: 9), represent the basic models of an Oriental aesthetics of pleasure, according to which gardens appear as loci of initiation into a world of wonders. See, for example, the story of King Schahriar and his brother Schahzenan ('Introductory Tale'), as well as 'The Loves of Zain al-Mawasif', in which lovers meet and commit adultery in a pleasure garden. In the first story, the Queen has sexual intercourse with a black slave in the palace garden, which is characterised by 'a great pond, which was one of the chief ornaments of the garden' ('Introductory Tale': 4). In the second story, the merchant Masrur daydreams about a garden 'filled as far as the eye could reach with harmonious terraces, flowered arbours and thickets of roses, [. . .] jasmine, violet and narcissus' (Mardrus 2005: 269–70), which is able to awaken love in its observers.

Likewise, the 'Story of the Prince Camaralzaman and the Princess Badoura' and the 'Story of Taj-elmolouk and the Lady Dunia' are set in luxuriant pleasure gardens where magic takes place. While working in a garden in a fishing village, Camaralzaman finds a cave in the ground containing a number of jars filled with red gold. Thanks to this magical discovery, he is able to reunite with Princess Badoura, monarch of the country of Ebony. Equally mesmerising is the garden pavilion decorated by Taj-elmolouk with dream-like illustrations, which are able to convince the Lady Dunia to reconsider her disillusioned attitude to men and thereby to accept the Prince's advances.

But more than this, Oriental gardens are inhabited by *jinn* or genii, 'supernatural creatures with bodies of flame', as Irwin called them (2004: 203), who are malevolent spirits kidnapping princes and princesses in order to imprison them in gardens of heavenly pleasures. This is the case with handsome, brave Prince Sayf al-Muluk, who features in the story 'Sayf al-Muluk and Princess Badi'at al-Jamdl'; while walking in the palace garden, which is rich in fruits and trees, he is assaulted by a *jinni*. Since a match of *jinn* and men is ill omened, Shahyal Ibn Sharukh, king of the *jinn*, orders the kidnap of Sayf al Muluk, with whom the Princess Badi'at al-Jamdl has fallen in love.

Image Schemas of the Orient: Rossetti's Illustrations and Paintings of the *Arabian Nights*

Similar to Christina Rossetti's poem 'The Dead City' (1847), John Everett Millais's illustrations for 'The History of Zobeide' (1865) and Aubrey Beardsley's cover designs for *The Forty Thieves* (1897), Rossetti made a series of sketches in 1840 illustrating episodes from the *Arabian Nights*. This series of fifteen drawings,[4] whose importance critics have under-estimated, was published in the second volume of *The Journal of Pre-Raphaelite and Aesthetic Studies* (1991), specifically in the section devoted to illustrations for literary works.

Of particular interest are the first and fourth drawings, which reproduce the Eastern universe of marvels as inhabited by magical figures such as *jinn*, fairies and demons. In both 'The Genius Threatening to Kill the Merchant' and 'The Black Overturning the Fish, in Presence of the Sultan & Vizier', Rossetti represents the figure of the malicious *jinni*, 'metaphor for metamorphosis and uncontrollable change' (Marzolph et al. 2004: 536) in the *Arabian Nights*. These giant-like, shape-shifting beings, so praised by Dickens[5] and Stevenson,[6] are always depicted by Rossetti as pitiless killers intent on threatening merchants, fishermen, viziers and magicians, but despite their strength and transformative capacities, *jinn* can be outsmarted by human resourcefulness and cleverness. Both the merchant who saw an enormous *Ifrīt* (the most powerful and dangerous *jinni* in Middle Eastern stories), white with rage and coming towards him with a scimitar in his hand, and the fisherman who is asked by the *jinn* how he wants to die, save their own lives, as Ulysses did. To Rossetti, who remediates the Orient into frames of violence and terror, EAST IS MAGIC, confirming Michelet's assertion that 'the Orient advances, invincible, fatal to the gods of light by the charm of its dreams, by the magic of its chiaroscuro' (Said 1977: 74).

This juvenile interest in what Todorov calls 'the pure marvellous' (1975: 44), based on hyperbole, the exotic and the instrumental, reveals Rossetti's first attempts at applying a blending mode of narration, as clearly explained by Jerome McGann:

> Rossetti's goal was not equivalence, it was imitation. This procedure led him to develop an art of pastiche and ritual form, and to explore the possibility that imaginative work possesses wondrous and terrifying powers of transrational understanding. (McGann 2000: 58)

Seduced by the 'wondrous and terrifying powers' of the *Arabian Nights*, Rossetti started to conceive his own mode of Orientalising the Orient by translating into images a world of fate, crime and violence. Such a drawing as 'Sinbad's Bales Brought to Him by Order of the Captain', illustrating the Arabian tale 'The First Voyage of Sinbad the Sailor', exemplifies Rossetti's projection of the East as a magic land in which fate, or *quadar*, plays a determining role. It is not a coincidence that Rossetti depicts the most significant episode in Sinbad's cycle: that is to say, the moment when the sailors of the city of Baghdad deliver to Sinbad the bales marked with his name.

The pen-and-ink sketch, whose title is inscribed beneath the image, faithfully and delicately reproduces the episode and its pivotal elements – the inscribed bales – decorating both sides of the image. In this small drawing (approximately 9.5 × 11.5 cm), featuring the famous voyager who has sailed over all the seas under the sun, Orientalism is remediated in a perfect balance between words and images, *studium* and *punctum*, written material and ornamental design. Through a conscious interplay between media, verbal and pictorial, Rossetti is able to remediate the Arabian tale in which fate, as Irwin underlines, is 'a thoroughly literary affair' (2004: 197). Like Scheherazade, Aladdin and Ali Baba, Sinbad cannot be separated from his story, as, in Novalis's words, 'character is destiny' (1802: 125), and Rossetti's Sinbad is a 'story-man'. The fearful symmetry of fate in the Muslim universe of the *Arabian Nights* is echoed in Rossetti's illustration, whose Oriental iconographic style (turbans, scimitars and flowery pantaloons) is aimed at achieving an immediacy of presentation.

Of special value is the illustration for the tale 'The Slaves Beating Amine at the Command of Prince Amin', which shows Rossetti's interest in the violent Islamic world. The history of Amine, later reproduced by Millais for Thomas Dalziel's *Illustrated Arabian Nights* (1865), is widely known for its whipping incident and the uncovering of Amine's scarred cheek. If all mediation reproduces the real, then Rossetti's remediation of the Arabian tale projects the conceptual metaphor EAST IS VIOLENCE. Visually dynamic in its rendering of the act of whipping Princess Amine, Rossetti's illustration sheds light on the dramatic condition of women in medieval Arab society. Secluded and veiled, Princess Amine innocently and girlishly shows her face to an ugly old silk merchant who is pretending to want a kiss. To her amazement, the rude and impertinent merchant gives her such a bite that her lovely face is entirely covered with blood. Unable to hide the fearful scar from her new husband Amin, she is obliged to tell the truth at the expense of her very life. By violating the social taboo imposed by Prince Amin, son of Caliph Alraschid, Amine is whipped and sentenced to death for speaking to another man. Thanks to the fairy Zobeide, a Scheherazade-like character, Amine will be forgiven by Prince Amin and her scars will magically disappear.

Morbidly fascinated by this story of revenge, in which a beautiful woman's face is deformed by an outrageous man, Rossetti envisions the East as a harem-like dimension ruled by cruel and domineering males. The haunting image of the disfigured princess is reduplicated by Rossetti in another illustration for the 'History of the Three Calendars, Sons of Kings, and of Five Ladies of Bagdad'. This time Amine appears lying on a pile of cushions, overcome by the ardour with which she sang a lute song, but the most appalling thing is that her reclining neck, instead of being as smooth and white as her face, is a mass of scars. It is highly significant that Rossetti, the singer of bodily beauty,[7] of stately, towering necks and full lips, is obsessed with a dark, almost horrific Orientalism.

The most highly refined graphic illustration of the series, however, is 'Amgiad and Assad' (1843), a pen-and-ink drawing copied from Harvey in Lane's *1000 Nights* (1853), which features the protagonists of a strange adventure in which Amgiad was made vizier, while Assad was thrown into a dungeon. The following description of the two princes from Lane's translation seems to have enacted an identification process in Rossetti's mind:

They were like two shining moons: the elder of them was the son of the Queen Badoura, and his name was the Prince Amgiad; and the younger was the son of Haiatalnefous, and his name was the Prince Assad; and Assad was more lovely than his brother Amgiad. They were reared with magnificence and tenderness, and instructed in polite arts and accomplishments: they learned calligraphy and general science, and the arts of government and horsemanship, until they attained the utmost perfection, and became distinguished by consummate beauty and loveliness, so that the women were ravished by their charms. They grew up to the age of seventeen years, always in each other's company, eating and drinking together, and never separated one from another, and all the people envied them on this account. (Lane 1853: 327)

Notably, Dante Gabriel and William Michael grew up together sharing a daily routine and all kinds of formative experiences. As recalled by William Michael in *Some Reminiscences*, their bond was so intense that they even slept in the same bed ('We rose, talked, walked, studied, ate, amused ourselves, and slumbered, together'; W. M. Rossetti 1906: 57). Though the story may be ascribed to the criminal underworld of the *Arabian Nights* for its treachery motif, a sense of fraternal reunion is retained. Through the subtle use of light and shade to define facial features and accentuate the moment of intensity, the sketch illustrating the Oriental princely brothers, characterised by different turban designs, seems to be a portrait of the Rossetti brothers. The domineering, extravagant personality of Dante Gabriel, the greatly gifted and successful poet and painter, may well be associated with Amgiad, the most illustrious vizier who is seduced by a veiled lady. Likewise, William Michael, the 'average man' of the Rossetti family, is very similar to Assad, the virtuous brother who suffers the condition of imprisonment, which metaphorically might recall the financial constraints experienced by William Michael, who worked as a clerk at the Excise Office.

Rossetti's black-and-white drawings illustrating episodes in the *Arabian Nights* are valuable examples of a personal and juvenile representation of the Orient, which is associated with crime, murder, theft and treachery. This form of dark and magic Orientalism is clearly evident in sketches such as 'Sinbad's Bales Brought to Him by Order of the Captain', 'The Slaves Beating Amine at the Command of Prince Amin' and 'The Genius Threatening to Kill the Merchant', as mentioned above.

But the paramount example of magic Orientalism as envisioned by Rossetti is *Golden Water, or The Princess Parisad* (1858), an exquisite little watercolour, full of charm, that illustrates tale number 20 in the Lang (1898) translation of the *Arabian Nights*, entitled 'The Story of Two Sisters Who Envied their Younger Sister'.

This pictorial work, advocating the principle of mere gratification of the eye, represents the climactic scene of the tale, in which Princess Parisad holds the black barrel containing the golden water that can restore her petrified brothers to human form. In the distance stands the green mountain and behind her is the singing lilac tree with the scarlet talking bird fluttering in branches that are heavy with mauve blossom. This pictorial rendering of the Arabian marvel tale confirms what Gorlée calls 'informational loss' (Gorlée 1994: 168), which is highest in intersemiotic translation since the semiosis shows maximum degeneracy. Compared to the Oriental story, the picture only illustrates the moment preceding the magic metamorphosis without exploring it, corroborating the inequality between the verbal and the visual.

Except for the fact that Rossetti has painted Oriental treasures such as the talking bird and the singing tree behind (the talking bird whose voice draws all other singing birds to it, to join in chorus, and the singing tree whose every leaf is a song that is never silent), and the fact that the lady is endowed with sumptuous robes and flowing golden hair, there is little to suggest that this is a luxuriant Persian garden. A typical European beauty, Parisad, looking like Fanny Cornforth,[8] Rossetti's most sensual and fleshly model, with her harvest-yellow blonde hair, has pale skin and big expressive eyes, epitomes of amazement and inner exploration. But the Oriental robe, in whose yellow tone we may perhaps find the origins of the 'greenery-yallery' aestheticism of the later 1880s, as well as the winged decoration on the flask, activate dreamscapes of Persian cultural models of magic femininity. Rossetti took a syncretic approach to the *Arabian Nights*, experimenting with ways of expressing mythical and imaginary mental projections as part of Pre-Raphaelite Orientalism.

The East is Violence: Rossetti's Double Works of Art and Turkish Orientalism

Deeply influenced by the nineteenth-century excavations at Nineveh and Troy, and in particular by the Assyrian Winged Bull that was transported to the British Museum[9] in 1849, as well as by the obelisk known as 'Cleopatra's Needle' that was erected on the Thames Embankment in 1879, Rossetti emphasises the universal value of Eastern civilisations, as exemplified in the poems 'The Burden of Nineveh' (1856) and 'Tiber, Nile, and Thames' (1881). In these poems, which criticise Britain's imperial activities in the East, Rossetti makes a blending of past and present, East and West. The artefact of a winged beast from Nineveh, displayed in the British Museum among other Roman, Greek, Egyptian and Babylonian sculptures, is the central metaphor for conceptualising his thinking about imperialism and art. As a tangible sign of Eastern culture, the god of Nineveh is another relic covered with dust in the blended space of the British Museum, where the distinctions between the great empires of the world are unclear and insignificant, confused and confusing: 'While school-foundations in the act / Of holiday [. . .] / Shall learn to view thee as a fact / Connected with that zealous tract: "Rome, – Babylon and Nineveh"' (ll. 76–80).[10] By projecting the conceptual metaphor ORIENTAL GODS ARE RELICS, Rossetti fiercely criticises the cultural policies of British imperialism, disempowering Eastern cultures and depriving them of their mystic aura. Such a senseless exhibition of Oriental cultures, of 'images / Of awe and worship' (ll. 116–17), is attacked sarcastically by Rossetti, who continues to focus on the metaphor of the blended space:

> And now, – they and their gods and thou
> All relics here together, – now
> Whose profit? whether bull or cow,
> Isis or Ibis, who or how,
> Whether of Thebes or Nineveh?   (110)

Like Byron's 'Childe Harold's Pilgrimage' (1812), in which the achievements of Athena's mighty warriors become 'A schoolboy's tale, the wonder of an hour!' (II l. 15), or with Shelley's 'Ozymandias' (1818), recalling the British Museum's acquisition of a large fragment of a statue of Ramesses II as an act of usurpation, 'The Burden of Nineveh' pre-announces a future in which Oriental antiquities will become 'relic[s] of London' (l. 180), thereby losing their cultural identity.

A similar ironic meditation on British imperialism's false values can be found in 'Tiber, Nile, and Thames', originally titled 'Cleopatra's Needle' in reference to the Egyptian obelisk on the Thames Embankment. Imported from Alexandria, where it stood for 2,000 years in a temple built by Cleopatra in honour of Mark Antony, Cleopatra's Needle not only represents British colonial dominion over the Middle East but also is another crafty metaphor conceived by Rossetti to criticise imperialism. Mapping between cognitive models – that is, between Roman acts of violation and Egyptian stories of deprivation – Rossetti restructures the target domain (Cleopatra's Needle) using concepts transferred from the source domain. Rossetti's sentence metaphor CLEOPATRA'S NEEDLE HURTS NATIONAL PRIDE is characterised by such a complicated metaphorical pattern that we can even understand his philosophical view of imperialism as being founded on a set of metaphorical representations. Drawing a parallel between the violation of Cicero's corpse by Fulvia, Mark Antony's wife, who used to pierce Cicero's tongue with a needle as a macabre act of revenge, and the English neglect of some of Rossetti's favourite poets (Keats, Coleridge and Chatterton), Rossetti blends together Roman and British metaphors.

Of great value is the river 'megametaphor' (Stockwell 2002: 111), a conceptual feature that runs throughout the sonnet, crossing time and space, and above all mapping to such targets as DEATH, VENGEANCE, HOPE and SCORN. Specific metaphors in 'Tiber, Nile, and Thames' accumulate into the sense of the river megametaphor. For example, the recurrence of metaphors that map THE River TIBER AS DEATH, THE RIVER NILE AS SURVIVING DEATH and THE River THAMES AS DEATH is aimed at foregrounding the cognitive model of historical rivers. This includes metaphors of rise and fall, up and down, heat and cold, and others, as exemplified by the following lines:

> The head and hands of murdered Cicero,
>   Above his seat high in the Forum hung,
>   Drew jeers and burning tears. When on the rung
> Of a swift-mounted ladder, all aglow,
> Fulvia, Mark Antony's shameless wife, with show
>   Of foot firm-poised and gleaming arm upflung,
>   Bade her sharp needle pierce that god-like tongue
> Whose speech fed Rome even as the Tiber's flow.
>
> And thou, Cleopatra's Needle, that hadst thrid
> Great skirts of Time ere she and Antony hid   10
>   Dead hope! – hast thou too reached, surviving death,
> A city of sweet speech scorned, – on whose chill stone
> Keats withered, Coleridge pined, and Chatterton,
>   Breadless, with poison froze the God-fired breath?

Through many linguistic deviations – elliptical constructions, compound words, archaic expressions and creative metaphors – Rossetti achieves *foregrounding*: that is, drawing attention to some meaningful elements. This dynamic process involves the renewing of the reader's attention, which initially follows the deadly relation between Cicero and Fulvia, then shifts to Cleopatra's Needle, whose transportation by sea from Alexandria to London caused the death of many men, and finally focuses on neglected British poets who died without receiving the recognition they deserved for their literary works.

Rossetti's response to Oriental culture is also evident through his double works of art, which appear to be characterised by a blending of the traditional Western European canon of beauty and the Eastern notion of Oriental eroticism. Of particular interest are Rossetti's illustrations for the *Iliad*, dating back to the time when he and his brother were beginning to learn Greek at school. As William Michael recalls in his *Memoir*, in order to please his sister Maria, who had a temporary affection for the *Iliad*, Dante Gabriel undertook to illustrate the entire work in pen and ink, one drawing for every book:

> While the *Iliad* fit was at its height, Dante, to please her, undertook to do a series of pen-and-ink designs for the epic, on a small scale, one design to each Book. This was in February 1840, when he was eleven years of age. These drawings – they still exist – are not in any tolerable degree good, nor even distinctly promising; but they may count for something as showing the lad's ambitious temper in design, and his willingness to take up any attempt that offered, however ludicrously inadequate his means for coping with it. I may add that Dante at this time, although he had not that glowing love of the *Iliad* which his sister entertained, liked it highly, and read it much. In later years he knew, and he also preferred, the *Odyssey*. (W. M. Rossetti 1895: 81)

Similarly to the sketches illustrating episodes from the *Arabian Nights*, the juvenile illustrations of Homer's epic poem may be considered as the genealogy of Rossetti's mental pictures of the East. Particularly fascinated with the Trojan War, which, according to British archaeologist Frank Calvert (Allen 1995), took place across the plain of Scamander in northwest Anatolia (Turkey), Rossetti builds up image schemas of Troy in his mind and decides to share those particular image schemas with the community through his illustrations and drawings. See, for example, the illustration entitled *Jupiter Awaking Sees Neptune Rallying the Greeks* (1840), featuring Greek gods such as Neptune, Jupiter and Juno watching over the battle between Greek and Trojan soldiers. Visually dynamic in its rendering of the warfare, Rossetti's illustration projects the conceptual metaphor EAST IS VIOLENCE as envisioned twenty-one years later (1861) in another drawing entitled *Cassandra*, a pen-and-ink monograph of approximately 13 × 18 cm reshaping, with a more mature rendering of characters, the tense configuration of conflicting forms and elements. Both illustration and drawing appear to be a series of replications of similar divergent or conflicted lines of action confirming that the events of the mediated Trojan War are constituted by combinations of subjects, media and objects that do not exist in their segregated forms. H. C. Marillier describes the dynamism of *Cassandra* in the following terms:

> The incident is just before Hector's last battle. Cassandra has warned him in vain by her prophecies, and is now throwing herself against a pillar, and rending her clothes in despair, because he will not be detained longer. He is rushing down the steps and trying to make himself heard across the noise, as he shouts an order to an officer in charge of the soldiers who are going round the ramparts on their way to battle. One of his captains is beckoning to him to make haste. Behind him is Andromache with her child, and a nurse who is holding the cradle. Helen is arming Paris in a leisurely way on a sofa; we may presume from her expression that Cassandra has not spared her in her denunciations. Paris is patting her on the back to soothe her, much amused. Priam and Hecuba are behind, the latter stopping her ears in horror. One brother is imploring Cassandra to desist from her fear-inspiring cries. The ramparts are lined with engines for casting stones on the besiegers. (Marillier 1899: 108–9)

The figure of Cassandra, Princess of Troy, achieves visual prominence in the black-and-white drawing, thanks to her central position in the composition. She differentiates herself from the other figures by throwing herself against a pillar in a desperate act of warning. The viewer pays attention to her rather than to the surrounding figures since her long blonde hair, highly elaborate mantle, simple but refined robe and naked feet are attractors that steal attention away from other elements in the drawing. In Peter Stockwell's words, prominence is conferred on a figure when 'the figure will be more detailed, better focused, brighter, or more attractive than the rest of the field' (Stockwell 2002: 15).

Likewise, the sonnet written for the drawing, which is a faithful remediation of the scene depicting Cassandra prophesying among her kindred, is characterised by the same visual determinants of prominence: hair, garments, face and eyes. The first sonnet for Cassandra's drawing exemplifies Rossetti's strategy in his double works of art:

> Rend, rend thine hair, Cassandra: he will go.
> Yea, rend thy garments, wring thine hands, and cry
> From Troy still towered to the unreddened sky.
> See, all but she that bore thee mock thy woe: –
> He most whom that fair woman arms, with show   5
> Of wrath on her bent brows; for in this place
> This hour thou bad'st all men in Helen's face
> The ravished ravishing prize of Death to know.

> What eyes, what ears hath sweet Andromache,
> Save for her Hector's form and step; as tear   10
> On tear make salt the warm last kiss he gave?
> He goes. Cassandra's words beat heavily
> Like crows above his crest, and at his ear
> Ring hollow in the shield that shall not save.

This sonnet doubling the drawing reproduces the visual dynamism of images whose trajector[11] is the structural line that traces a path from an initial position (from Cassandra's raised left arm) to a final resting position (Hector's finger pointing at his heart). This image schema underlines many concepts involving not only movement (the shouted words addressed to Hector) but also the prophecy of death and the Fall of Troy.

In the sonnet, the first example in which the trajector and landmark are realised is at lines 2–3 ('and cry / From Troy still towered to the unreddened sky'), in which the trajector (Cassandra's prophecy) is moving towards its landmark (the sky). Described as a fair woman whose words beat heavily, the figure of Cassandra becomes the focal point of the sonnet, thanks to a dynamism expressed by verbs of movement such as *rend*, *wing*, *bear* and *beat*. Another very important trajector giving prominence to the figure of Cassandra is at lines 12–14, where her words are metamorphosed into crows beating above Hector's helmet. This is an image contained within the domain of death, an image of a chain of action in which a trajector (prophecy) moves along an existing path – Hector's body, helmet and shield: 'Cassandra's words beat heavily / Like crows above his crest, and at his ear / Ring hollow in the shield that shall not save' (ll. 12–14).

Rich in locative expressions using prepositions ('from', 'to', 'in', 'on' and 'above'), which in cognitive linguistics are understood as *image schemas*, the sonnet tries to visualise the dynamism of the drawing, as exemplified by the different paths taken by the trajector (Cassandra's cry) in relation to different landmarks (the sky and Hector):

Trajector (Cassandra's cries) takes a path reaching up the landmark (unreddened sky).

Trajector (Cassandra's words) comes to be in contact with the landmark (Hector's helmet and shield).

Of all the female characters in the *Iliad*, Rossetti also mentions Helen ('Helen's face', l. 8) and Andromache ('What eyes, what ears hath sweet Andromache, / Save for her Hector's form and step', ll. 9–10) without giving verbal prominence to their singular stories. For example, there is no mention in the sonnet of other figures such as Priam and Hecuba, or of one of Cassandra's brothers imploring her to desist from her fear-inspiring cries, a nurse holding the cradle of Andromache's child and all the soldiers marching round the ramparts on their way to battle. Despite its verbal dynamism, visual metonymies and conceptual metaphors (WORDS ARE CROWS), the sonnet is lacking the conceptual density of the picture, as well as the tension and energy of Cassandra's and Hector's figures.

A meaningful example of Rossetti's blending process is expressed in the painting entitled *Helen of Troy* (1863), whose female protagonist is commonly known as 'the face that launched a thousand ships' (Marlowe 1998, *Doctor Faustus*, l. 88). Compared to the ekphrastic poem 'Troy Town' (1869), the picture illustrates the mythical event of the destruction of Troy, without exploring its narrative complexity.

The poem was composed in the Autumn of 1869, while Rossetti was staying at Penkill in Ayrshire, and is based on the legend that Helen, wife of Menelaus of Sparta, dedicated a goblet to Venus that was moulded to the shape of Helen's breast – one of the antecedent acts of the Trojan War. As reported by Jan Marsh in a note on the sonnet (Rossetti 1999), Rossetti's main classical reference book was Lemprière's *Dictionary of Classical Mythology*, which he used for his mythological pictures.

The pictorial work, advocating the principle of mere gratification of the eye, projects the Oriental conceptual metaphor LOVE IS DESTRUCTION, as confirmed by David G. Riede, who refers to Rossetti's painting as the representation of 'the destructive female principle' (Riede 1992: 96). In H. C. Marillier's words, *Helen of Troy* appears to be a:

> full-face study, head and shoulders only, of a rather pretty model, with masses of rippling yellow hair. [. . .] Except that Rossetti has painted a burning town behind, and that the lady is fingering a crystal locket in which is a flaming torch, there is little to suggest that daughter of the gods divinely tall and most divinely fair for whom the towers of Ilium were sacked. (Marillier 1899: 130)

As confirmed by Marillier's comment, Rossetti under-translates the lines of the ballad 'Troy Town', since the picture lacks the presence of Paris, as well as the figure of Helen kneeling in the shrine and offering the carven cup to Venus. At the same time, however, the picture seems to over-translate the doom of Trojan civilisation, triggered by beauty, desire and destruction, which, according to George Landow, are 'all but equivalent' (Landow 2014: 191).

The picture depicting the 'destroyer of ships, destroyer of men, destroyer of cities' (Aeschylus 1824: 105), which is a companion to the artist's poem 'Troy Town', depicts a stunning woman shown in three-quarter length, whose sumptuous robes and long, flowing hair seem almost to glow like the shifting of the fire burning in visual metaphor in the background. A typical European beauty, Helen has pale skin, full, red lips and large, expressive eyes, epitomes of fatal beauty, but the Oriental town in flames, as well as the pendant decorated with a fire emblem, activate dreamscapes of Turkish cultural models of destructive seduction. Rossetti's conceptual metaphors, included in such lines as 'Dead at heart with the heart's desire, – / 'Oh to clasp her golden head! / (*O Troy's down, / Tall Troy's on fire!*)' ('Troy Town', ll. 95–8), are mapped on to Oriental abstractions such as beauty, desire and fate. The latter could be easily ascribed to Rossetti's reading of Homer's *Iliad*, whose dreadful mental obsession is that the beauty of one woman destroyed entire nations.

Rossetti's double work of art entitled 'Troy Town' shows a situation in which, as Marek Zasempa maintains, 'the poetic has the advantage over the pictorial' (Zasempa 2011: 31). The ballad was originally accompanied by a black-chalk drawing, *Troy Town* (1870), which renders just a part of the mythological event: Helen is kneeling in a shrine, offering the carven cup to Venus. Thus, the drawing, which is far more faithful to the ballad than the painting, illustrates only lines 8–28 of the ballad 'Troy Town', which embraces the whole of the poetic concept, thereby disregarding the figure of Paris introduced in the final two stanzas:

> Cupid took another dart,   85
>   (*O Troy Town!*)
> Fledged it for another heart,
> Winged the shaft with the heart's desire,
> Drew the string and said, 'Depart!'
>   (*O Troy's down,*
>   *Tall Troy's on fire!*)
>
> Paris turned upon his bed,
>   (*O Troy Town!*)
> Turned upon his bed and said,
> Dead at heart with the heart's desire, —   95
> 'Oh to clasp her golden head!'
>   (*O Troy's down,*
>   *Tall Troy's on fire!*)

Although the oil painting *Helen of Troy* does not form part of a double work, it relates directly to the Matter of Troy that Rossetti took up in the drawing *Troy Town* and which he pursued as a double work. All of these works interconnect because Rossetti took a syncretic approach to the Matter of Troy, experimenting with ways of expressing mythical and imaginary mental projections of the East as part of Turkish Orientalism.

Rossetti's Deviations from Biblical Orientalism

Among Rossetti's biblically derived double works of art, *The Girlhood of Mary Virgin* (1849) envisions the East as a blended space in which there is a mapping of properties and domains between the biblical and medieval worlds, as well as between Eastern symbology and Western physiognomy. It is a picture that is fully encoded in a symbol system that can be scrutinised, and Rossetti wrote two sonnets (one ekphrastic poem and one explanatory sonnet) that were printed on a slip of gold-covered paper and fixed to the frame of the picture. Set in Nazareth in Galilee, as attested to by the first sonnet ('she / Was young in Nazareth of Galilee', ll. 2–3), the picture represents a medieval indoor scene whose holy figures (St Anne and the Virgin Mary) are captured in the medieval practice of embroidering a lily and are surrounded by medieval objects (a stack of books with titles relating to the medieval scheme of the virtues, a portable organ with the inscription *O sis, Laus Deo*, and a trellis forming a cross). The device of incorporating linguistic forms in the canvas that are nevertheless strictly related to the New Testament is also medieval. From the names of the virtues on the book spines to the legend *Tot dolores tot gaudia* appearing on the golden scroll binding the seven-thorned briar and the seven-leaved palm, Rossetti employs *foregrounding* according to his intention to defamiliarise the holy subject matter.

His *deviations* from the expected and ordinary representation of the Virgin Many are many: for example, instead of reading a book, she is engaged in the ordinary task of embroidering some vestment under the supervision of her mother. Rossetti's strategy of humanising the Virgin by representing her everyday routine is also confirmed by his decision to use his own family members as models in the Pre-Raphaelite painting. Deliberately painting the Virgin using his sister Christina as a model, Rossetti, as Lorraine Janzen Kooistra's observes, aims at 'foregrounding the personal and relegating the religious subject matter to an allusive, subsidiary role' (2002: 173). Looking like a seventeen-year-old Christina, the Virgin, light-skinned and endowed with extremely long, blonde hair in accordance with the medieval tradition, achieves prominence through her light-grey robe. The image schema of the Virgin – that is to say, the mental picture that the common reader shares with the community – is completely neglected. Rossetti seems to neglect what cognitive linguists call *redundancy* – stereotypical and expected features – in order to focus the viewer's attention on features that are new.

In the visual field, figures are more attractive than backgrounds because *perceptual grouping* (Stockwell 2002: 19) attracts attention more effectively than *locational grouping* (19). In *The Girlhood of Mary Virgin*, however, there is a rich complex of potentially interesting objects to attract the viewer's attention: the red vase of lilies, the oil lamp and the red cloth hanging from the window frame, the trellis cross twined with ivy, and the naturalistic, brightly lit landscape. Looking at Rossetti's double work of art is a dynamic experience, involving a process of renewing the attention in order to follow the relations between figures and ground. The Oriental *attractors* painted by Rossetti draw the attention away from one element and on to another in a dynamic process. Therefore, the spotlight moves, depending on which object is the most interesting for the viewer.

Apart from the decorated amphora of white lilies, the oil lamp and the colourful Oriental decoration on the window frame, there is little to suggest that the scene is set in Israel. Even the view from the large window appears to be deliberately medievalised, since the foregrounded ivy-covered trellis recalls a medieval garden. Furthermore, the white building over the hill is much more similar to a medieval castle than to the Church of Multiplication on the northwest shore of the Lake of Galilee, which is portrayed in the background of the painting. All these deviations from biblical Orientalism can be explained in Hunt's words:

> Rossetti treated the Gospel history simply as a storehouse of interesting situations and beautiful personages for the artist's pencil, just as the Arthurian legends afterwards were to him, and in due course to his younger proselytes at Oxford. (Hunt 1905: 172)

The sonnets inscribed on the back of the picture almost completely lack the Orientalism envisioned in the painting, since there is no reference to the aforementioned Eastern attractors. The Oriental symbology is replaced by Marian and Christian references. The verbal remediation of *The Girlhood of Mary Virgin* is based mainly on the process of *figuring*, which focuses the attention on figures rather than ground. Foregrounding of the education of the Virgin within the text is achieved by a variety of devices, such as rhyme, anaphoric repetitions, creative syntactic ordering ('wise in charity; / Strong in grave peace / in duty circumspect'; I ll. 7–8) and compound words ('An angel-watered lily', I l. 10; 'The seven-thorned briar and the palm seven-leaved', II l. 10). In both sonnets, the Virgin Mary is the figure and the dominant image schema is one of WAITING FOR ANNUNCIATION. In this conceptual structure, the trajector traces a path from an initial position (girlhood) outside the landmark to a final position in which the landmark contains the trajector (womanhood). This image schema underlies many concepts involving not only evolution but also identity and holiness. The following lines, taken from both sonnets, exemplify Rossetti's use of this image schema:

> [. . .] Till one dawn, at home,
> She woke in her white bed, and had no fear
> At all, – yet wept till sunshine, and felt awed;
> Because the fullness of the time was come.   (I ll. 11–14)

> Until the time be full, the Holy One
> Abides without. She soon shall have achieved
> Her perfect purity: yea, God the Lord
> Shall soon vouchsafe His Son to be her Son.   (II ll. 11–14)

The concluding lines of the first ekphrastic sonnet seem to describe another painting entitled *Ecce Ancilla Domini!* (1849–50), in which the Virgin, clad in white, is awakened by the Angel Gabriel. This interrelation between media (pictorial and verbal) is a peculiar trait of Rossetti's double works of art, which are continually commenting upon, reproducing and replacing each other. For Rossetti, 'all mediation is remediation' (Bolter and Grusin 1996: 22) because each act of mediation depends on other acts of mediation. From this perspective, *Ecce Ancilla Domini!*, whose attractors are the dominance of the whiteness, the lily held by the angel and the stand holding the long, red cloth embroidered with a white lily (visual reminders of *The Girlhood of Mary Virgin*), appears to be a more Oriental version of the Marian subject than the oil painting. Apart from the redundant paraphernalia of Christianity (the dove and the white lily), it is the whiteness that achieves prominence, thereby foregrounding the uncanny and inexplicable nature of the event. The extreme simplicity of the interior decoration, along with the white walls and ceilings, makes this painting a more realistic and Oriental representation of the house of the Virgin Mary.

Another deviation from biblical Orientalism is exemplified by *The Beloved, or The Bride* (1865), a painting that is unique in Rossetti's series of 1860s beauties, not only for including a black figure, the only one he ever painted, but also for applying a blending mode in the process of intersemiotic translation. It was originally intended to represent Dante's Beatrice, and Rossetti inscribed the frame with lines from *The Song of Solomon* (Old Testament) and *The Psalm of David*, psalm 45:

> My beloved is mine and I am his. (*The Song of Solomon* 2: 16)
> Let him kiss me with the kisses of his mouth: for thy love is better than wine. (*The Song of Solomon* 1: 2)

> She shall be brought unto the King in raiment of needlework: the virgins her companions that follow her shall be brought unto thee. (*Psalm* 45: 14)

As Figure 1.1 suggests, the relation between *The Song of Solomon* and *Psalm* 45 is forged by conceptual integration.

From the biblical source domain of individual female member or prototypical female member we can map on to classes of persons in the Rossettian target domain. However, when we map from a category's prototype (Solomon's bride) to other members of the class (Rossetti's Beloved), two more domains are introduced: that is, mapping from a person to a virtue, and from a prototype to a class

<table>
<tr><td colspan="2" align="center">Generic space

Women

Beauty, eroticism and exoticism</td></tr>
<tr><td>Specific source
Solomon's bride

The King's bride</td><td>General target
Erotic woman

Virginal woman</td></tr>
<tr><td colspan="2" align="center">Blend
Rossetti's Beloved, a European beauty endowed with Oriental sensuousness, is like Solomon's and the King's brides
A class member is the prototype</td></tr>
</table>

Figure 1.1 Conceptual blending network for *The Beloved, or The Bride*.

member, suggests four domains are involved. This is when blending theory[12] can be useful as an integration in the mental network within which input mental spaces are projected into a separate, blended mental space.

If *The Song of Solomon* (Old Testament) and *The Psalm of David* are the source texts, then Rossetti's portrait represents the intersemiotic blended text whose female allegories bring to life the metaphorical source domain through parabolic mappings. In Solomon's parable of love, the poet suggests a movement from courtship to consummation ('As the lily among thorns, so is my love among the daughters'; *The Song of Solomon* 2: 2) and introduces the black servant ('I am black, but comely, O ye daughters of Jerusalem, as the tents of Kedar, as the curtains of Solomon', 1: 5) as a symbol of exoticism. The black African girl, probably inspired by the figure of the black servant in Manet's *Olympia*, which Rossetti saw during a visit to the French artist's studio in November 1864, was intended to add a note of exoticism and a decorative contrast with the pale complexion and auburn hair of the bride. In a letter to his patron, George Rae, written in March 1865, Rossetti explained, 'I mean the colour of my picture to be like jewels' (qtd in Surtees 1971: 105). The visual rendering of the mulatto girl is a case of what Umberto Eco would call intersemiotic irony or intertextual irony, since only the cultured observer will be able to capture the biblical references to Solomon's black and comely servant, who is not mentioned in the lines inscribed on the picture frame.

In this pleasure garden Rossetti projects his prototypical love story in which LOVE is closely associated with other concepts, such as DESIRE, RESPECT and DEVOTION. Though moved by intense desire on seeing his beloved, the male observer is convinced to postpone erotic fulfilment by a fair-skinned, red-haired bride, whose Western European canon of beauty is blended with her Japanese robe, intricate Peruvian leather headdress and Chinese hair ornaments. According to the Middle Eastern custom, her face is unveiled for the bridegroom so that he (the King) sees her for the first time. This is the exact moment shown in the painting – she draws back her veil to reveal her beautiful face. From this perspective, Rossetti the *pasticheur* transmutes two biblical texts (Solomon's and David's) that project such conceptual metaphors as ORIENTAL LOVE IS EROTICISM and ORIENTAL LOVE IS PURITY, by employing a blending mode of translation.

From this perspective, Rossetti employs what Sherry Simon calls 'aesthetics of cultural pluralism' (Simon 1996: 154), of Oriental pluralism, as exemplified by the presence of the four bridesmaids, whose varying shades of dark Caucasian skin tones (Jewish and Romany) convey a range of different racial types of beauty. Seen as a celebration of racial diversity, *The Beloved, or The Bride* is the quintessential representation of intersemiotic translation as a sign of fragmentation and cultural negotiation.

Another paramount example of Rossetti's double works of art aimed at defamiliarising biblical Orientalism is *Astarte Syriaca* (1876), one of his most disturbing and sinister pictures, whose ekphrastic poem depicts, according to Theodore Watts-Dunton, 'one of the Oriental Venuses – (Al Husa, perhaps – or else the Syrian Venus) who, growing less and less mystical as she travelled, became the Aphrodite of Western poetry' (Watts-Dunton 1883: 412). The poem was written for the painting with the same title that was reproduced in 1876–7; it depicts Astarte, one of the names given to the classical goddess Aphrodite/Venus. According to Herodotus, the religious community of Aphrodite originated in Phoenicia, and in particular at Ascalon in Syria, where the Phoenicians erected the oldest sanctuary to the goddess, called 'Aphrodite *Ourania*' (1992: 1.105.2–3). Therefore, the Latin feminine nominative singular word 'Syriaca', meaning 'Syrian', denotes the goddess's origins in the ancient Middle East.

Both picture and poem project the conceptual metaphor LOVE IS A MYSTERY, as epitomised by this arcane Syrian dominatrix, endowed with 'love-freighted lips and absolute eyes that wean' (Rossetti, 'Astarte Syriaca', l. 7) and whose abundant sea-green robe reinforces the appearance of massive proportions and inscrutable feminist power. In this case of recodification of non-linguistic codes into linguistic signs, Rossetti employs the translation strategy of fidelity in order to render a detailed version of the Oriental myth of seduction.

Without breaking the balance between under- and over-translation, Rossetti reproduces a Semitic goddess of fertility and sexual love whose appearance recalls Jane Burden's[13] stately enigmatic figure, characterised by glowing, mysterious and steadfast eyes looking from under the shadows of her ample brows and abundant masses of bronze–black hair, shadows that add to the mystery and wonder of her face.

As suggested by Jan Marsh (Rossetti 1999: xxiv), Rossetti responds to a momentary emotion by raising a correlative poetic figure or motif as a conceit on which to structure the poem. From this perspective, *Astarte Syriaca* appears to be determined by Oriental schemas that Rossetti manipulates, highlighting his creativity as a translator, inevitably engaged in a complex creative process. Astarte's Oriental robe girdles twice, just beneath her breasts and again around her hips with a chain of alternate links of roses and pomegranates, symbolising passion and sexual regeneration ('In silver sheen / Her twofold girdle clasps the infinite boon / Of bliss whereof the heaven and earth commune'; 'Astarte Syriaca', ll. 3–5). From this perspective, it is worthwhile mentioning the amulet appearing above her hair, between the sun and crescent moon ('Amulet, talisman, and oracle, – / Betwixt the sun and moon a mystery', ll. 13–14), an eight-pointed star of Venus trembling in a purple atmosphere. Visually recalling the Muslim crescent moon, which became affiliated with the Muslim world during the period of the Ottoman Empire and the Turkish conquest of Constantinople in 1453, the picture is none the less imbued with Christian symbology, since the amulet may be easily misunderstood as the Holy Spirit.

This blending mode is also confirmed by the two ministering attendants bearing torches, compared by Alastair Grieve (1969) with William Blake's angels in several of his engravings for the Book of Job. Once again, seductive female figures, portrayed as Western European beauties, are characterised by mystic Oriental signs, as exemplified by the torches whose flame is bent by a mysterious wind ('Torch-bearing, her sweet ministers compel / All thrones of light beyond the sky and sea / The witnesses of Beauty's face to be', 'Astarte Syriaca', ll. 9–11).

There exists another double work of art strictly connected with *Astarte Syriaca*, which is imbued with a deviant kind of Orientalism. Begun as an oil study for *Astarte Syriaca*, *Mnemosyne* (1881), representing the Greek goddess of memory, remembrance and language, appears to be a replica of the Venus Astarte subject due to the extreme resemblance between the two female figures. Both stunning black-haired, green-clad women are portrayed with the distinctive features of Jane Morris, whose hands achieve prominence because they hold highly detailed objects that are part of the visual field. Seen as symbols of their divinity, Astarte's golden chain of roses and pomegranates and Mnemosyne's winged chalice and ornate oil lantern are small but prominent items in the viewer's visual field that receive attention and focus, thereby becoming the figures in the ground. In *Mnemosyne*, the attention is first focused on the goddess's blank, emotionless face and then on objects that are presented in strategic positions. Visually and verbally speaking, elements such as 'the winged chalice of the soul' (l. 1) that Mnemosyne holds in her right hand and the 'fire-winged [. . .] lamp' (l. 2) of memory that she touches with her left hand are selected for the viewer's attention. The relation between these two luminous objects with different Oriental designs is explained in the lines inscribed on the picture's frame:

> Thou fill'st from the winged chalice of the soul
> Thy lamp, O Memory, fire-winged to its goal.
>   (Rossetti 1999: 458)

The locative expressions 'from' and 'to' involve a dynamic movement and a final resting position resulting from that movement. In the FROM image schema, the moving figure (Mnemosyne), who is filling the lamp of memory with soulful images, can be seen to follow a path. From this perspective, Mnemosyne is the trajector that comes to be in contact with both the chalice of the soul and the lamp of memory. Moreover, the chalice and the lamp seem to be composite parts of the same Oriental object, since the circular base of the chalice suggests that the chalice can be inserted on the circular lamp with flame-like petals. The Orientalism of this double work of art is all the more evident if we analyse closely the similarities and differences with respect to *Astarte Syriaca*. Through the cognitive process of *restructuring*, Rossetti seems to change a few variables of the Astarte schema in order to allow for new interpretations of the painting. From a Syrian goddess Rossetti creates a Greek goddess by modifying Oriental schemas and replacing some of the variable components (that is, Astarte's golden chain is substituted by Mnemosyne's chalice and lamp). From this view, the Greek goddess schema can be created by patterning it on the Syrian goddess schema, and by substituting some variable figures and objects with other items. Unlike Astarte, who is surrounded by a pair of angels, Mnemosyne appears to be the sole figure in the painting and is immersed in a naturalistic scenario. But the most strikingly different variable in the Astarte schema is exemplified by Mnemosyne's altar, on which a pansy flower (symbol of remembrance) and a sprig of yew (symbol of immortality) lie alongside the lamp of memory. These minor visual items seem to Orientalise the painting, which lacks any sign of Greek culture. Notably, the yew tree (*Taxus baccata*) is a conifer native to northwest Africa, northern Iran and southwest Asia. Likewise, the pansy is a hybrid resulting from a wildflower of western Asia known as heartsease. All variables employed by Rossetti are associated with Oriental schemas and tend to foreground Rossetti's blending mode of conceptualising the East.

To conclude, like Aladdin and Mnemosyne, Rossetti is enlightened by his wonderful lamp of translation, a foreignising translation, preserving the alterity of the source text and recognising cultural pluralisms by drawing attention to mythology, ethnography and history. His Oriental illustrations, paintings and double works of art are blended spaces combining different visions of the Orient, thereby allowing new insights to appear, along with a new understanding of Orientalism, in order to alter our original cognitive models.

Notes

1. Lakoff and Johnson (1980) were the first to assert that metaphor is not a matter of mere language but is something conceptual. As they suggest, conceptual metaphors typically project experientially basic categories on to more abstract ones. For example, the source domain of WRITING IS HEALING is a dimension of our everyday experience: we are constantly writing at work. The target domain, by contrast, is something more abstract: a dimension of social relations.

2. The use of small capitals to indicate conceptual metaphors has become conventional in Cognitive Stylistics and other fields, so is used here for clarity.

3. In *Some Reminiscences*, William Michael Rossetti recalls that his brother kept a menagerie of animals in his Cheyne Walk back garden, including wallabies, wombats and a Brahmin bull: 'Between "pots" and "beasts" a good deal of Dante Gabriel's time and attention was shared at Cheyne Walk; "pots" being his generic term for blue china, and "beasts" for animals that he kept in the garden, or sometimes in the house. [. . .] There were quadrupeds, birds, and reptiles. From contemplating a Japanese salamander in a tank or a white mouse nursing her brood, in the studio, and hearing a wood-owl hoot or a parrot talk in the corridor, you could pass into the garden, and see a kangaroo skipping, a racoon washing and swallowing a biscuit, or an armadillo pacing his rounds not to speak of a zebu chasing (on one occasion not unfrequently [sic] reported) Dante Gabriel Rossetti round a tree' (W. M. Rossetti 1906: 285).

4. As reported in *The Rossetti Archive*, edited by Jerome J. McGann (2008), each drawing is dated 1840 on the back, and the number of the story and the title of the episode are provided for each illustration. Here is the list of individual titles: Story 1 – 'The Genius Threatening to Kill the Merchant'; Story 2 – 'The Steward's Daughter Disenchanting the First Old Man's Son'; Story 3 – 'The Second Old Man's Surprise on Discovering his Wife to Be a Fairy'; Story 4 – 'The Black Overturning the Fish, in Presence of the Sultan & Vizier'; Story 5 – 'The Head of Douban Speaking to the King, After It Had Been Cut Off'; Story 6 – 'The Husband Asking the Parrot About his Wife's Behaviour'; Story 7 – unlocated; Story 8 – 'The Young King of the Black Isles Killing the Moor'; Story 9 – 'Amine Fainting After Having Played on the Lute'; Story 10 – unlocated; Story 11 – 'The 1ˢᵗ Calendar Seized by Order of the Caliph's Vizier, who had

Usurped the Crown'; Story 12 – 'The Third Calendar Killing the Young Man by Accident'; Story 13 – 'Zobeide Discovering the Young Prince Reading the Koran'; Story 14 – 'The Slaves Beating Amine at the Command of Prince Amin'; Story 15 – 'Sinbad's Bales Brought to Him by Order of the Captain'.

5. In Chapter 45 of *Martin Chuzzlewit*, Dickens alludes to an enchanted lamp that recalls the lamp possessed by Aladdin in the Oriental tale, 'The Story of Aladdin, or, the Wonderful Lamp': 'And as if, in the course of this rubbing and polishing, he had rubbed an enchanted lamp or a magic ring, obedient to which there were twenty thousand supernatural slaves at least, suddenly there appeared a being in a white waistcoat' (Dickens 2009: 590). For an interesting study of Dickens's literary imagination see Christensen et al. (2015).

6. Stevenson's 'The Bottle Imp' (1891) is a darker version of 'The Story of Aladdin, or, the Wonderful Lamp', the story being imbued with narrative elements taken from 'The Fisherman and the Jinni'.

7. On this topic see Psomiades (1997) and Bullen (1998).

8. Rossetti's mistress, Fanny Cornforth, modelled for Oriental figures such as Princess Parisad, the siren Ligeia and Sidonia von Bork. She is also portrayed in *The Blue Bower* (1865) playing a Japanese stringed instrument (the *koto*), and in *Woman with a Fan* (1870) holding an Oriental feather-fan.

9. For a thought-provoking study of literary representations of museums see Patey and Scuriatti (2009).

10. All quotations from Rossetti's poems are taken from the Dent edition edited by Jan Marsh (1999).

11. In cognitive studies, the element that is the figure is called the trajector, and the element it has a grounded relationship with is called the landmark. For an interesting study of foregrounding see Douthwaite (2000).

12. Blending theory, also known as conceptual integration theory or conceptual blending theory, was developed to account for the online construction of meaning in terms of networks of 'mental spaces'. As Elena Semino maintains, 'blending theory explains the production and comprehension of specific metaphorical expressions in terms of conceptual networks involving four mental spaces' (Semino and Culpeper 2002: 114).

13. Jane Morris, née Jane Burden and known as Janey, is the legendary Pre-Raphaelite muse who was married to William Morris for thirty-seven years.

Toward a Corporeal Orientalism: Foregrounding Arabian Erotic Figures in Algernon Swinburne and Aubrey Beardsley

Hur al-ayn and *hammam*: Swinburne, Beardsley and Burton's Uncensored Translation of the *Arabian Nights*

Of all forms of Orientalism, Algernon Swinburne and Aubrey Beardsley appear to be representing what Said terms the 'eminently corporeal' (Said 1977: 184). Like Nerval, Flaubert, Gautier, Baudelaire and Huysmans, Swinburne and Beardsley belong to a community of authors depicting 'the imagery of exotic places, the cultivation of sadomasochistic tastes [. . .] a fascination with the macabre, with the notions of the Fatal Woman' (180). Swinburne and Beardsley seem to project into their works such a conceptual metaphor as EAST IS SEXUAL FREEDOM, inscribing their texts in corporeal Orientalism. In their view, the East is a sexual dimension inhabited by such female figures as Cleopatra, Salome and Isis, evoking the strong sensual, even pornographic, content of the *Arabian Nights*.

As followers of the fleshly school of poetry, which combines aestheticism and immorality, Swinburne and Beardsley exhibit female carnality as a realistic feature of sensual love. It is not by chance that they both read the *Arabian Nights* in the plain and literal translation by Sir Richard F. Burton, the Victorian explorer and Orientalist who exalted the ethnographical and anthropological nuances of the East, and who is most remembered for his perilous journey to the sacred city of Mecca in 1853.

Unlike Ruskin, the Rossetti brothers, Morris and Ford, who used to read Lane's translation of the *Arabian Nights*, Swinburne and Beardsley privileged Burton's uncensored version, which revealed the erotic customs of the Orientals. According to Said, Burton's form of Orientalism occupies a median position between Lane and Chateaubriand, and between science and imagination:

> He was preternaturally knowledgeable about the degree to which human life in society was governed by rules and codes. All of his vast information about the Orient, which dots every page he wrote, reveals that he knew that the Orient in general and Islam in particular were systems of information, behavior, and belief, that to be an Oriental or a Muslim was to know certain things in a certain way, and that these were of course subject to history, geography, and the development of society in circumstances specific to it. (195)

What stirred Swinburne's and Beardsley's interest was Burton's personal, authentic, sympathetic and humanistic knowledge of the Orient, deriving from 'systems of information, behavior, and belief'. If the *Edinburgh Review* and the *Pall Mall Gazette* criticised Burton's work for the 'degrading customs and statistics of vice' (Reeve 1886: 83) emerging from the notes, as well as for the revolting obscenity of the translation, then Swinburne and Beardsley emphasised the same shocking qualities that were fiercely criticised by the leading organs of the purity campaign.

Swinburne's appreciation of Burton's translation is clearly exemplified by the poem entitled 'To Sir Richard F. Burton: On His Translation of "The Arabian Nights"' (1886). In this poem, Swinburne paid homage to the darkly exotic and rakish adventurer, with whom he shared a common interest in the erotic that resulted in a dissolute friendship characterised by a ruinous form of alcoholism. Swinburne literally adored Burton for what Deborah Lutz calls 'the kind of fascinating larger-than-life qualities found in certain Victorians' (Lutz 2011: 73). Morbidly fascinated with sex, and in particular with the sexual liberty of the Muslim races, Burton was to Swinburne an irresistible source of temptation, the latter praising the former for his 'wider soul than the world was wide' (Swinburne, 'On the Death of Richard Burton', l. 41).[1]

Likewise, Beardsley, the erotic Victorian illustrator famous for his black-and-white drawings of Oscar Wilde's *Salome* (1894), received a copy of Burton's *Arabian Nights* from Leonard Smithers, publisher of decadent artists, who soon became Beardsley's loyal and devoted friend. Beardsley's gratitude to Smithers for sending him the *Arabian Nights* is attested to in a letter (10 July 1896) in which he expresses his intention of illustrating 'The Story of Ali Baba and the Forty Thieves Destroyed by a Slave': 'Many thanks for the *Nights*. I will take great care of the tome. *Ali Baba* will make a scrumptious book' (Maas et al. 1970: 143). The drawings for *Ali Baba*, commissioned by Smithers in 1896 and intended as part of a set of illustrations for the Arabian tale, were never completed, however.

Swinburne's and Beardsley's interest in Burton's translation was kindled at a critical moment in the age of sexual repression. Female sexuality, prostitution and homosexuality were all taboo issues for the establishment, which welcomed the Criminal Law Amendment Act (1885), aimed at protecting women from sexual offences and strengthening existing legislation against prostitution and homosexuality. Amidst this socio-cultural turmoil, Burton's unexpurgated translation of the *Arabian Nights*, along with his translations of the Kama Sutra and other love manuals, are to be seen, in Dane Kennedy's words, as a 'mirror to his own society, exposing its various imperfections to itself' (2000: 339). Such a provocative form of Orientalism deeply affected Swinburne's irreverent imagination and Beardsley's desire to shock. For this reason, all versions of sensual Orientalism in Swinburne's and Beardsley's selected writings seem to reproduce and pervert the erotic and direct nature of the Arabian tales, as embodied by the Arabian *hur al-ayn*, the prototype of carnal female temptation. According to Irwin, 'a woman who is *hur al-ayn* has eyes in which there is strong contrast between the black and the surrounding white. To be *hur al-ayn* is one of the attributes of houris in paradise' (2004: 164).

Such epitomes of Oriental beauty, eyes of lively white and black, are one of the most tangible signs of Swinburne's and Beardsley's women who resemble the *hur al-ayn* prototype in *The Masque of Queen Bersabe* (1862) and *Under the Hill* (1896). Both writings appear to distort and pervert the Arabian representation of female sensuality externalised in toilet scenes that recall the Muslim public baths (*hammam*) depicted in the *Arabian Nights*.

Notably, in Burton's translation there is a final section entitled 'The Tale of Scheherazade Concluded',[2] in which Scheherazade and her sister Dunyazad enter the *hammam*-bath scented with 'rose-water and willow-flower water and pods of musk' (Mondschein 2011: 678). The *hammam*-bath scene is a good example of the Oriental beauty from which Swinburne and Beardsley took inspiration. Burton's translation of this final sensual scene is rich in metonymic references to corporeal beauty, focusing in particular on Scheherazade and Dunyazad as women of paradise – namely, *hur al-ayn*:

> And the imagination was bewildered at their charms, for indeed each of them was brighter than the sun and the moon. Before them they lighted brilliant flambeaux of wax in candelabra of gold, but their faces outshone the flambeaux, for that they had eyes sharper than unsheathed swords and the lashes of their eyelids bewitched all hearts. Their cheeks were rosy red and their necks and shapes gracefully swayed and their eyes wantoned like the gazelle's. (678)

This description of Scheherazade's and Dunyazad's bodily beauty is based on metonymic images of light. Both sisters can be seen as luminous figures against the ground of the setting (*hammam*-bath) and they evolve specific personal traits of Oriental beauty. Defined as 'brighter than the sun and the moon' for their luminous faces and their sharp eyes, whose lashes are able to ravish human hearts, Scheherazade and Dunyazad achieve cognitive prominence. The reader pays attention to them, to their brilliant faces, gazelle-like eyes, rosy cheeks and graceful necks, rather than to the surroundings. In Ronald W. Langacker's words, prominence refers 'to the directing of attention within the conceived situation. The concept draws upon the notion of *figure* and *ground*, originating within gestalt psychology and which has exerted an extensive influence within cognitive linguistics' (qtd in Harrison et al. 2014: 6).

This Oriental toilet scene may have influenced Swinburne's and Beardsley's representations of *femmes fatales*, who are often displayed in partial or complete nudity. This is clearly exemplified by Swinburne's 'Laus Veneris' (1864), 'Atalanta in Calydon' (1865), 'Hymn to Proserpine' (1866), 'Anactoria' (1866) and *The Masque of Queen Bersabe: A Miracle Play* (1866), as well as by Beardsley's *The Toilet of Salome* (1894), *The Toilet, from The Rape of the Lock by Alexander Pope* (1895–6) and *Venus at Her Toilet* (1896), in which the exhibition of the female body is always associated with intimate toilet scenes.

Seen as methods of cleansing and relaxation, *hammam*-baths became very popular during the Victorian era. By 1860, over 600 Turkish baths could be identified in the British Isles and eminent personalities such as Ford Madox Brown,[3] John Everett Millais,[4] Burne-Jones[5] and Ford Madox Ford[6] frequently visited the public baths. Swinburne himself had a penchant for *hammam*-baths and wrote a very long essay on Baudelaire's *Fleurs du mal* in a Turkish bath in Paris.

The Turkish bath is not only, in Billie Melman's words, 'a *locus sensualis* of the imaginary Orient' (1992: 131) but also a blended space mixing gender categories and social classes that are all unified by public nudity. Apart from its curative properties, the public bath, defined by J. L. W. Thudichum as an 'immersion of the whole body in hot common air' (1861: 40), raises social and moral issues. If nudity is the norm at the Turkish baths, then the frequent use of the *hammam* may, from a Western perspective, destroy British manliness. Supposed to foster effeminacy and indolence, the Turkish bath is stigmatised for perverting nature, for relegating private activities to the public sphere.

Because of the complexity of inputs deriving from the *hammam*, it is easy to think that both Swinburne and Beardsley relied heavily on the provocative power of this Oriental practice by transposing it into their textual and visual worlds. The aim of this chapter is to investigate how they recreated and extended the Oriental world of the *Arabian Nights* with its customs and traditions. Swinburne's and Beardsley's texts seem to lift Oriental characters, plots, settings and themes out of their original environment and place them into new blended spaces with the intent of provoking their readers by exposing their fears and anxieties.

'[T]o live as an Oriental': The Cognitive Prominence of Burton's Sensual East in Swinburne's Poems

Commonly known as a wild, outrageous and blasphemous poet, Swinburne was first and foremost a Pre-Raphaelite sympathiser and disciple who was initiated into the Brotherhood by D. G. Rossetti, with whom he took up residence at Tudor House on 24 October 1862. In this cultural milieu, Swinburne made the acquaintance of Burton,[7] with whom he later spent a wonderful holiday in Vichy (France), where they used to make excursions in the countryside. As reported by Edward Rice, they 'went hiking, climbed various peaks, and sat with their feet swinging into formidable abysses. By dusk both would be exhausted, Swinburne by his natural frailty and Burton from his long years of hard living and his advancing age' (2001: 507).

It was all the more evident that Swinburne was completely dependent on Burton's Byronic personality. Burton's first contact with the East was when he served in the army of the British East India Company from 1842 to 1853. After seven years in India, where he studied

Hindu culture and Muslim customs and behaviours, Burton crossed the Arabian Peninsula disguised as an Arab in order to embark on a pilgrimage from Alexandria to Mecca.

But it was in 1885, when Burton's ten-volume edition of the *Arabian Nights* was published, that Swinburne publicly aligned himself with Burton's literary interests. Swinburne's response to Burton's work was such that he celebrated it as the most faithful translation of the *Arabian Nights*, imbued with what he calls 'all that glorious orient glow[ing] / defiant of the dusk' ('To Sir Richard F. Burton: On His Translation of "The Arabian Nights"', ll. 11–12). Swinburne, like Borges, praised Burton's translation for its cultural weight, despite the intricacies of his language, which was characterised by archaic and forgotten words. In Irwin's words, 'the range of vocabulary is wider and stranger than Payne's, lurching between the erudite and the plain earthy, so that Harun al-Rashid and Sinbad walk and talk in a linguistic Never Never Land' (2004: 31).

Lauded by Borges too as the best of the English translations of the *Arabian Nights*, Burton's edition appears to be a blended space mixing different styles: 'the hard obscenity of John Donne, the gigantic vocabulary of Shakespeare [and] Swinburne's tendency to archaism' (Borges 1981: 74). Burton's translation changed the way readers saw the *Arabian Nights* and how they conceptualised the Orient, and was regarded not simply as a cultural translation of the Muslims' customs but also as a challenge to a set of Victorian values.

From a cognitive perspective and at a parabolic level, Burton's translation is a blend of other translations, of Antoine Galland's and John Payne's earlier versions, allowing new insights to appear and a new understanding to be formed of the elements of the input spaces (that is, the translations by Galland and Payne). Seen as a blended space, as a 'complete new work of literature' (Mondschein 2011: xvi), Burton's version allows readers to apply inferences, arguments, concepts and emotions back into the input space in order to alter their own original cognitive model.

Published in *The Athenaeum* in 1886, 'To Sir Richard F. Burton: On His Translation of "The Arabian Nights"' is a luminous poem, imbued with solar and stellar images, projecting the conceptual metaphor THE ORIENT IS LIGHT, as exemplified by such phrases as 'glorious orient' and 'splendour as of orient spears', locative adverbials ('westward', 'eastward' and 'toward kindling star') and verbs of movement ('the sun skins' and 'the sundawn breaks') that activate spatial metaphors underlying mental spaces.

If the 'meaning' of a literary work can be found in the minds of readers, configured there partly from readerly processes and individual experiences, then the meaning of Swinburne's lines can be found in the epistemic world created in the poem, revealing the truth about the explorer and translator, defined as 'he that hearkens eastward [and who] hears / Bright music from the world where shadows are. / Where shadows are not shadows' (258: ll. 7–9). Such a description of Burton as an Orientalist of extraordinary sensitivity and capacities, able to decode the sensual signs of the East, its stars, sundawn, music and shadows, confirms Swinburne's view of Burton as an immortal being endowed with 'the jaw of a devil and the brow of a god' (qtd in McMichael Nurse 2010: 115).

If the explorer is able to hear 'bright music' from the East, a world believed to be inhabited by shadows, then the translator is endowed with the power of words, which reveal the truth about the Eastern world. Behind the metonymic line 'Where shadows are not shadows' there lies Swinburne's attempt at exalting Burton's anthropological approach to the Orient, and his interest in Muslims as human beings with their own customs and traditions.

As an exemplary poem of Swinburne's aesthetics, 'To Sir Richard F. Burton: On His Translation of "The Arabian Nights"' is characterised by what Swinburne called 'the identity of contraries [. . .] the latent relations of pain and pleasure, the subtle conspiracies of good with evil, the deep alliances of death and life, of love and hate' (455). As demonstrated by the first stanza, the West exists in accordance with the East, in a relation of cyclical alternation, of life and death:

> Westward the sun sinks, grave and glad; but far
>   Eastward, with laughter and tempestuous tears,
>   Cloud, rain, and splendour as of orient spears,
> Keen as the sea's thrill toward a kindling star,
> The sundawn breaks the barren twilight's bar   5
>   And fires the mist and slays it. Years on years
>   Vanish, but he that hearkens eastward hears
> Bright music from the world where shadows are.

If the sun sinks westward, then the sundawn breaks eastward with the immense power of light that 'fires the mist and slays it' (l. 6). Thanks to such binary world-builders as westward versus eastward, twilight versus sundawn, our twilight land versus glorious Orient, Swinburne builds a dualistic world characterised by epistemic sub-worlds: that is, East and West as envisioned in the concluding lines emphasising the power of Oriental love. In such lines as 'but all the heaven is all one rose, / Whence laughing love dissolves her frosts and snows' (ll. 13–14), there is a metaphorical reference to the desert rose, a flowering plant native to the Arabian Peninsula, which is able to grow in the seemingly most barren landscapes. This glorious Eastern icon of love is employed by Swinburne to suggest a universal truth: to see the world in a grain of sand, in a desert rose that reunites East and West under the same heaven. From this perspective, Swinburne's poem seems to suggest a kind of corporeal and sensual Orientalism, a kind of love that is able to dissolve the 'frosts and snows' of the Western world.

Likewise, the poem entitled 'On the Death of Richard Burton' (1890), Swinburne's farewell to his beloved friend, represents a dualistic world of life and death projecting the conceptual metaphor LIFE IS THE SHADOW OF TIME. In Swinburne's view, the line that separates life from death is almost invisible, since 'life may vanish in death' (l. 15). Burton is celebrated as an outcast 'who found not on earth his kin' (l. 4), an in-between figure lurking between night and day because his death occurred at midnight.

Burton died from a heart attack in Trieste on 19 October 1890. On that day he was engaged on the last page of the twentieth chapter of *The Scented Garden*. In order to show how unexpected his death was, his biographer Thomas Wright reports the sentence Burton addressed to his wife: 'To-morrow I shall have finished it and then I will begin our biography' (1906: 94). Swinburne describes his friend as a 'living soul' among 'heartless souls', a man rich in vitality ('alive with a life more clear') and endowed with a vision ('clear-eyed'), with whom he shared ideas and experiences. In the fifth stanza, the narrative voice shifts from the more impersonal third-person singular to the more inclusive first-person plural:

> But not for us is the past a dream
> Wherefrom, as light from a clouded stream,
>   Faith fades and shivers and ebbs away,
> Faint as the moon if the sundawn gleam.   (ll. 17–20)

In this poem, we can project the deictic centre – that is, the speaker, and place and time of utterance – that says 'one' in the fourth line, and then projects the viewpoint of the heartless souls within the narrative speech. Then the poem projects another embedded deictic centre describing life, faith and England, in order to understand that 'us' and 'him' refer, respectively, to Swinburne's and Burton's friends and to Burton himself.

We can follow three different persons (Burton, the heartless people and Swinburne) and three different entities (life, faith and England), as well as one place (here) and three different times (present, past and metaphorical time): the day of Burton's death, the time in which Burton was alive, and the deictic projection to the metaphorical time of life, faith and England.

All of the locative expressions follow the deictic centre in each case: 'wherein' (l. 1) is spatially related to Burton's dead body; 'here' (ll. 6, 38) is understood relative to the earth, inhabited by heartless souls, as well as to the world in which Burton is considered the bravest; and 'from afar or near' indicates the resonance of Burton's genius. However, the deictic elements of Swinburne's poem go beyond person, place and time. There is a relational aspect to the participants within the text, in terms of how they are metaphorically related to each other, and how each deictic centre seems to regard the other participants. This is a matter of deixis in the sense that characters in a scenario are anchored not absolutely but in relation to each other. For example, the poet calls Burton 'one who found not on earth his kin', 'a living soul', 'boldest born of the bravest' and 'a wider soul than the world was wide', summarising him by his roles rather than by his personal name, which appears only at line 50.

Swinburne uses certain metaphorical expressions like LIFE IS THE SHADOW OF TIME, FAITH IS THE MOON, FAITH IS A TREE, ENGLAND HAS ITS STARS and BURTON IS LIGHT to encode his feelings towards the other man, whose fame is connoted in luminous terms. There are expressions of evaluation of Burton the bold, the brave and the bright that make it clear how much Swinburne admired him, setting him in turn into a fame hierarchy with respect to Raleigh: 'A fame outshining [England's] Raleigh's fame, / A light that lightens her loud sea's rim' (ll. 47–8). There is also a stellar deictic dimension to be considered. The poem draws attention to Burton as a luminous figure in a variety of ways. The poem inscribes the light of stars and refers to the 'light', its flame and gleam, and ends with the simile 'as dawn on a tideless sea', creating a parallel between Burton and the light of the rising sun, which is the star at the centre of the solar system.

It can be argued that, unlike 'To Sir Richard F. Burton', which is a prototypical example of a sonnet, 'On the Death of Richard Burton' represents in its form a celebration of Burton's vision of the Orient. The latter is formally an Oriental poem, since it appears as a series of quatrains following the Rubáiyát stanza (*aaba*) with a few changes in the rhyming scheme. As already used in 'Laus Veneris', the rhyme scheme of the Rubáiyát stanza is maintained but the third line of each stanza rhymes with the first, second and fourth lines of the following stanza (*aaba, bbcb, ccdc* and so on). Swinburne's fascination with the *Rubáiyát* is summarised in his *Studies in Prose and Poetry*: 'every quatrain [. . .] is [. . .] the sublimation of elegance, the apotheosis of distinction, the transfiguration of grace' (Swinburne 1894: 105). Other Pre-Raphaelites, such as Ruskin,[8] Morris[9] and Burne-Jones, deeply admired the *Rubáiyát*, a collection of sceptical and hedonistic poems by Omar Khayyám, a Persian poet, mathematician and astronomer, whose verse was propagated by Edward FitzGerald. It is no coincidence that in 1880 Burton published his best original poetry, *The Kasidah*, written under a pseudonym and patterned after the *Rubáiyát of Omar Khayyám*. Thus, the Orientalism of form in Swinburne's poem is matched by the kind of personal Orientalism envisioned by Burton, who, in Said's words, was 'able to live as an Oriental' (1977: 196) by 'shak[ing] himself loose of his European origins' (196).

Like Burton, Swinburne envisioned the East as a sexual dimension inhabited by Aholibah, Cleopatra, Myrrha, Amestris and many others, royal female representatives of the strongly sensual, even pornographic, content of the *Arabian Nights* and Eastern erotic manuals. The 'master of literary imitation', as Riede calls Swinburne (1978: 85), seems to restructure the Oriental erotic schemas by perverting the sensual and direct nature of the Arabian tales in *The Masque of Queen Bersabe* (1860). The latter is a miracle play, whose eponymous Persian female protagonist, wife of Uriah (whom King David caused to be murdered in order to be able to marry Bersabe himself), is the object of desire for a multitude of men who are hypnotised by her 'goodly body bare' (253: l. 394).[10] This adulterous queen activates the process of desire through the exhibition of her flowing hair: in Elisabeth Gitter's words, 'the more abundant the hair, the more potent the sexual invitation' (1984: 938).

Originally addressed to an all-male audience, as attested to by Irwin (2004: 160), the *Arabian Nights* are characterised by a frame story in which the two kings Shahriyar and Shahzaman discover that their wives are adulterous. Similarly to this libertine vision of the East, Queen Bersabe seems to embody the Oriental adulteress, a plot-mover whose story of seduction projects a conceptual metaphor like the EAST IS SEXUAL FREEDOM. King David derives great pleasure and sexual excitement from observing Bersabe's long, abundant hair, falling down to her feet, 'round her lap and round her knee / Even to her small soft feet / Shod now with crimson royally / And covered with clean gold' (*The Masque of Queen Bersabe*, ll. 96–100).

But the most sensual moment of this celebration of sex occurs when David voyeuristically observes Bersabe bathing herself in the water in which her bodily beauty is entirely externalised; this is an echo of the Muslim public baths (*hammam*) and recalls Scheherazade's bath, surrounded by wax candles, fruit and food, on the fifty-ninth night. As already mentioned earlier in this chapter, Scheherazade's beauty is characterised by solar brightness, distributed all over her body and conferring cognitive prominence on her. Likewise, Bersabe's body is described as 'waxen white' (236: l. 416) and its brightness becomes the determinant of her prominence, as attested to by the male observer:

> With all her body waxen white
> I woxe nigh blind to see the light
> Shed out of it to left and right;
> This bitter sin from that sweet sight
>   Between us twain began.   (ll. 416–20)

In this conceptual structure, the trajector is the light that traces a path from an initial position (from the left side of the female body) to a final resting position (the right side of Bersabe's body). This image schema underlines many concepts involving not only movement (the shedding of light on Bersabe's white body) but also sin (voyeurism) and Oriental sensuality. Essentially, the figure becomes part of the ground (the bath). In the poem, the first example in which the trajector and landmark are realised is at lines 417–18 ('the light / Shed out of it to left and right'), in which the light trajector is moving towards its landmark: that is, the female body. Exactly like Scheherazade and Dunyazad, who are described as 'moons, bending and leaning from side to side in their beauty and loveliness' ('The Tale of Scheherazade Concluded', 651), the figure of Bersabe becomes part of the ground due to her luminous white body.

Another very important trajector giving prominence to the figure of Bersabe is her hair, which not only functions as a towel, drying her wet body, but also takes the form of a 'drawing net' (l. 405), decorating her body with a sensual tattoo. This is an image contained within the domain of Oriental sensuality, an image of an action chain in which a trajector (hair) moves along an existing path: that is, the sensual curves of Bersabe's body. Similar to Scheherazade, who 'veiled her face with her hair like a chin veil' ('The Tale of Scheherazade

Concluded', 652), Bersabe dries her body 'with her owen hair' (l. 395). Furthermore, the eroticism lurking within Bersabe's apparently innocent body care involves the production of a juncture between two surfaces: the place where naked flesh meets a garment is the focus of erotic pleasure.

To put it in Barthes's words, 'A naked body is less erotic than the spot "where the garment leaves gaps"' (qtd in Culler 1983: 99). The sweet sight of transparencies excites King David's mind, in the same way as Scheherazade's veiled body ('Enveils her hips the blackness of her hair – / Beware of curls that bite with viper bite!', Mondschein 2011: 653) excites the two kings Shahriyar and Shahzaman, whose minds remain fixed on the idea of sin. Bersabe's hair, as Anne Hollander observes, 'displays some of the false, drapery-like qualities of Botticelli's hair, in having an extravagant existence separate from the face and head, like a lowering heavy turban when it is bound up' (1993: 73). Swinburne's beautiful unveiled infidel, like Flaubert's Kuchuk, Salambo and Salome, represents the prototype of carnal female temptation, a kind of corporeal Orientalism that may be summarised by the Queen of Sheba's words, 'Je ne suis pas une femme, je suis un monde' (Flaubert 1913: 222).

Blending the Sacred and the Profane: Beardsley's Oriental Remediations of Pre-Raphaelite Art

Another sensual Orientalist who fell under the spell of Pre-Raphaelite artists is Aubrey Beardsley, the great admirer of D. G. Rossetti's female figures and of Morris's art of book design,[11] as well as of Burne-Jones's medieval style and androgynous males.[12] Defined by Snodgrass as a 'dandy of the grotesque' (1995), whose aim was to restructure previous works of art in parodic black-and-white drawings, Beardsley may be considered as the inventor of an original style imbued with a perverted form of Orientalism.

There are many examples of Pre-Raphaelite paintings that inspired Beardsley's satirical pen-and-ink drawings. Notably, Morris's *La Belle Iseult* (1858) is turned into Beardsley's *La Beale Isoud at Joyous Garden* (1893–4), and Burne-Jones's *King Cophetua and the Beggar Maid* (1884) is mockingly reproduced in a lithograph entitled *Ex-Libris by John Lumsden Propert* (1894). Likewise, the series of biblical paintings composed of Rossetti's *Ecce Ancilla Domini!* (1850), Burne-Jones's *The Annunciation* (1879) and William Holman Hunt's *Light of the World* (1854) are all fused together and refashioned with

Oriental decorations in *The Mysterious Rose Garden* (1895), the drawing that appeared in volume IV of *The Yellow Book*.

What distinguishes all the aforementioned parodic remediations of Pre-Raphaelite paintings is a disruptive mimicry, rebelling against Beardsley's artistic fathers. Even though Burne-Jones and Morris appreciated Beardsley's drawings, deeming them 'full of thought, poetry, and imagination' (Snodgrass 1995: 21), as well as his 'feeling for draperies' (Vallance 1898: 364), they encouraged him to improve his style by following some school of art. As a reaction against his mentors' critical comments, Beardsley seems to remediate the principles of Pre-Raphaelite art into satirical replicas aimed at distorting the very essence of Pre-Raphaelite beauty with Oriental eroticism. By way of illustration, the sensuality of Morris's *La Belle Iseult* is embellished with grotesque features in Beardsley's drawing, in which the female figure is wearing a huge white cloak decorated with the repeating pattern of stylised peacock feathers. Almost like a metamorphic witch strolling in her medieval walled garden, which is characterised by flame-like trees whose leaves decorate the horror-vacui borders, Beardsley's Iseult is eroticised through her curvilinear silhouette and the ripe fruit surrounding the figure. As Barbara Tepa Lupack's notes, 'the circular clasp of her cloak and the roundness of her bosom repeat the circular and sexual characteristics of the fruit that forms the border of the picture' (Lupack and Lupack 2008: 87).

Beardsley's pornographic remediation of Morris's *La Belle Iseult* appears to be a perversion of goodness, since his black-and-white drawing, aimed at illustrating, borrowing and repurposing the Pre-Raphaelite queen, is imbued with overt sexuality. In search of his own style for representing a world of nothingness (black) and silence (white), Beardsley becomes a remediator of Oriental schemas who sometimes remediates Pre-Raphaelite works of art so aggressively that they may lose much of their cultural significance. Focusing on Orientalising the West and de-Orientalising the East, Beardsley carries out an actual change in the very categories of Oriental schemas. Thus his restructuring involves more than merely an addition or minor modification to bring Oriental categories in congruence with his revolutionary demands. His schema creation allows for new interpretations of Western knowledge of the East.

In *La Beale Isoud at Joyous Garden* the viewer may detect Oriental abstract decorations such as the flame-like leaves decorating the borders and the geometric platform with a sundial standing in the middle of the garden. If the unnaturally bent and convoluted leaves epitomise Tristan's and Isoud's burning passion, which ultimately leads them to death, then the Babylonian sundial, encircled with flowers and throwing no light on to the dial plate, recalls a tombstone. According to the legend, Isoud arrives in Brittany only moments too late to save Tristan, who dies in despair at the false news that Isoud is not coming to see him. From this perspective, Oriental variables are introduced in a Western scenario through the process known as *schema adding* or *accretion*, aiming to Orientalise a medieval Western legend.

Likewise, Burne-Jones's *King Cophetua and the Beggar Maid* appears to be restructured in *Ex-Libris by John Lumsden Propert*, in which a timid *pierrot* is kneeling at the feet of a *femme fatale*, whose voluminous black robe occupies almost half of the drawing. Following Bolter and Grusin's theory of remediation, Beardsley seems to start a conscious interplay between media because his grotesque remediation of Burne-Jones's painting can be considered an act of mediation that depends on Burne-Jones's act of mediation.[13] By taking property from one medium (painting) and reusing it in another (drawing), Beardsley, in his drawing for the bookplate of John Lumsden Propert,[14] intends to disempower the masculinity of King Cophetua and pervert the pure and humble Pre-Raphaelite maid. A gigantic and sullen-looking dark lady, far from resembling the pretty and delicate beggar maid, remediates her predecessor by trying to subvert the older version entirely, so that the discontinuities between the two are maximised. However, the new medium remains dependent on the older one in parodic ways.

If the implicit, and sometimes explicit, goal of remediation is to refashion or rehabilitate other media, then *The Mysterious Rose Garden* appears to be an innovative form of remediation. Following the rhetoric of remediation, which claims that a new medium makes a good thing even better, in terms of immediacy and hypermediacy, than its predecessor, the female subject in *The Mysterious Rose Garden* is the result of a succession of grotesque relationships with various female figures in different media: that is, three paintings reproducing the Annunciation and the Temptation of Eve. By blending the sacred and the profane, Beardsley aims to achieve an immediacy of representation by combining biblical, pagan and Oriental traditions. This multicultural form of remediation is also confirmed by Stanley Weintraub, who maintains that 'Beardsley's unusual creatures [are] borrowed from several cultures' (2000: 29).

Like Rossetti, the *pasticheur* who mixed together Western and Oriental categories, Beardsley places no limit on the number of cultural spaces that can be set up in the course of blending. In the latter's mind, multiple paintings can be related to each other and integrated into a single conceptual network through the construction of a blended and grotesque space. Through a strange sense of fusion between different conceptual domains, Beardsley is able to refashion an older medium and make the viewer reflect on the vices of society.

Beardsley scandalously combines ANNUNCIATION with TEMPTATION and, in terms of conceptual metaphor theory, combines three different mappings. On the one hand, there is a mapping from Rossetti's and Burne-Jones's painterly reproductions of the Annunciation on to Beardsley's naked Eve. On the other hand, there is a mapping from Hunt's Christ holding the lamp of redemption, as featured in *The Light of the World*, on to Beardsley's Satan carrying the lamp of sin and tempting those looking at him. The two mappings seem to be fused together in a single image whose blasphemies are visually reiterated in the naked body of Eve, who appears to be pregnant, and even more so in the satanic version of Hunt's Christ. This pagan seducer wearing winged sandals may be identified not only with Hermes, the messenger of the pagan gods and patron of liars, but also with a satanic Japanese figure of temptation through his kimono-like robe whose lower edge is on fire. In particular, Beardsley's effeminate corrupter, with long, flowing hair and curling moustache, recalls James Abbott McNeill Whistler, whose notorious moustache gave him a devilish appearance.

In my own view, Japanese art had a huge impact on Beardsley's *The Mysterious Rose Garden*, as exemplified by the rose trellis in the background that seems to echo Kitagawa Utamaro's *Teahouse Maidens Under a Wisteria Trellis* (1795), as well as other Utamaro prints representing young women wearing kimonos decorated with flower patterns. In Weintraub's words, 'Aubrey began to seek out Japanese art wherever he could find it, and experimented with a personal amalgam of Burne-Jones and Utamaro' (2000: 22).

From this perspective, a fourth mapping takes place, from Utamaro's erotic domain on to Beardsley's grotesque one. Interestingly, Beardsley decorated his bedroom with Utamaro prints and, as reported by Patrick Bade, owned 'the finest and most explicitly erotic Japanese prints in London' (2001: 57). Therefore, the lighted lantern is a visual reminder of sin, not only illuminating the innocent's path to sin but also attracting men to the pleasures of sex, in the same way as Utamaro's lighted lanterns in *Teahouse Maidens Under a Wisteria Trellis* are aimed at illuminating the charming Japanese courtesans waiting for their clients. This blending mode is summarised by Crane, who recalls how Beardsley had 'a strong

mediaeval decorative feeling, mixed with a curious weird Japanese
like spirit of *diablerie* and grotesque' (Crane 2014: 221).

Mapping from Oriental Text Worlds: A Conceptual Metaphor Analysis of Beardsley's *Under the Hill* and Illustrations for *Ali Baba*

Beardsley's Orientalism became all the more evident with his illustrations of Wilde's *Salome*, ten full-page drawings and a cover design
that remediated Wilde's Byzantine play in the form of Japanese
drawings. Between 1893 and 1895, Beardsley experimented with
Japanese eroticism, blending together the abstract decorations of
Islamic places with Japanese representations of fashionable women
in the Whistlerian manner.

The Peacock Room at the London town house of Frederick Ley-
land, decorated by Whistler in 1876, represented to Beardsley the
perfect blending of English and Japanese styles, his artistic mind
becoming obsessed with the peacock motif, which he finely reproduced in *The Peacock Skirt* (1892) and *The Black Cape* (1894). The
latter are Oriental blended spaces in which the Far East is combined
with the Middle East, in that Japanese female sensuality is foregrounded through Byzantine atmospheres. In R. A. Walker's words,
'the concern of Beardsley was not to create an illusion of reality, but,
like the Eastern artist, to make a beautiful design or pattern within
a given space' (1948: 54).

Of all the illustrations for Wilde's play, the first version of *The
Toilet of Salome* is considered to be the most scandalous of the series
because of the exposed nudity of Salome, who is surrounded by
naked attendants and phallic furniture. Like the bookplate for John
Lumsden Propert, the first version of *The Toilet of Salome* seems to
de-Orientalise the scene that precedes the dance of the seven veils.
Instead of an Oriental *coiffeur*, Salome's closet figures a masked *pierrot*, causing cognitive embarrassment to the viewer who does not
expect to see such a stock pantomime character in a biblical story.

It is only the decorative objects, such as teapot and cups, vases,
perfume bottles, cosmetic boxes and a hexagonal stool, that reveal
their Oriental origins through their highly elaborated design. The
blending of contemporary Western design and Oriental patterns is
all the more evident in the Art Nouveau dressing table, on which
Oriental decorative objects are exhibited. As visual reminders of Orientalism, projecting the conceptual metaphor EAST IS DECORATIVE

ARTS, perfumes, bottles and vases are located on the upper and lower bookshelves.

Sexuality is visualised everywhere in the drawing, not only in the naked bodies of Salome and her attendants but also in the books stocked on the middle shelf of the dressing table. Among the naked or semi-naked Oriental figures there are books from Western culture, such as Baudelaire's *Fleurs du Mal* (1857) and Zola's *La Terre* (1887), some of the most sexually explicit writings of the nineteenth century.

Obsessed with female toilet scenes, Beardsley, 'the only artist who knows what the dance of seven veils is' (Hart-Davis 1962: 348), seems to take inspiration from the Oriental sensuality of the *Arabian Nights*. Evidence of his indebtedness to the *hammam*-bath scenes depicted in 'The Second Kalandar's Tale' and 'The Tale of Scheherazade Concluded' can be found in *Under the Hill* and 'The Ballad of a Barber'.

Defined as 'the most exotic of all Beardsley's hot-house growths' (Weintraub 2000: 165), *Under the Hill* is an unfinished and fragmentary erotic tale combining picture and prose. By remediating the legend of Tannhäuser into visual and verbal media, Beardsley grotesquely refashions the older story entirely, while still marking its presence and therefore maintaining a sense of multiplicity. Despite its rococo style, *Under the Hill* is a blended space in which cultures collide in what Bernard Muddiman has termed settings 'unrolled before us like priceless tapestries' (1921: 32). Apart from the attested influences of Wilde, Max Beerbohm, Laforgue and Wagner, *Under the Hill* and, in particular, 'The Toilet of Helen' are imbued with Orientalism.

Japanese sculptures, eyes and dogs are mentioned in the story of the Abbé Fanfreluche, a handsome knight who, after many wanderings, finds the Venusberg. The portal to the kingdom of Venus is carved with loving sculptures, which 'surpassed all that Japan has ever pictured from her maisons vertes' (Beardsley 1974: 8). In the same Japanese vein, Sporion, the protagonist of 'The Bacchanals of Sporion', the book found by the Abbé in Venus's library, is endowed with Japanese eyes. And when Venus and the Chevalier enter De La Pine's studio, they start admiring a little canvas representing a lady in white frock, at whose feet lies a tiny Japanese dog.

It is, however, the chapter entitled 'Of the Manner in Which Venus was Coiffed and Prepared for Supper' that best represents the Orientalism of the *Arabian Nights*. Beardsley's Venus, extravagantly renamed Helen,[15] is depicted in both words and images as surrounded

by many attendants, pageboys and manicurists, helping her to pre-
pare for supper. A similar toilet scene is found in the *Arabian Nights*,
when Scheherazade enters the *hammam*, which has been perfumed
by eunuchs with rose-water and willow-flowers and where slave-girls
play musical instruments:

> Then the eunuchs went forth, that they might perfume the Hammam for
> the brides, so they scented it with rose-water and willow-flower water
> and pods of musk and fumigated it with Kakili eagle-wood and amber-
> gris. ('The Tale of Scheherazade Concluded', 651)

Of all the figures inhabiting the hill of Venus, the coiffeur Cosmé,
who is looking after Helen's *chevelure*, is visually the most Oriental character in the drawing. Gifted with a skilled expertise in hair
styling, Cosmé is able to make 'delicious intelligent curls that fell
as lightly as a breath about her forehead and over the eye-brows,
and clustered like tendrils round her neck' (Beardsley 1974: 14).
If Salome's *coiffeur* is a masked *pierrot* figure de-Orientalising the
scene, then Helen's *coiffeur* becomes an Oriental veiled lady, covered
from head to foot with a black robe that recalls a *burka*, the Islamic
women's garment. The *coiffeur* is the most mysterious and Oriental
figure of the scene, in which Helen's white body chromatically con-
trasts with the blackness of her attendant's robe. From this perspective, black-veiled Eastern femininity is contrasted with white naked
Western beauty, as if to crystallise the cultural differences between
East and West.

But aesthetic similarities can be found between Scheherazade and
Helen, who are both connoted for their luminous bodies. As already
emphasised, Scheherazade achieves cognitive prominence for her
bright complexion, 'brighter than the sun and the moon' ('The Tale
of Scheherazade Concluded', 651), and Helen is likewise metonymi-
cally described for her naked beauty, and for her neck, shoulders,
breasts, arms, hands and legs: 'Never before had Helen been so radiant and compelling' (Beardsley 1974: 17). Scheherazade's and Helen's
private toilet activities become disproportionately significant to the
attendants and the viewers, who share the pleasure of exhibiting the
body in public. The smallest features of their bodily beauty are seen
as small yet prominent items that attract attention and become the
focus, creating proximity and intimacy. The latter provide much of
the texture of these texts, which prototypically involve face-to-face
discourse participants.

Like Scheherazade and her attendants, Helen and her favourite boys and girls construct a text world of erotic sensuality. Figure 2.1 illustrates the text world elements of both texts, revealing a similarity in terms of world-building elements and function-advancing propositions.

World-builders	*Arabian Nights*	*Under the Hill*
Time	Before supper	Before supper
Location	*Hammam*-bath: 'When they came forth of the *hammam* bath, they donned raiment and ornaments'	Toilet: 'Before a toilet that shone like the altar of Notre Dame des Victoires, Helen was seated in a little dressing-gown'
Characters	Scheherazade, her sister, eunuchs and slave-girls	Helen, Cosmé, favourite girls, favourite boys, dwarves, doubtful creatures, Mrs Marsuple, the manicurist
Objects	Rose-water, willow-flowers, dresses, jewels, candelabra	Slippers, gloves, frock, jewels, flowers, sweets

Figure 2.1 Text world elements in the *Arabian Nights* and *Under the Hill*.

The function-advancers in both texts are propositions propelling the sensual dynamic within the text worlds. Any actions and arguments are made in relation to Scheherazade, Helen and their embellishing garments. If Scheherazade is offered a great variety of dresses (seven dresses of surpassing beauty), then Helen may choose the most exquisite shoes from a range of all varied colours: grey, black, brown, white, rose, velvet, sea-green, red, silvery, ivory and so forth (Figure 2.2).

On the one hand, Scheherazade's attendants bring and display dresses; on the other hand, Helen's favourites bring trays of shoes. Both Scheherazade and Helen, who utter performative verbs (*request* and *command*), are intent on choosing the best garments to embellish their bodies in order to come 'forward swaying from side to side and coquettishly moving' ('The Tale of Scheherazade Concluded', 653) and to rise 'before the mirror in a flutter of frilled things' (Beardsley 1974: 30).

Function-advancing propositions in 'The Tale of Scheherazade Concluded'	*Function-advancing propositions in* 'Of the Manner in which Venus Was Coiffed and Prepared for Supper'
Dresses → 'Presently they brought forward Scheherazade and displayed her, for the first dress, in a red suit.'	Pantoufles → 'The tray was freighted with the most exquisite and shapely pantoufles, sufficient to make Cluny a place of naught.'
Dresses → 'Then they returned to Scheherazade and displayed her in the second dress, a suit of surpassing goodliness, and veiled her face with her hair like a chin veil.'	Pantoufles → 'there were shoes of grey and black and brown suède, of white silk and rose satin, and velvet and sarcenet.'

Figure 2.2 Function-advancing propositions in 'The Tale of Scheherazade Concluded' and 'Of the Manner in Which Venus Was Coiffed and Prepared for Supper'.

In such text worlds, based on hyperboles and metonymies, Scheherazade and Helen share the cult of bodily beauty, which, like the *Arabian Nights* and in particular 'The Second Kalandar's Tale'[16] and 'The Third Kalandar's Tale', must be celebrated before supper time. 'The Second Kalandar's Tale' is the story of a prince disguised as a lowly forester in the kingdom of one of his father's enemies. After twenty-five years of wandering, the Prince reaches a large palace, inhabited by a lady of extraordinary beauty who is being held captive by a hostile genie. Like Beardsley's Helen and the Abbé, the beautiful lady and the Prince soon become romantically involved, and after a sensual *hammam* scene recalling the erotic toilets of both Helen and the Abbé, the Arabian protagonists enjoy a talkative and exquisite supper.

> Hereat she was glad and, springing to her feet, seized my hand and carried me through an arched door-way to a Hammam-bath, a fair hall and richly decorate. I doffed my clothes, and she doffed hers; then we bathed and she washed me; and when this was done we left the bath, and she seated me by her side upon a high divan, and brought me sherbet scented with musk. When we felt cool after the bath, she set food before me and we ate and fell to talking; but presently she said to me, 'Lay thee down and take thy rest, for surely thou must be weary.' ('The Second Kalandar's Tale', 117)

This description exemplifies the intimacy and proximity of the characters experiencing the pleasures of bathing, toileting, dressing and eating. All function-advancing propositions describe the sensual scene, whose function-advancers express predications that are relational and descriptive, and others represent intimate actions and events:

> she → seized the kalandar's hand and carried him to a *hammam*-bath
> he → doffed his clothes
> she → doffed her clothes
> they → bathed and washed
> they → ate and talked

It is likely that Beardsley took inspiration from the *hammam* scenes in the *Arabian Nights* by perverting and eroticising the Islamic world-builders. A case in point is provided by the toilet of the Abbé Fanfreluche, depicted in Chapter VII and entitled 'How Tannhäuser Awakened and Took His Morning Ablutions in the Venusberg', which seems to rewrite grotesquely the *hammam* scene in 'The Third Kalandar's Tale'. The latter is the story of a prince who, after surviving a shipwreck, is carried off and deposited by a giant bird at a strange castle, where he lives with forty beautiful young ladies. All world-builders (time, location, characters and objects) and relational predications and material actions that can be found in 'The Third Kalandar's Tale' are remediated by Beardsley in his visual and narrative text world by refashioning and perverting the original text world. Defined as a 'triumph of excess' (Weintraub 2000: 171), *Under the Hill* is a blending of eroticism, obscenity and perversity. Not only is Fanfreluche a parodic, effeminate version of the medieval knight Tannhäuser ('His hand, slim and gracious as La Marquise du Deffand's in the drawing by Carmontelle, played nervously about the gold hair that fell upon his shoulders like a finely-curled peruke'; Beardsley 1974: 25) but also he is the protagonist of perverted bath and toilet scenes recalling the sensual practices of the Turkish baths depicted in the *Arabian Nights*. This involves a mapping from two source text worlds – the Tannhäuser legend and the *Arabian Nights* – into a new blended and perverted text world. Figure 2.3 points out the similarities and differences between the world-builders in 'The Third Kalandar's Tale' and Chapter VII of *Under the Hill*.

The text world that is built in *Under the Hill* is more than simple predications ('those beautiful boys who stood ready with warm towels and perfume'; Beardsley 1974: 59), since all of these elements

World-builders	'The Third Kalandar's Tale'	'How Tannhäuser Awakened and Took His Morning Ablutions in the Venusberg'
Time	Morning	Morning
Location	*Hammam*-bath	Bathroom
Characters	Prince Agib, servants and handmaids	Abbé Fanfreluche, boys, barber and dressers
Objects	Trays, flowers, fruit, wine and robes	Towels, perfume and chocolate

Figure 2.3 World-builders in 'The Third Kalandar's Tale' and 'How Tannhäuser Awakened and Took His Morning Ablutions in the Venusberg'.

have been enriched by the reader's ongoing knowledge of the *Arabian Nights* and inferences that the reader draw from the bath scene. If Prince Agib is surrounded by beautiful handmaids who in turn spend the night with him, then Fanfreluche enjoys the company of beautiful boys who, while washing him and carrying out his toilet, perform 'quasi-amorous functions' (59). Agib's *hammam*-bath scene confirms the inherent patriarchal Oriental culture according to which women were subalternised in domestic spaces: '"This day thou art our lord and master, and we are thy servants and thy handmaids, so order us as thou wilt"' ('The Third Kalandar's Tale', 155).

The material actions performed by the Oriental damsels may be summarised as follows: they carry Agib to the bath; they bathe him; they dress him; they serve him food; and one of them has sexual intercourse with him —

> when it was morning, the damsels carried me to the Hammam-bath and bathed me and robed me in fairest apparel. Then they served up food, and we ate and drank and the cup went round till nightfall when I chose from among them one fair of form and face, soft-sided and a model of grace. ('The Third Kalandar's Tale', 156)

The same sequence of sensual actions seems to be repeated in *Under the Hill*, in which homosexual practices become the norm in the bath and toilet scenes. Instead of forty damsels, sumptuously dressed and ornamented, Beardsley describes beautiful boys jumping into the water and playing erotically with Fanfreluche. Like the Oriental damsels, the pageboys bathe Fanfreluche and one of them has sexual intercourse with him. Described as 'valets de bain' (1974: 59) and 'tried attendants' (59), the pageboys are turned into erotic performers who are able to dispel any sickness. After such sensual rites, Fanfreluche starts sipping chocolate while waiting for his morning toilet:

> After he had rested a little, and sipped his chocolate, he wandered into the dressing-room. Daucourt, his valet de chambre, Chenille, the perruquier and barber, and two charming young dressers, were awaiting him and ready with suggestions for the morning toilet. [. . .] The two dressers, under Daucourt's direction, did their work superbly, beautifully, leisurely, with an exquisite deference for the nude, and a really sensitive appreciation of the Chevalier's scrumptious torso. (60)

Beardsley's obsession with toilet scenes, as suggested by Allison Pease, is an 'evocation of the artificial beauty to which he aspires' (2000: 102). Firmly convinced that 'beauty is difficult' (Yeats's 'Upon a Dying Lady'; Yeats 1919), Beardsley mockingly reproduces the vanity of the Victorians in ridiculous toilet scenes whose ultimate representation is exemplified by 'The Ballad of a Barber' (1896). Seen as a parable of decadence, this poem projects the conceptual metaphor BEAUTY IS DEATH by blending together Eros and Thanatos in a story of fatal attraction. A demon barber, probably inspired by the ballad of Sweeney Todd, the barber of Fleet Street, is so ravished by the beauty of a princess of thirteen that he feels a sudden impulse to cut her throat with a smashed bottle of cologne.

Originally intended to form part of *Under the Hill*, the poem was published separately in *The Savoy* (July 1896), accompanied by an exquisite drawing characterised by concealed signs of Orientalism. All objects and figures are placed within the outline of an imaginary pyramid, at whose apex there is the figurine of the Virgin and Child on the sideboard in the background. The presence of these small religious statues, looking more Oriental than Occidental with their voluminous cape and pointed crowns, seems to leave no space for the visual representation of evil. Such a discrepancy between the verbal and the visual, between sex-crime and religious iconicity, and between fantasy and reality, confirms Beardsley's delight in scandalising the middle classes by blending together the sacred and the profane.

Like Rossetti's double works of art, combining different cultures into minor and major pictorial details, Beardsley's illustration appears to be a remediation of cultures, Art Nouveau furniture, and Oriental figurines and footstools. The Orientalism of Beardsley's ballad is all the more evident when compared with the *Arabian Nights*, and in particular with the tales narrated by the barber, whose brothers deserve punishment for their lust and foolishness. Published in July 1896, when Beardsley received a copy of Burton's *Arabian Nights* from Smithers, 'The Ballad of a Barber' seems to tune the violence and magic atmospheres of the *Barber* cycle and in particular of 'The Story of the Barber's Fourth Brother', in which a butcher is supposed to sell the meat of humans rather than that of sheep.

Like a malevolent sorcerer, holding 'a magic wand' (Beardsley 1921: 50, l. 23), the demon barber practises ritual magic, a method of casting a spell based on the performance of specific gestures and actions:

> Three times the barber curled a lock,
>   And thrice he straightened it again;
> And twice the irons scorched her frock,
>   And twice he stumbled in her train.   (ll. 46–9)

After this ritual, the barber commits an act of sexual violence against a young princess of delicate beauty, who seems to be a fantasy character because of her extremely long hair ('Her gold hair fell down to her feet'; l. 41), as well as because of her sweet and lyrical voice. The moment preceding the crime is characterised by uncanny events and inexplicable physical reactions:

> His fingers lost their cunning quite,
>   His ivory combs obeyed no more;
> Something or other dimmed his sight,
>   And moved mysteriously the floor.   (ll. 50–3)

The supernatural appears in an experience of limits, in a trance-like state that is the prelude to crime, characterised by the following function-advancing propositions:

> his fingers → lost their cunning
> his combs → obeyed no more
> something → dimmed his sight
> something → moved the floor.

The ultimate expression of Beardsley's Orientalism is exemplified by the drawing for the front cover design (1899) of a never-produced Smithers publication of *The Forty Thieves*. Similar to Ruskin's appropriation of the Arabian tale and its conceptual metaphors, with the aim of promoting new corn laws, Beardsley grotesquely remediates the figure of Ali Baba into a 'vast and impotent eunuch' (Zatlin 1990: 37), whose opulent jewels and exhibited obesity reveal a lust for wealth rather than sex. Firmly convinced that 'vice is terrible and it should be depicted' (Benkovitz 1981: 66), Beardsley seems to criticise the materialism and corruption of the nineteenth-century industrial middle class. All ornamental details – a black coat, a jewelled turban, an ornate belt with jewels, necklaces and bracelets – seem to remediate into images the happy ending of Ali Baba's story:

> Thus Ali Baba and his household lived all their lives in wealth and joyance in that city where erst he had been a pauper, and by the blessing of that secret treasure he rose to high degree and dignities. (Mondschein 2011: 431)

The excerpt projecting the conceptual metaphor WEALTH IS JOY is grotesquely perverted into a hyperbolic version of the robber, whose Whistlerian moustache and obese jewelled figure express the conceptual metaphor WEALTH IS CORRUPTION. Compared with another illustration for the abortive *Forty Thieves* entitled 'Ali Baba in the Wood' (1897), which represents the skinny protagonist hiding from the thieves, the front cover design perversely remediates the positive character of Ali Baba with the help of Japanese blacks and whites, and the obese silhouette of the figure whose almost naked flesh achieves visual prominence. Beardsley was completely satisfied with this drawing, which he described as 'a quite a sumptuous design' in a letter of 7 May 1897 to Marc André Raffalovich (Maas et al. 1970: 315). *The Forty Thieves* was conceived as a Christmas book, and the artist admitted to having great fun and deriving great pleasure from illustrating it.

The two very different illustrations demonstrate not only Beardsley's blending mode but also his stylistic evolution and search for perfection. As attested to by a letter of 6 July 1896 sent to Smithers, he was convinced that *The Forty Thieves* was 'his best choice' (Maas et al. 1970: 142), adding his intention of doing the pictures 'in a very superior *Mortedarthurian* manner' (142). The stylistic traits of the front cover confer prominence on the figure, which is differentiated from the white background through the contrast with the black coat and the highly elaborate jewels. Similarly, albeit with different effects, the figure of Ali Baba emerges from the black wood, achieving prominence through the whiteness of his ragged clothes.

To conclude, Swinburne and Beardsley appear to be the most original representatives of a corporeal Orientalism. Through a process of restructuring of Oriental schemas as envisioned in the *Arabian Nights*, they reshape, remediate and pervert the stories of Scheherazade, Ali Baba, the Kalandar and the Barber. As forms of aggressive and sensual remediations, Swinburne's and Beardsley's Oriental works throw the source text into relief, creating a new Oriental space concealing relationships with Arabian tales. A shared trait of corporeal Orientalism is exemplified by the exhibited and displayed nakedness of the characters, aimed at exciting the viewer, in *hammam*-bath scenes of the utmost eroticism. The obsession with water and all the ritual practices associated with cleaning and performing the toilet always derive from personal and autobiographical events.

As a 'sea-worshipper' (Rooksby 1997: 5), Swinburne relies on the aesthetic qualities of water, which emphasise female nudity in its ecstatic vision. The prominent role played by water is also demonstrated in a letter from Swinburne to his sister, in which he writes of the euphoria generated by being naked in the sea:

> I ran like a boy, tore off my clothes, and hurled myself into the water. And it was but for a few minutes – but I was in Heaven! The whole sea was literally golden as well as green – it was liquid and living sunlight in which one lived and moved and had one's being. And to feel that in deep water is to feel – as long as one is swimming out, if only a minute or two – as if one was in another world of life, and one far more glorious than even Dante ever dreamed of in his Paradise. (Lang 1959: V, 275)

The ecstasy felt by Swinburne in swimming off the coast of the Sussex Downs convinced the French philosopher and psychologist Gaston Bachelard to name the Swinburne complex after him.[18]

Likewise, Beardsley, who always worked indoors by artificial candlelight with his sister Mabel as his only model, was obsessed with personal care, good taste and fashion. As Sturgis observes, 'the demands of the toilet were always scrupulously observed; [. . .] he was spotlessly clean & well-groomed – one was impressed by his cleanliness' (1998: 97). His visitors and friends also recall that Beardsley used to 'dress with scrupulous care to be in the severest good taste and fashion' (Weintraub 2000: 85). If one of Beardsley's distinguishing characteristics was cleanliness, then it is likely that, due to his intimate relationship with his sister, he used to observe her while she was performing her toilet and dressing up. When Mable became a professional actress, Beardsley 'was to observe rather than participate' (15). Not only was Mabel the one who gave Beardsley his first lessons in sex but also she was his first model.

As suggested by B. Reade (1967), Malcolm Easton (1972) and Frank Harris (1963), Beardsley was engaged in an incestuous relationship with Mabel that resulted in an expected pregnancy. There are many examples of Mabel appearing disguised in the persons of the erotic women depicted in Beardsley's drawings (see Eve in *The Mysterious Garden*, the flagellant in the drawing for the frontispiece of John Davidson's *A Full and True Account of the Wonderful Mission of Earl Lavender*, the naked girl in the frontispiece to *Plays* by John Davidson and so forth).

Both Swinburne and Beardsley, keen readers of Burton's *Arabian Nights*, applied a blending of their own fleshly poetry and corporeal Orientalism, creating not just a new mental space but also a new sensual and perverted universe in their works. Sometimes Swinburne and Beardsley rely heavily on a single Arabian tale through a direct citation or through the transposition of plot into a different world and epoch. Sometimes they recreate and extend the same Arabian world, by undermining the ideology of the original. In any case, they lift characters, plots, settings and themes out of their original environments and place them into new blended spaces where an emergent structure develops independently. This is the mechanism by which, through erotic parables, Swinburne and Beardsley are able to alter our perspective on, knowledge of and way of thinking about the Eastern world.

Notes

1. All quotations from Swinburne's poems are taken from the Chatto & Windus edition (1904).
2. All quotations from 'The Tale of Scheherazade Concluded' are taken from Burton's translation of the *Arabian Nights*, edited by Ken Mondschein (2011).
3. Brown installed a Turkish bath at home, which he used on a daily basis.
4. As reported by Francis Spufford, Mrs Millais was obliged to take a steam treatment at the bathhouse owned by Captain Trelawny when they were both modelling for Millais's *The North-West Passage* (1874).
5. Burne-Jones used to visit the Turkish baths to recover his health and drew a few humorous sketches there (1880). See Christian 2011.
6. A Turkish bath was one of Ford's real luxuries. Many of his fictional characters experience this Oriental practice: Mr Todd in *Mr Apollo: A Just Possible Story* (1908), Mr Sorrell in *Ladies Whose Bright Eyes* (1911), Mr T. in *Women and Men* (1923) and so on.

7. On his return to London from the United States in 1865, Burton was invited to breakfast by Richard Monckton Milnes, an English poet, patron of literature and politician who became a personal friend. Among the guests were Algernon Swinburne and Coventry Patmore. For a critical insight into the life and work of Burton see Antosa (2013).

8. In the 1860s the *Rubáiyát* was still believed to be an original composition written in English by an anonymous author. On 2 September 1863, Ruskin, who was deeply impressed by those Oriental verses, wrote a letter of admiration that he entrusted to Burne-Jones, begging him to transmit it to the author of the *Rubáiyát*.

9. Among Morris's calligraphic masterpieces there is the *Rubáiyát of Omar Khayyám*, which he produced with illustrations by Burne-Jones in 1872.

10. All quotations from *The Masque of Queen Bersabe* are taken from the first volume of *The Poems of Algernon Charles Swinburne*, published by Chatto & Windus (1904).

11. In a letter to G. F. Scotson-Clark, Beardsley describes Morris's *The Earthly Paradise* as 'simply enchanting' (Maas et al. 1970: 25).

12. Beardsley's work has been defined as 'Burne-Jones with acid' (Lang 1975: xix).

13. Burne-Jones's *King Cophetua and the Beggar Maid* is the painterly reproduction of the legend of an African king who falls in love with a beggar.

14. John Lumsden Propert was a well-known doctor of medicine who proved to be an accomplished engraver, most notably producing etchings and reproductions of works by J. M. W. Turner.

15. The name Helen, of Greek origin, sounds more Oriental than the Roman name Venus.

16. All quotations from 'The Second Kalandar's Tale' and 'The Third Kalandar's Tale' are taken from the first volume of Burton's *The Book of the Thousand Nights and a Night* (1885).

17. Marc André Raffalovich (1864–1930) was a wealthy Russian who had become Beardsley's patron in April 1895 when the latter lost his post as art editor of *The Yellow Book*.

18. For a definition of the Swinburne complex see Bachelard (1991: 228).

The Cognitive Process of Parable: John Ruskin, William Morris and the Oriental Lure of the Forbidden

Projecting Parables of Poverty: Ruskin, Morris and the *Arabian Nights*

Along with other Pre-Raphaelite and Orientalist artists, John Ruskin and William Morris appear to sympathise with what Said calls 'the primitive simplicity' (Said 1977: 230) of the Asian people, revealing the same fellow feeling experienced by Karl Marx. Notably, with the theory of the Asiatic mode of production[1] dating back to the early 1850s, Marx investigated Asiatic village communities that were held in thrall by a despotic ruling class in charge of public works. Furthermore, Marx was firmly convinced that colonies were a form of 'primitive accumulation' (Marx 2007: 847). In his view, the beginnings of the conquest of India, as well as the exploitation and enslavement of Africans, are to be seen as the first attempts at capitalism, at what he defined as 'the dawn of the era of capitalist production' (823).

Almost a decade later, in 1859, Ruskin published *The Two Paths*, in which he depicted the Arabians and the Indians as savage people who none the less excelled in the decorative arts. According to him, as reported in the lecture 'The Unity of Art', 'the art whose end is pleasure only is pre-eminently the gift of cruel and savage nations, cruel in temper, savage in habits and conception' (Ruskin 1869: 66). As opposed to the producers of European art, whose motto is 'truth first and pleasure afterwards' (66), denoting thoughtful, sensitive and earnest men, the Arabians and the Indians are savage people exalting primitive drives like violence and pleasure.

Morris, who was well acquainted with the art of carpet-making and defined Persia as 'the mother of beautiful art' (Mackail 1995: 5), likewise opposed the rough work of the Asian tribes to the modern, hand-made Western carpets that, in his view, should equal the Oriental ones in terms of material and durability. The following words exemplify Morris's vision of Asian people and the decorative arts:

> The traditions of excellence of the Indian Carpets are only kept up by a few tasteful and energetic providers in England with infinite trouble and at a great expense [. . .] As for Persia, [. . .] nothing could mark the contrast between the past and the present clearer than the Carpets, doubtless picked for excellence of manufacture [. . .] we people of the West must make our own handmade Carpets, if we are to have any worth the labour and money such things cost; and these while they should equal the Eastern ones as nearly as they may be in material and durability, should by no means imitate them in design. (Mackail 1995: 5)

Similarly to Ruskin, Morris profoundly admired Indian and Persian carpets, characterised as they were by their excellence of manufacture that was the result of a hundred years' experience. Morris's invitation to emulate the Asian art of carpet-making by trying to find an original style in order to distinguish Western from Eastern hand-made products seems to echo Ruskin's fascination with Asian decorative arts.

Regarded as a highly innovative pattern-designer, Morris looked to the East, the land between the Tigris and Euphrates, for inspiration. In his lecture 'The History of Pattern Designing', delivered on 8 April 1879 to the Trades Guild of Learning at the Co-operative Institute in Oxford Street, London, he admits that, to him, 'Persia has become a holy land' (Morris 1910–15: 206) and that 'there is nothing to do but to imitate, and again to imitate, and to pick up what style the gods may give us' (217). Behind these words lies Morris's admiration for archaic, elaborate Byzantine art, which, according to him, contributed to the splendour and magnificence of Eastern art.

In Morris's view, Byzantium represents the utmost expression of civilisation, not only because of its unified culture celebrating the Church of the Holy Wisdom but also because of its majestic decorative motifs of the Tree of Life and the Holy Fire. Seen as 'the most meaningful and creative phase in the cyclical history of civilization' (McAlindon 1967: 309), Byzantium appears to be a conceptual metaphor to both Ruskin and Morris, blending together earth and fire, architecture and decoration, past and present.

If Morris is an enthusiastic admirer of Byzantine pattern motifs, then Ruskin, who devotes four chapters of *The Stones of Venice* (1851) to the Byzantine arch and capital, must be remembered for rediscovering its magnificent architecture. As J. B. Bullen says:

> [Ruskin's] lyrical, impassioned, almost erotic account of the view of San Marco from across the piazza [. . .] opened the eyes of thousands of readers to the beauty of Byzantine art and helped to place it securely in the history of post-classical architecture and culture. (Bullen 2006: 54)

Like Morris, who visited the baptistery of Ravenna in 1878 and insisted on preserving its beauties from ruin, as witnessed in a letter to the editor of *The Times* (9 June 1880, in Kelvin 1996: I), Ruskin started to appreciate Oriental art when he visited the surviving treasures of Italy's Byzantine heritage (the mosaics, paintings and sculpture in churches, palaces, catacombs, grottoes and museums from Milan and Venice). Both artists, as Dimitra Kotoula has summarised, 'were pioneers in teaching Victorian audiences to appreciate Gothic art and architecture' (2015: 78).

Ruskin was firmly convinced of the Arabic impact on Venetian architecture, as seen in the first volume of *The Stones of Venice*, in which he distinguishes two periods of influence: the Byzantine phase from the ninth to the eleventh centuries, and the transitional period after 1180 when the Arabs introduced exquisite refinements in the style called Arabesque. As Deborah Howard has suggested in her book on *Venice and the East: The Impact of the Islamic World on Venetian Architecture 1100–1500* (2000), Arabic and Venetian cultures are related by virtue of their savageness. The latter is not only the supreme quality of Venetian art, 'a [mental] element in many other healthy architectures [. . .] as in Byzantine' (Ruskin 1867: 172) but also the unfinished or unperfected nature of all animate things.

Cognitively speaking, both Ruskin and Morris describe the East as an imaginative container in which all conceptual metaphors associated with art and beauty flourish in the reader's mind. Following Lakoff (1993), the conceptual metaphor EAST IS MARVEL that is often referred to is simply one specialisation of what he calls the event structure metaphor, an interlocking set of very general metaphors such as STATES ARE LOCATIONS, CHANGES ARE MOVEMENTS, PURPOSES ARE DESTINATIONS and MEANS ARE PATHS. According to J. E. Grady (1999), there exists an underlying level of a very general metaphor such as EAST IS MARVEL that is called *primary metaphor*.

As exemplified by Ruskin's and Morris's works, the primary metaphor defining the very essence of the East is grounded in correlations of other metaphors such as EAST IS DECORATIVE ARTS, EAST IS SAVAGERY and EAST IS POVERTY.

Unlike Rossetti, Swinburne and Beardsley, who privileged the sensuousness of all Eastern experience, Ruskin and Morris were more concerned with the artistic and economic conditions of the Asian people. They were both amazed and concerned to see such a blending of superb artistry and abysmal poverty. If Marx's economic analyses demonstrate his sympathy for the misery of people from Asia, then Ruskin's and Morris's lectures, poetry and fiction are imbued with Oriental conceptual metaphors projecting the image of Asians as ordinary people dealing with extraordinary events.

It is not by chance that Ruskin and Morris were morbidly fascinated with Arabian stories of peasant and low life, always dealing with forbidden places and taboo objects. This is exemplified by Ruskin's rhetorical use of Oriental metaphors, inspired by the stories of 'The Fisherman and the Jinni', 'The Barber's Sixth Brother' and 'The Story of Aladdin, or, the Wonderful Lamp', which appear in his letters, lectures and novels.

Notably, Ruskin spent the winter of 1867–8 in Denmark Hill, South London, enjoying the company of many friends, among whom were Edward and Georgiana Burne-Jones. As reported by Lady Burne-Jones, Ruskin was an avid reader of Lane's *Arabian Nights* and in particular of the story of 'The Barber's Sixth Brother', for which 'he expressed great admiration' (Cook 2009: 143). The reiterated invocations of God by Shakalik, the brother of the title, who is the victim of terrible misfortunes such as bodily mutilation, destitution and exile, seem to amuse Ruskin and his guests:

> Edward read aloud, from Lane's *Arabian Nights*, the Story of the Barber, in which there is scarce a paragraph without some mention of God, the High, the Great, and at its conclusion Ruskin expressed great admiration for it. 'God forgive you, my child,' said a pitying voice from the fireside. (143)

As a story of a rise and fall, 'The Barber's Sixth Brother' projects the conceptual metaphors LIFE IS CRIME and LIFE IS POVERTY, as exemplified by the Arab robbers attacking and mutilating Shakalik, as well as by the invisible meal offered by the Barkamid family.

Such exclamations as 'by Allah! by Allah!' seem to characterise almost any utterance spoken by Shakalik and his wealthy host, who pretend to be eating all kinds of delicious food (white bread, *sikbaj*,[2] chickens stuffed with pistachio nuts, and different kinds of viands and *kataif*[3]) in an invisible banquet. The following excerpts show the use of these invocations:

> If thou desire, O my guest, to eat more, and to delight thyself with extraordinary dainties, by Allah! by Allah! remain not hungry. (Lane 1853: 169)

> By Allah, I will do to him a deed that shall make him repent before God of these actions! (169)

In order to punish his irreverent host for playing such a cruel game, Shakalik decides to feign drunkenness and assault the master of the house by landing a slap on his neck. It is probable that Ruskin admired this act of clever rebellion against the cruelty of wealthy people. Despite all the times God's name is taken in vain, provoking the moral reproach of Ruskin's mother ('God forgive you, my child'; Cook 2009: 143), 'The Barber's Sixth Brother' is a thought-provoking parable of poverty.

Through the process of parabolic projection, developed by Mark Turner in the 1990s, the story of Shakalik is magnified, helping us to make sense of the other stories. This projection, of one story on to another, is thus what is commonly known as a parable and is the basic cognitive ability that helps us to understand a broad range of communication. See, for example, Dickens's 'The Thousand and One Humbugs', published in *Household Words* during April and May 1855, whose narrative projection of the story of Shakalik is based on blending: that is, a cognitive notion whose operation is central to how parable works. The parable demands conceptual integration of the poor Arab into the general category of desperate people, among whom Shakalik becomes the prototype. From this perspective, Dickens, who uses the satirical device of the invisible meal in 'The Thousand and One Humbugs', seems to be operating a blending. A blending is a kind of meeting point between two conceptual structures, known as input spaces, which are mapped into generic spaces where shared information becomes evident.

As a form of political satire of aristocratic insolence, Dickens writes three articles entitled 'The Thousand and One Humbugs' in 1855. In the first of the articles, Dickens announces the discovery of a new Arabic manuscript whose stories seem to be a mocking echo of those in the *Arabian Nights*. The Sultan's Grand Vizier, Parmastoon (or Twirling Weathercock), seeks to alleviate his master's distress at his inability to find a suitable wife, by persuading him to listen to some legends told by the fair Hansardadade. The legend that seems to emulate 'The Barber's Sixth Brother' is 'The Talkative Barber', a mocking reference to Lord Palmerston, the Prime Minister, who embodied England's aristocratic governing class. In Dickens's words, Palmerston was 'the barber of mischief, the barber of sin, the barber of false pretence' (Dickens 1855: 314). The conceptual blending shown in Figure 3.1 illustrates the parable of poverty of Dickens's beggar, intentionally named Publeek, who desperately seeks asylum and food in a rich man's house.

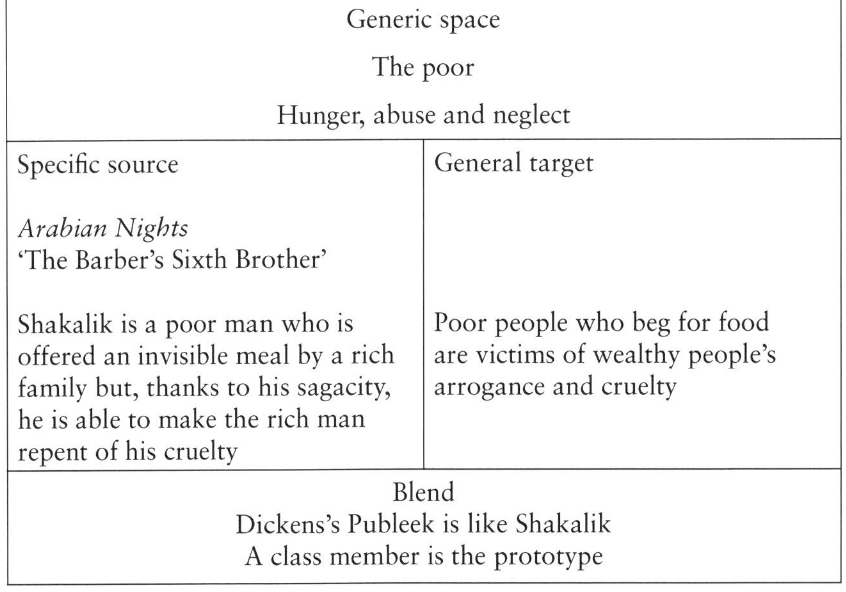

Figure 3.1 Conceptual blending network for Dickens's Publeek.

Information from the generic space of poor people includes hunger, abuse and neglect. The generic background informs the construction of Shakalik's story, which is of the utmost importance for conceptualising the parable of poverty. Indeed, we can see the blending of the generic with the specific if we consider Shakalik as a member of the poor category. In other words, the parable demands conceptual integration of Dickens's beggar into the general category of poor people and his specific situating among Shakalik, the prototype of that category.

Dickens's allegorical version of Shakalik's story is imbued with satirical references to British politics such as 'a smoking dish of Reefawm', 'Educational Kabobs' and 'the ragout, called Law-of-Partnership'. Unlike the happy ending of the Arabian story, in which Shakalik befriends the Barmakid family, Dickens's parable of poverty[4] ends in physical abuse and public punishment. Guld Publeek is humiliated by the rich barber Barmecide, who instructs his slaves to blacken Publeek's face, shave his beard and eyebrows and, last but not least, publicly expose him with the following inscription round his neck: 'This is the punishment of Guld Publeek who asked for nourishment and said he wanted it' (316).

As with Dickens's adaptation of 'The Barber's Sixth Brother', Ruskin, who was deeply concerned by the conditions in which the poor were living, believed that the life of the barber was a life worth living and had the same value as that of any other higher-class worker. In *Unto This Last* (1860), a book on anti-industrial utopianism comprised of five essays, which changed Gandhi's ideas about life,[5] Ruskin outlines his belief that 'The rich and the poor have met, God is their light' (1920: 63) by implying that the interaction between wealth and poverty is one of the laws of power interchange and that God, seen as the embodiment of justice, is able to illuminate their paths to salvation.

In the essay entitled 'Qui Judicatis Terram', Ruskin seems to take inspiration from the incipit of 'The Barber's Sixth Brother', narrating the story of a very rich man who inherited a hundred silver drachmas from his father. Like Ruskin's Jewish merchant, who 'made one of the largest fortunes of his time' (61) and left behind some general maxims on wealth and poverty, Shakalik's parable of poverty, begging and starvation provides a didactic message about justice. The moral lesson given by Shakalik, who pays back the outrageous behaviour of the powerful and rich Barmekis, is echoed in Ruskin's essay on what he calls 'the economics of justice' (1920: 82) because, according to him, 'People will be happy in so far as they learn to do justice and be righteous. All else is not only vain but leads straight to destruction' (83).

After taking into consideration the oppression, robbery and starvation of the poor, caused by vain and wicked wealthy people, Ruskin focuses on the laws of justice and the perils of enrichment that act as a curse, thereby poisoning all human intercourse. For this reason, the Arabian tale about a poor and hungry man who is welcomed by a rich family by offering him an invisible meal as a form of satirical mockery appealed so much to Ruskin, who appears to mention the Barber cycle and other tales in a few letters to Charles Eliot Norton.[6]

Of particular interest is the letter sent on 23 January 1872 to Norton, in which Ruskin reveals the pleasure he derives from reading the *Arabian Nights*. Not only do the stories please Ruskin, who is granted euphoria in moments of discomfort, but also his pleasure in reading extends to bliss when he happens to read exemplary stories of justice:

> I've been reading the *Arabian nights* again, with a little – the Caliph being able to hang forty Barmecides whenever he likes is balm to my wounded spirit. To be able to hang bad men – would be glorious, but to have power to hang good ones – if one was in the 'humour'. There – What a bliss! (Bradley and Ousby 1987: 255)

In the story of 'The Three Apples', Caliph Haroun Alraschid threatens to kill his grand vizier and forty other Persian nobles because of their failure to solve a mysterious murder. This story of crime and punishment becomes a text of bliss, satisfying Ruskin's deep need for justice. Defined as a 'balm to [his] wounded spirit', the story of the caliph who has the power to hang bad and good men is an exciting thought for Ruskin, whose sense of morality appears to be experiential: that is to say, acquired from direct experience of pain and pleasure.

According to Lakoff and Johnson, morality is the experience of emotions, of pain and pleasure, of praise and shame. Ruskin's blissful reaction to the parable of justice may be explained in cognitive terms, since morality is a feeling and part of the brain itself. As Lakoff and Johnson maintain, 'We may very well experience emotions in the same way we experience certain physical forces' (1999: 72). In Ruskin's case, the emotions he feels while reading these Arabian stories of justice range from pleasure to bliss, giving him physical comfort and soothing his pain, which is caused by the miserable conditions of the poor.

Tuning Oriental Schemas: Sinbad, Aladdin and Ruskin's Metaphorical Language

Another Arabian story that appealed to Ruskin's sense of morality is 'Sinbad the Sailor's Second Voyage', a tale that he clearly mentions in one of his lectures in *The Ethics of the Dust* ([1866] 1908a). Taking the form of ten dialogues between an old lecturer (Ruskin) and a group of twelve female students, *The Ethics of the Dust* blends together theatre and autobiography, deriving from Ruskin's experiences from 1859 to 1868 at the Winnington school (Cheshire), directed by Margaret Bell, whose liberal programme of education deeply interested him. Ruskin's interaction with nine-year-old girls is characterised by its theatrical hue, as reported by Georgiana Burne-Jones, who recalled girls clad in white dancing around Ruskin in the gallery. Likewise, Ruskin's dramatic speeches on the issue of education reveal a theatrical stance, as exemplified by his metaphorical language, whose Oriental lure is particularly evident in the first lecture, entitled 'The Valley of Diamonds'.

With Florrie, Isabel, May, Lily and Sibyl, Ruskin starts playing a rhetorical game of imagination inspired by 'Sinbad the Sailor's Second Voyage', one of the most famous stories in the *Arabian Nights*, which would have been familiar to the girls in both print and pantomime forms. After describing a real valley of diamonds 'covering the grass in showers every morning, instead of dew' ('The Valley of Diamonds', 1908a: 12), Ruskin starts to muse about the difference between reality and fancy. In a series of questions and answers about Sinbad's forbidden valley of diamonds, inhabited by huge and horrible snakes that emerge from the caverns by night, Ruskin tries to educate the girls from Winnington to resist such temptations as pride, lust, envy and anger. By blending reality with fancy and promising to tell the truth no more than 'the man who wrote the *Arabian Nights*' (13), Ruskin develops the pupils' rhetorical skills in narrating invented stories, parables of morality teaching to avoid the sins of the whole world. In Sharon Aronofsky Weltman's words, Ruskin 'breaks down the barriers between being and performing, between adult and child, between real and play' (2007: 77).

Through parabolic projection entailing other mental phenomena such as metonymy, metaphor and blending, Ruskin narrates his own version of the valley of diamonds, projecting the conceptual metaphors EAST IS MAGIC, EAST IS CORRUPTION and EAST IS SIN. The metonymic expressions of wealth – diamonds and gold – are constantly referred to as corruptors of human morality. As Ruskin explains:

> once fix your desire on anything useless, and all the purest pride and folly in your heart will mix with the desire, and make you at last wholly inhuman, a mere ugly lump of stomach and suckers, like a cuttle-fish. [. . .] So, the practical, immediate office of gold and diamonds is the multiplied destruction of souls, (in whatever sense you have been taught to understand that phrase); and the paralysis of wholesome human effort and thought on the face of God's earth [. . .] . (Ruskin 1908a: 19–20)

If the girls were initially craving possession of the diamonds that Sinbad was able to take up from the forbidden valley full of horrible snakes, then they all become eager to know something more about the origin of diamonds, about the fatal dust of glittering minerals. Seen as 'the worst enemies of mankind, the strongest of all malignant physical powers that have tormented our race' (18), diamonds are metaphorically imbued with a moral lesson. Unlike the story of Sinbad, who bestows large sums of money on the poor, Ruskin's lecture projects the conceptual metaphors DIAMONDS ARE CORRUPTION, since they have corrupted the souls of any civilised nation.

Interestingly, Ruskin's version of Sinbad's valley of diamonds becomes a blended space in which serpents and snakes – the most fearsome Oriental beasts, perceived as dangerous throughout the *Arabian Nights* – become singing animals, whose delightful melodies recall the cicadas in Italy. Like a snake-charmer, Ruskin is able to turn his pupils' fear of snakes ('I couldn't pick up the least little bit of a diamond, I was so frightened', 12) into amazement at the renewed beauty of the aforementioned disempowered creatures: 'they keep good time [. . .] and most of them have seven heads, with throats which each take a note of the octave; so that they can sing chords – it is very fine indeed' (16). The forbidden treasure, guarded by fearsome animals, is turned by Ruskin into a diamond sand among hills whose forests are inhabited by anthropomorphised snakes with singing abilities. Thanks to his rhetorical skills, rich analogies and the metaphors with which he speaks of reality in Oriental terms, Ruskin denounces modern industrial capitalism, as does Dickens,[7] who described his Coketown as a 'town of machinery and tall chimneys, out of which interminable serpents of smoke trailed themselves for ever and ever' (Dickens 1998: 27).

As reported by Irwin, the *hawi*, or snake-charmer, was one of the entertainers who, together with the storytellers, contortionists, jugglers and wrestlers, were listed by Ibn Khaldun, the fourteenth-century thinker, in the treatise on the philosophy of history entitled the *Muqaddimah*. In medieval Arab lands, the snake-charmers competed with the aforementioned low-life entertainers for 'the attention and money of the crowds' (Irwin 2004: 108).

Ruskin's fascination with reptiles, as attested to by his many dreams about beautiful women linked with venomous snakes, as well as by his lecture at the Royal Institution on 17 March 1880 entitled 'A Caution to Snakes', during which he exhibited a fine anaconda skin, may be connected with his attraction to the East.

According to Edward Williams Byron Nicholson, librarian of the London Institution, Ruskin's lecture on St Patrick's Day was so successful that he was asked to repeat it on 23 March 1880. The great mass of people who flocked to hear Ruskin's speech demonstrates how fascinating the East was to British people in the Victorian age, and in particular to William Morris who attended the lecture,[8] in which Ruskin offers a spiritual version of the development of the species, in opposition to that offered by Thomas Henry Huxley, one of the first adherents to Darwin's theory of evolution by natural selection.

The blending of female and reptile, as exemplified by Ruskin's dream of snakes with womanly breasts (on 1 November 1869) that slid into his room, and another dream in which he showed his cousin Joanna a beautiful snake (on 9 March 1878), also becomes evident in the lecture 'The Valley of Diamonds' when Ruskin tells little Florrie that she might turn into a snake:

L. You would like it very much indeed, Florrie, if you were there. The serpents would not bite you; the only fear would be of your turning into one!

Florrie. Oh, dear, but that's worse.

L. You wouldn't think so if you really were turned into one, Florrie; you would be very proud of your crest. (Ruskin 1908a: 15)

Ruskin's obsession with snakes is well documented in the book chapter entitled 'The Dream of the Dragon: Ruskin's Serpent Imagery' by Marc A. Simpson (1982), who, despite the detailed overview of Ruskin's real and fictional representations of snakes, does not mention the *Arabian Nights* as a possible source of inspiration. The possibility of a woman metamorphosing into a snake, as in an Arabian tale such as 'The Story of Zobeide', is a fearful thought to Florrie, while Ruskin finds this transformation particularly alluring. All the evidence suggests that Ruskin was deeply influenced by 'The Story of Zobeide', commonly known as 'The Story of the First of the Three Ladies of Baghdad', in which a fairy transforms Zobeide's jealous sisters into black dogs in order to punish them for their infringement of the patriarchal laws that govern the conduct of women. While sailing on the Prince's vessel, Anime and Safie, who were jealous of their sister's good fortune, decide to throw Zobeide and the Prince overboard. Unfortunately, the Prince drowns in the Persian Gulf, while

Zobeide is able to reach an island, where she saves a large, long, winged serpent from another giant snake who is chasing the former in order to devour it. To Zobeide's great surprise, the winged serpent is revealed to be a fairy, 'a black woman [. . .] of lively and agreeable complexion' ('The Story of Zobeide', 132), who, as in Persian myths, was metamorphosed into a serpent.

Of all the Arabian tales, 'The Story of Aladdin, or, the Wonderful Lamp', 'The Fisherman and the Jinni' and 'Ali Baba and the Forty Thieves' were the ones that most influenced Ruskin's rhetorical language. References to Aladdin's lamp, trapdoor, palace, ring and genie appear in Ruskin's letters, lectures and other writings. The first use of the Aladdin metaphor dates back to *Modern Painters* (1843–60), in which Ruskin associates Aladdin's genie in a bottle with the creative imagination itself. Ruskin seems to create an alternate possible world in which windows are 'jewelled like Aladdin's' (Ruskin 1858: 250), magic formulas are able to open the treasure house of knowledge, and *jinn* released from magical lamps grant people's wishes for wealth.

According to possible world theory, Ruskin's possible world of Oriental magic is clearly exemplified by the promise of a cultural harvest in *Sesame and Lilies* ([1865] 1900):

> Try if you cannot get corn laws established for it, dealing in a better bread; – bread made of that old enchanted Arabian grain, the Sesame, which opens doors; – doors not of robbers' but of Kings' Treasuries. (Ruskin 1900: 73)

By employing the sesame metaphor, leitmotif of the story 'Ali Baba and the Forty Thieves', Ruskin hopes to see new corn laws established within the British Constitution. Ruskin's textual universe is a dynamic combination of an actual text world and a different type of alternate possible world provided by corn laws that deal with bread made of sesame, a magic Arabian grain endowed with the power of opening the doors of knowledge.

Ruskin describes this alternate possible Oriental world as an upside-down Wish world in which all wishes are granted. By projecting the wish for new corn laws, Ruskin creates a conflict between the Wish world on the one hand and, on the other, the poverty-stricken world of the Victorian age. The following extract, taken from the letter sent to Charles Eliot Norton on 23 January 1870, provides a paramount example of Ruskin's alternate possible world:

If I had Aladdin's lamp my first rub of it should be to call the genius to restore and more than restore your loss. Why do we who could spend money so well have to suffer from the errors of those who can only gain it? It is a far nobler thing to spend money wisely than to accumulate it rapidly. (Bradley and Ousby 1987: 184)

In order to introduce the mechanics of mental space analysis, I will briefly outline Gilles Fauconnier's account (1997: 42–3) of the comprehension of the following sentence:

> If I had Aladdin's lamp my first rub of it should be to call the genius to restore and more than restore your loss.

Fauconnier's diagrammatic representation of the mental space configuration relevant to this sentence is reproduced as Figure 3.2.

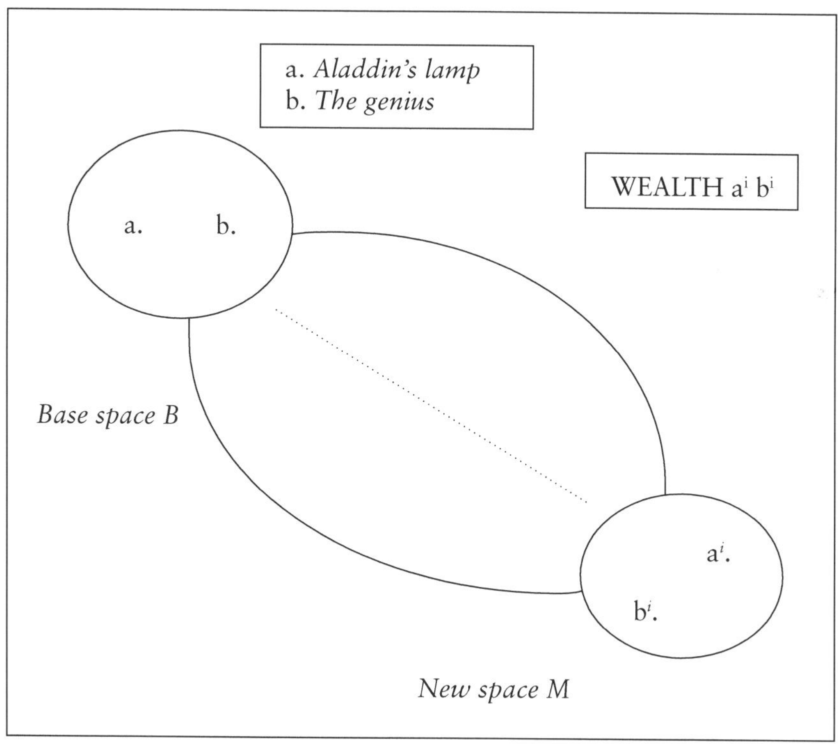

Figure 3.2 Diagrammatic representation of Ruskin's mental space configuration relevant to the letter sent to Charles Eliot Norton (23 January 1870).

Comprehension of this sentence, according to Fauconnier, involves the construction of two mental spaces. The first mental space, the 'Base' (B), includes two elements, 'a' and 'b', which are accessed by the names 'Aladdin's lamp' and 'the genius'. This space is linked with information about the two entities that is part of our background knowledge, or information that has been derived from the preceding co-text. The Base is the space that functions as the starting point of each network of spaces, and is always accessible for the addition of further material for the construction of new spaces.

The second mental space is derived from the Base via the conjunction 'if', which functions as a 'space-builder'. Space-builders are linguistic expressions that trigger the construction of new spaces and indicate the nature of the connection between each new space and the one from which it is constructed. The conjunction 'if' sets up the new space as a 'possibility' space: that is, as corresponding to a condition that may or may not be true in relation to the Base. The possibility space contains two entities, 'a^i' and 'b^i', which are counterparts of 'a' and 'b' in the Base, and are accessed by means of the same names. This is what Fauconnier calls the 'Access Principle'. In the possibility space, a^i is restoring b^i. This space is also structured by background knowledge triggered by the expression 'more than restore'. While B is the Base space of the structure, M is the 'Focus' space: that is, the space to which material is being added by the sentence. The space-builder is marked for temporal distance from the Base, making what Fauconnier calls 'reality within fiction' (1997: 50).

From this perspective, Ruskin's rhetorical language is imbued with Oriental references, as neatly summarised by Jane Carlyle, wife of essayist Thomas Carlyle, who praised Ruskin's art of naming, which recalls the magic atmosphere of the *Arabian Nights*. In a letter sent on 15 July 1865, Mrs Carlyle writes to Ruskin the following words:

> What a talent for naming you have!
> *Of King's Treasuries*
> *Of Queen's Gardens*
> the names lift me already into the sphere of *Arabian Nights*.
>   (Cate 1982: 111)

The intertextual activation of the parable of Aladdin on to Ruskin's lectures, entitled *Of King's Treasuries* and *Of Queen's Gardens*, restructures Mrs Carlyle's ongoing conviction about Ruskin's Oriental imagination. In this example, we see that the *Arabian Nights* is not a monolithic entity; rather it is characterised by a potential intertextual input space that can be projected in the elaboration of Ruskin's lectures to facilitate the meaning-making process.

Of King's Treasuries projects the conceptual metaphor KNOWLEDGE IS A TREASURE, which, in Ruskin's view, refers to the hidden treasure in books. In order to advance in life and to form a good society, Ruskin enumerates virtues such as honesty, generosity and benevolence, deriving from reading books. It is not by chance that the epigraph chosen by Ruskin is highly evocative of the story of 'Ali Baba and the Forty Thieves Destroyed by a Slave', in which a poor woodcutter discovers a thieves' den, a cave filled with 'heaps of gold and silver' (766), whose door opens at the command contained in the magical incantation 'Open Sesame'.

The epigraph is taken from Lucian's[9] *The Fisherman*, an account of his conception of poetics that takes its inspiration from Old Comedy, in contrast with more recent philosophical schools. With its epigrammatic simplicity, the paratextual sentence from Lucian, 'You shall each have a cake of sesame' (Ruskin 1900: 26), seems to suggest that Ruskin's schema has to do with Lucian and the *Arabian Nights*, which are frequently applied as metaphorical source domains to construct a range of experiences. The OPEN SESAME domain has a high multivalency[10] or a very wide scope,[11] due to its salience, its positive emotional associations. As far as conceptual structure is concerned, therefore, Ruskin's mind style is characterised by a systematic mapping between the OPEN SESAME domain and the TREASURE domain, or possibly the domain of KNOWLEDGE in general. This mapping includes correspondences between behaviour and virtues appropriate to the constitution of a good society. Originally employed as a component of religious ceremonies (Bedigian 2010: 14), sesame in Ruskin's mind becomes a metaphor for knowledge, blending together the Oriental magic domain and the economic domain in a parable of poverty, in which the poor become wealthy, thanks to good fortune and magic.

Similarly, Ruskin's second lecture, entitled *Of Queens' Gardens*, is imbued with Oriental references, as exemplified by the epigraph '"Be thou glad, oh thirsting Desert; let the desert be made cheerful, and bloom as the lily; and the barren places of Jordan shall run wild with wood" – ISAIAH xxxv, I. (Septuagint.)' (Ruskin 1900: 77). If *Of King's Treasuries* metaphorically introduced the issue of how and what to read in Oriental terms, the second lecture explains the reasons for reading books by introducing the Oriental metaphor of the desert. In this case, the DESERT metaphor functions as a fairly successful tool for Ruskin's thoughts on the role of women. There is a cross-space mapping between source and target inputs: to Ruskin, the mind is a thirsting desert that we must nourish in order to make it blossom with ideas. It is highly significant that Ruskin celebrated the middle-class wife, her beauty and her role as her husband's assistant, with the help of the DESERT metaphor. Ruskin implies that the desert is like a woman's garden, which must be tamed and nourished. From this perspective, reading books helps us possess 'a power over the ill-guided and illiterate' (Ruskin 1900: 72), a power that he defines as 'kingly', since all education is useful, beneficent and therefore kingly. In Ruskin's view, a kingly education is required for a beautiful queen: that is to say, for a Victorian woman who was thought to be 'the shadow and attendant image of her lord' (Ruskin 1900: 74). Such a patriarchal vision of society seems to echo the *Arabian Nights*, whose frame story about two kings, Schahriar and Schahzenan, who are obsessed with the idea of their wives' adultery, projects the idea of women's subjugation. Unlike the queens' Oriental garden, a place of sexual pleasure in which queens and princesses secretly meet their black lovers, the queens' garden depicted by Ruskin is a locus of peace and learning.

In Ruskin's garden, flowers flourish properly if someone loves them, since flowers have thoughts and lives like humans do. In the *Arabian Nights*, gardens, as already mentioned in Chapter 1, are sensual and erotic dimensions that can be explained with the contextual frame theory,[12] focusing on how contexts within fictional worlds are constructed. The plot reversals in the story of Schahriar and Schahzenan depend on situations transferred from another context. One example is when Schahzenan places himself near the windows of his apartment in order to see all that passes in the garden. This is an off-stage projected frame, since it describes a context occurring elsewhere at the time of the action without the action actually switching to that other place. Schahzenan only observes the persons and the black servants accompanying the sultaness in the garden without knowing exactly what occurred in that place. According to Emmott (1997), these are mental representations of contexts that are embedded within the primed context, but are not themselves developed in sufficient detail for the reader to feel that they are primed.

In Schahriar and Schahzenan's story, the description sets up this projected frame, and no one actually leaves the palace to check whether Schahzenan's suspicions of treachery are true. Both the King of Tartary and the reader infer that the Queen of Samarcande has sexual relations with the black servant Masoud in the garden, but the reader's 'deictic centre' (Duchan et al. 1995) remains at the palace and the garden is therefore not primed. The following excerpt illustrates the notion of an off-stage projected frame:

> He observed, that the persons who accompanied the sultaness threw off their veils and long robes, that they might be at more freedom; but he was wonderfully surprised when he saw ten of them blacks, and that each of them took his mistress. The sultaness, on her part, was not long without her gallant. She clapped her hands, and called Masoud, Masoud; and immediately a black came down from a tree, and ran to her in all haste.
>
> Modesty will not allow, nor is it necessary, to relate what passed betwixt the blacks and the ladies. It is sufficient to say, that Schahzenan saw enough to convince him, that his brother had as much cause to complain as himself. ('Introductory Tale', 4)

From these words, it is clear that the reader maintains information about who is present in this specific narrative context in mental representations termed contextual frames. These enable the reader to take contextual information from each sentence and cognitively construct the remaining context around it, thereby inferring that the sultaness is unfaithful to her husband. The sultaness, Masoud, the ladies and the blacks are primed in the reader's attention, facilitating the process of inference-making, which depends on how much contextual information is given.

Praeterita as a Mental Journey to the East and *The King of the Golden River* as an Oriental Tale of the Forbidden

Another meaningful example of Ruskin's fondness for the *Arabian Nights* is provided by *Praeterita* ([1885–9] 2012), a peculiar kind of autobiography that blends together landscapes and mental states.[13] As Ruskin clearly explains, 'we did not travel for adventures, nor for company, but to see with our eyes, and to measure with our hearts' (Ruskin 2012: 78).

From this perspective, *Praeterita* seems to be mapping Ruskin's experiences in cultural space through time. Ruskin's cognitive map[14] – that is, his mental representation of environment – is determined by the landmarks in the countries that he visited. All the experiences and travels described in *Praeterita* form Ruskin's cognitive map, which is an appropriate model to adopt in order to make sense of his life. The Piazza del Popolo in Rome, Milan cathedral, the great

Certosa of Pavia, the Campo Santo of Pisa, l'Hôtel du Mont Blanc, the Alps, the pine forest on the Cenis Road, St Bernard's birthplace at Fontaines-lès-Dijon, Lake Geneva, the mountains of Chamonix, the Grand Canal or St Mark's Square in Venice and so on are only a few examples of Ruskin's landmarks that place his actions within a cultural whole.

If a cognitive map is characterised by a fixed orientation, then Ruskin's *Praeterita* appears to be a mental journey, a journey to the East where the Old World lies: that is, the history, art and literature of the past. As a pilgrim of hope looking for artistic and architectural truths, Ruskin nourishes his soul with walks and visions, confirming Henry David Thoreau's philosophy of walking (Emerson and Thoreau 2012), according to which our real treasure, our property, is the quantity of representations that we have taken in and conserved, the sum of all the individual spaces experienced in a lifetime.

Apart from the more conventional aspect of the Grand Tour that preached the unity of morality and taste, Ruskin's motive for going on a trip to Europe was to study works of art and literature. It is not by chance that Ruskin mentions the *Arabian Nights* and Aladdin's story several times in *Praeterita*, as if to invite the reader to start a journey eastward in order to discover the marvels of the old Arab world. The first reference to Aladdin projects the conceptual metaphor EAST IS FORBIDDEN, providing a kind of prototypical Oriental concept in order to understand the description of his first journey to Switzerland. As Ruskin explains, the travelling carriage chosen for this journey was equipped with strong wheels in order to ensure steady and safe transit of persons and luggage. But among all the luxuries it provides, Ruskin is particularly fascinated with the distribution of storage cellars under the seat, secret drawers and invisible pockets 'accessible only by insidious slits, or necromantic valves like Aladdin's trap-door' (Ruskin 2012: 70).

As is well known, in the story of 'The Story of Aladdin, or, the Wonderful Lamp', the entrance to the cave is under a trapdoor in the desert. Aladdin passes through that trapdoor and finds the magic lamp with the help of a brass ring, which magically raises the huge stone:

> take hold of the ring, and only pronounce the names of your father and grandfather, and lift it up, and you will find it will come easily. Aladdin did as the magician bade him, and raised the stone with a great deal of ease, and laid it by. ('The Story of Aladdin, or, the Wonderful Lamp', 658)

In Ruskin's view, a travelling carriage becomes a magic vehicle, what Todorov called the 'instrumental marvellous' (Todorov 1975: 56), which serves to communicate with other worlds. In Ruskin's words, his journey to Switzerland in the luxurious chariot 'was an imaginary journey in itself, with every pleasure, and none of the discomfort, of practical travelling' (Ruskin 2012: 70). Such a feeling of marvel is also experienced by Ruskin when he describes illuminated manuscripts in noblemen's houses. He clearly admits his admiration for illuminated prayer books, his love of embroidery and treasures, as exemplified in a sentence like 'I was never tired of numbering sacks of gold and caskets of jewels in the *Arabian Nights*' (Ruskin 2012: 315). But even more than that, he expresses his feelings of pride and happiness about his own very first missal, which he explains in Oriental terms: 'the feeling was something between the girl's with her doll, and Aladdin's in a new Spirit-slave to build palaces for him with jewel windows' (491). To possess and gaze at a well-illuminated missal is like playing with a doll or giving orders to a genie, resulting in an immense joy. All the evidence suggests that there is a metaphorical structure to Ruskin's knowledge of happiness deriving from the art of illuminated manuscripts and illustration. The metaphorical aspects of joy include the verbs of *gazing*, *playing* and *giving orders* in the illumination scenario generated by Ruskin's words.

To Ruskin, a missal is like a pocket cathedral 'full of painted windows, [. . .] with the music and the blessing of all its prayers besides' (491), thereby projecting the conceptual metaphor ILLUMINATED MANUSCRIPTS ARE CATHEDRALS. For him, illuminated books are centres of considerable density of meaning and emotion. Not only are books able to open new worlds but also their ornamental designs, their letters and golden arabesques, induce positive emotions of joy and pleasure:

> The new worlds which every leaf of this book opened to me, and the joy I had, counting their letters and unravelling their arabesques as if they had all been of beaten gold, – as many of them indeed were, – cannot be told, anymore than – everything else, of good, that I wanted to tell. (491)

According to Oatley and Johnson-Laird's cognitive theory of emotions (1987), positive emotions occur when a goal is achieved or when subgoals are achieved because a plan is progressing well. From this cognitive perspective, Ruskin's enjoyment arises when he is fully engaged in reading and admiring illuminated books, a creative activity through which he becomes conscious of his fondness for Oriental design. Ruskin's positive emotions deriving from ornamental design enhance motivation, the power of affect to elicit artistic behaviours that increase his happiness.

Like Rossetti, Ruskin was deeply affected by the prototypical Oriental story of unjust oppression and triumphant reward entitled 'The Story of Two Sisters Who Envied Their Younger Sister', with which Scheherazade succeeds in removing Schahriar's prejudice against all women. As Ruskin admitted in *Praeterita*, the Cinderella-like story of Princess Parisad not only was his favourite Arabian tale but also deeply influenced his literary imagination: 'the story of "Golden Water" [. . .] is a quite favourite story with me, and has had an immense power over my own life' (Ruskin 1908b: 639).

Ruskin's fondness for the story led him to purchase the beautiful drawing by Rossetti, *Golden Water*, illustrating the story of Princess Parisad, which was hung on the walls of his house at Denmark Hill; it was later deposited at the ladies' school in Winnington, only because, as Ruskin explained in a letter, he 'went there often, and enjoy[ed] [it] more than if it was hanging up here [in his house]' (W. M. Rossetti 1903: 133).

Praised by Ruskin as 'the most precious in the old series' (Ruskin 1908b: 639) of the *Arabian Nights*, the story of Princess Parisad must be considered as a source of Ruskin's *The King of the Golden River* (1851), with illustrations by Richard Doyle. Even though Ruskin admitted that he had taken inspiration from the Brothers Grimm and Dickens, 'mixing with a little true Alpine feeling of [his] own' (Ruskin 1908b: 304), there is evidence to suggest that *The King of the Golden River* is patterned on the Oriental schemas of 'The Story of Two Sisters Who Envied Their Younger Sister'. Written merely to entertain and amuse, Ruskin's *The King of the Golden River* is, according to U. C. Knoepflmacher, 'the first Victorian literary fairy tale for children' (2016: 874), whose element of imaginative experience is the golden water of a river flowing across the mountains that is endowed with the immense power of fertility:

> And when he [Gluck] came in sight of the Treasure Valley, behold, a river, like the Golden River, was springing from a new cleft of the rocks above it and was flowing in innumerable streams among the dry heaps of red sand. (Ruskin 1860: 67)

As the excerpt demonstrates, the supernatural quality of the golden water originates in a figurative image, in what Todorov calls the 'hyperbolic marvellous' (1975: 77). If exaggeration leads to the supernatural, then the innumerable streams of golden water flowing in the valley, making fresh grass spring, creeping plants grow and young flowers suddenly open, are all expressions of hyperbole shifting to the fantastic.

A systematic use of this procedure is also evident in 'The Story of Two Sisters Who Envied Their Younger Sister', whose Yellow Golden Water is believed to form a perennial fountain wherever it is poured. At the end of the story, Parisad pours the yellow water into a large marble basin, 'which increased and swelled so much, that it soon reached up to the edges of the basin, and afterwards formed a fountain twenty feet high, which fell again into the basin, without a drop running over' ('The Story of Two Sisters Who Envied Their Younger Sister', 868). Here, again, the quantity of water splashing in the fountain twenty feet high leads to the supernatural, activated by hyperbolic representations of golden water.

From a cognitive perspective, Ruskin's *The King of the Golden River* is repatterned on 'The Story of Two Sisters Who Envied Their Younger Sister' because of the similarity between their goals (such as mutual goal pursuit: searching the golden river), conditions (such as outside opposition) and specific features (such as brothers and sisters, cruelty toward our fellow human beings). During text understanding there are two high-level processing mechanisms that allow readers to establish connections between different texts and discover similarities between them. As described in Chapter 1, these are *memory organisation packets* (MOPs) and *thematic organisation packets* (TOPs). MOPs are processing structures that allow people to relate new information to existing expectations in order to generate reasonable predictions about events narrated in books. TOPs are not static memory representations of abstract prototypical categories, but rather processing capabilities that allow readers to be creative in their understandings of narrated events in literary texts.

Analysis of Ruskin's *The King of the Golden River* demonstrates the power of MOPs and TOPs to provide coherence for the Arabian tale. See, for example, the differences and conflicting beliefs between Parisad and Gluck, a Persian princess and a farmer from Stiria who start a perilous journey to find a magic fountain. If Parisad's journey is intended to find golden water for reasons of vanity, in order to embellish her house with such an ornament, then Gluck's mountain climbing is aimed at regenerating the Treasure Valley with water from a pure and magical stream. This contradiction of intent differs from the reader's expectation that the protagonists of the *Arabian*

Nights search for treasures in order to achieve a goal: that is, to bestow money on the poor. But readers resolve this contradiction by creating a meta-MOP, 'Charity', in which the prototype and the expectations usually associated with it are not fulfilled. In this way, readers assemble a new concept with its own prototypical structure.

Thanks to TOPs, however, readers establish connections between apparently unconnected schemas (vanity versus charity), establishing a novel connection between two fantastic situations: one where the magic fountain serves to be admired, another where the golden fountain is able to restore fertility to a valley and turn it into an earthly paradise.

From this perspective, readers create an analogy between Parisad and Gluck, especially if we consider the metamorphosis of Parisad's and Gluck's brothers into black stones. Both transformations are perceived as thematically related and negative. While searching for the golden river, Prince Bahman and Prince Perviz are turned into black stones because they forget the dervise's advice and turn about for 'the noise and clamour of the terrible threatening voices, which they heard on all sides of them, without seeing anybody' ('The Story of Two Sisters Who Envied Their Younger Sister', 877). Likewise, Hans and Schwartz are metamorphosed into black stones since, failing to heed the King of the Golden River's warning, they pour unholy water into the river after refusing to help some beggars (a grey-haired old man and a lovely child), who are moaning for water:

> Shuddering he [Hans] drew the flask from his girdle and hurled it into the center of the torrent. As he did so, an icy chill shot through his limbs; he staggered, shrieked, and fell. The waters closed over his cry, and the moaning of the river rose wildly into the night as it gushed over THE BLACK STONE. (Ruskin 1860: 59)

> And when Schwartz stood by the brink of the Golden River, its waves were black like thunder clouds, but their foam was like fire; and the roar of the waters below and the thunder above met as he cast the flask into the stream. And as he did so the lightning glared in his eyes, and the earth gave way beneath him, and the waters closed over his cry. And the moaning of the river rose wildly into the night as it gushed over the TWO BLACK STONES. (63)

In both examples, Ruskin seems to employ the Oriental frame of the forbidden, according to which the protagonists must observe only one rule in order to save their lives. The Oriental words of warning 'not to look behind' become, in Ruskin's tale, the warning 'not to cast unholy water into the river', but the punishment for violating the rule of the fantastic is the same. This analogy between Parisad's and Gluck's brothers, who are turned into black stones, reflects a parallelism that is recurrent in the *Arabian Nights* and is explicitly pointed out as the forbidden and its punishments. Notably, the forbidden door cycle is exemplified by Arabian tales such as 'The House with the Belvedere', 'The Man Who Never Laughed Again for the Rest of His Life', 'The Third Kalandar's Tale', 'The Story of Janshah' and 'The Adventures of Hasan of Basrah'. The lure of the forbidden is neatly summarised by William Alexander Clouston:

> there are certain rooms which the fortunate mortal who has entered the enchanted palace is expressly forbidden to enter, or doors which he must on no account open, or cabinets which he must not unlock, if he would continue in his present state of felicity. (Clouston 1884: 308)

By violating the forbidden, Gluck's brothers lose not only their state of felicity but also their human form for the rest of their lives. Unexpectedly, Gluck, depicted as a positive character who is fair, 'blue-eyed, and kind in temper to every living thing' (Ruskin 1860: 16), the only one who passes the test of the Golden River because he risks thirst by giving water to beggars on the way there, decides not to restore human form to the petrified black brothers.

Unlike Gluck, who is only able to ask the cruel king the reason why he transformed his brothers into stones, Parisad is a most determined heroine who decides to spill a little of the miraculous water on every large black stone cast along the path to the river in order to save her brothers. The incongruity of this analogy helps us figure out the adaptive character of many aspects of text understanding. According to R. C. Schank (1982), and more recently Raymond W. Gibbs, Jr (2006), skilled readers do not comprehend texts simply by activating pre-existing prototypes; rather they activate their TOPs in combination with MOPs because understanding arises as the product of dynamic meaning construction processes.

The role of prototypical Arabian stories in the construction of meaning in Ruskin's writings is of utmost importance, since he seems to draw on a whole set of Arabian experiences to flesh out an ongoing reading experience. Ruskin's *The King of the Golden River*, as well as his other lectures, letters and writings, is imbued with references to

Oriental stories, and thus readers understand experiences and ideas by making reference to what they already know about the *Arabian Nights*. In Schank's words, 'expectations are the key to understanding' (1999: 79) because they are stored in our memory awaiting the call to action. This is the power of *Arabian Nights*, whose unforgettable stories and storytelling become fundamental to Ruskin's communication and interaction with others.

Forbidden Doors, Treasures and Words: A Cognitive Poetic Analysis of Morris's *The Earthly Paradise*

Morris's interest in the East is clearly exemplified by the art of carpet-making and in particular by Persian rug-weaving. He set up a hand-loom in Kelmscott House, Hammersmith, West London, in 1877–8, and hired a carpet-knotter from Glasgow to teach his young workers how to knot properly. The result was that hand-knotted Hammersmith rugs and carpets were very expensive (in 1883 Alexander Ionides paid £113 for a 16 foot by 13 foot carpet) and were sold in relatively small numbers. Despite such business problems, Morris's carpets were unique for their design, quality and colour because, as Charles Harvey and Jon Press have summarised, 'they were conceived as the central element in an ambitious decorative scheme' (Harvey and Press 1991: 108).

Firmly convinced that people should have nothing in their houses that was not either useful or beautiful, Morris praised the usefulness of the lives of weavers from Persia who

> in their own way [. . .] meant to tell us how the flowers grew in the gardens of Damascus or how the tulips shone among the grass in the mid-Persian valley, and how their eyes delighted in it all and what joy they had in life. (Morris 1994: 112)

These words exemplify how Islamic art is true to nature, with its curving sinuous arabesques and geometric patterns reproducing Persian gardens as bi-dimensional earthly paradises. In such an Oriental cosmos, people rejoiced at the beauty of life.

Another paramount example of Morris's enthusiasm for Eastern art is provided by a letter to his daughter May (21 March 1878), to whom he reports the pleasure he derived in attending an exhibition of Eastern artefacts. To Morris's wonder, Vincent Joseph Robinson, author of the book *Eastern Carpets* (1882), recreated a room from

Damascus with its walls, ceiling and window, and above all with its wonderful colours: vermilion, gold and ultramarine. Such a chromatic combination reminded him of the *Arabian Nights* or, in his words, 'was just like going into the *Arabian Nights*' (Kelvin 1996: 465).

Furthermore, as a considerable admirer of Oriental carpets, Morris decorated his house in Hammersmith with beautiful Oriental ornaments. In 1880 George Bernard Shaw recalls his first visit to Kelmscott House, whose walls were papered in the Morris pattern, *Pimpernel*, and hung with an Oriental carpet: 'There was an Oriental carpet so lovely that it would have been a sin to walk on it; consequently it was not on the floor but on the wall and half way across the ceiling' (Shaw 1936: 20).

It is no surprise, then, that, due to his keen knowledge of the history of carpet manufacture, Morris became adviser on carpets to the South Kensington Museum[15] in 1883. He supported the acquisition of the Ardabil carpet from the shrine of the Safavid Sheikh Safi, whose descendants founded Persia's sixteenth- and seventeenth-century Safavid dynasty. As one of the largest carpets in the world, dating from 1539–40, the Ardabil carpet was praised by Morris in a letter to Thomas Armstrong (13 March 1893) as a 'remarkable work of art' (Kelvin 1996: IV, 23) with a design of 'singular perfection' (23).

In almost the same period, Morris started a campaign against the restoration of St Mark's Basilica in Venice, 'the wonder of the civilized world' (Morris 1996: 180), whose balustrade capitals epitomised their root – all Byzantine Arab capitals. Ruskin, notably, in *The Stones of Venice*, had pinpointed the Arab influence on Venetian architecture, retracing the origins of the Venetian–Arab school. Defined as 'a new gospel and a fixed creed' (Mackail 1995: I, 38), Ruskin's aesthetic manifesto was, for Morris, the most influential piece of writing with regard to his own theory of art and society. Along with the notions of art as the expression of man's pleasure in labour, and the whole moral being of the artist, Morris was inevitably affected by Ruskin's analysis of the Oriental character of Venice:

> a rich, luxuriant, and entirely original Gothic, formed from the Venetian–Arab by the influence of the Dominican and Franciscan architecture, and especially by the engrafting upon the Arab forms of the most novel feature of the Franciscan work, its traceries. (Ruskin 1851: 22)

Ruskin's words on the Venetian–Arab, on the distinctive architecture of Venice as embodied by its churches and palaces, had an undeniable impact on Morris's perception of Venetian art. The effect of this influence was visible in Morris's campaign against the restoration of St Mark's Basilica. As founder of SPAB, Morris was particularly concerned by the proposed restoration of the church's west front, along with its mosaics. For that reason, he sent a letter to the editor of the *Daily News* on 31 October 1879, lamenting the perils and follies of restoration. To Morris, the idea of pulling down St Mark's was unbearable from both an aesthetic and a historical point of view. The uniqueness of the church derives from 'the solemnity of tone, and the incident that hundreds of years of wind and weather have given to the marble' (Morris 1996: 180), making it 'a monument of history, and a piece of nature' (180).

The campaign against the restoration of St Mark's continued for almost thirty years and Morris was able to sensitise such eminent personalities as Ruskin, Burne-Jones, G. E. Street[16] and another 2,000 people who signed a petition to be presented to the authorities in Italy. This was only one of the battles that Morris fought in the name of our cultural heritage, trying to preserve the integrity of historic buildings and avoid all 'treason[s] to the cause of civilisation and the arts' (180).

Morris's interest in the East, however, does not extinguish itself in the preservation of ancient monuments, buildings and works of art in general, a cause that, at that time, was promoted by SPAB. As reported by his daughter, Morris used to read aloud much of Lane's *Thousand and One Nights* to his family.[17] Evidence of his indebtedness to the *Arabian Nights*, which to him 'was a kind of Bible' (Caracciolo 1988: 31), can be found in *The Earthly Paradise*, whose utopian dreamland and narrative design recall the rare combination of magic and realism, as well as the inner-frame narratives of the *Arabian Nights*.

Morris was attracted by the moral message and, above all, by the warning lurking within such marvel tales as 'The Story of Aladdin, or, the Wonderful Lamp', 'The Man Who Never Laughed Again' (from the Fifth Wezeer's Tale) and 'The Adventures of Hasan of Basrah'.[18] Similarly to Marx's ideological Orientalism, Morris sympathises with the misery of the people, with their material life and with the Arab townsfolk, and thereby with the criminal underworld. From this perspective, Morris envisions the Orient as a conceptual metaphor, projecting an alternative world of marvels wherein the low and the high, the real and the unreal, are successfully integrated.

For this reason, he seems to restructure three Arabian tales that are highly representative of the forbidden, the tabooed and thus the sacred that represents the core of traditional Arab religious beliefs and esoteric folk practices. Forbidden treasures, forbidden words and forbidden doors are the schema variables of Morris's 'The Writing on the Image',[19] 'The Land East of the Sun and West of the Moon' and 'The Man Who Never Laughed Again'. The Sicilian scholar, John the Shepherd and Bharam, the protagonists of Morris's Oriental poems, are all strongly affected by hubris and greed, leading them to lose their earthly paradises: namely, the land east of the sun and west of the moon and the swan-maiden's realm. These protagonists live a failure experience that seems to echo the frustrating Arabian treasure-hunting leitmotif. As observed by Irwin in his companion to the *Arabian Nights* (2004), treasure-hunting was both an occult science and a professional occupation. As a science, it demanded from its students a knowledge of ancient lore and sorcery. As a profession, it demanded courage because the *mutalib* (treasure hunter) was engaged in a high-risk occupation fraught with narrow passages, firetraps, maps, talismans and, above all, lamps. The cognitive map shown in Figure 3.3 exemplifies the blending process activated in Morris's mind.

Despite the Italian setting, 'The Writing on the Image', whose sorcerer protagonist is well acquainted with Egyptian and Babylonian lore, seems to reverse and satirise the story of 'The Story of Aladdin, or, the Wonderful Lamp'. Morris's narrative poem, praised

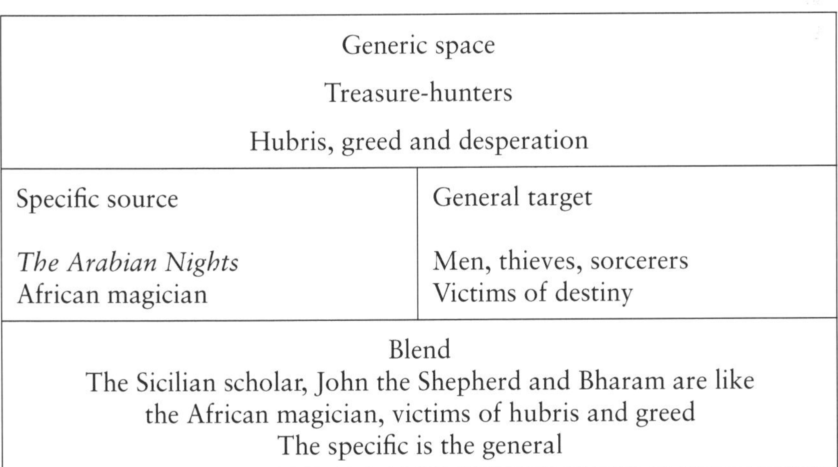

Figure 3.3 Conceptual blending network for the protagonists of Morris's narrative poems.

by Florence Boos for being a 'brief, compact, well-told, shockingly direct tale of utter failure' (Boos 1991: 87), involves parabolic mapping and invites the reader to become consciously aware of the connections it makes from the Arabian source story to the others. If the magician in the *Arabian Nights* tale is safely waiting outside the cave for Aladdin to bring him the wonderful lamp, in 'The Writing on the Image' Morris's African magician personally descends into the cave to find the wonderful green stone. As soon as he seizes the jewel, this releases an arrow, which then seals the vault irrevocably. In the dark cave, the Morrisian sorcerer is surrounded by the dead bodies of other treasure-hunters, by kings, queens, guards, serving-men and minstrels, as if to show that treasure-hunts in medieval Egypt were not just the stuff of fantasy and fiction.

There are numerous references to Aladdin's lamp in 'The Writing on the Image' ('lamps [. . .] hung up here and there / Of strange device', ll. 148–9; 'lamps upon the stair', l. 163) but one lamp in particular attracts the master's attention by illuminating the great hall, 'although no flame / Was burning there' ('The Writing on the Image', ll. 201–2). This magical lamp also appears *mutatis mutandis* in the late romance *The House of the Wolfings* (1890), in which a holy lamp is always kept burning by the Celtic druidess, Hall-Sun:

> a wondrous lamp fashioned of glass; yet of no such glass as the folk made then and there, but of a fair and clear green like an emerald, and all done with figures and knots in gold, and strange beasts, and a war-rior slaying a dragon, and the sun rising on the earth. (Morris 1913: 13)

Despite its medieval manufacture, Morris's magic, eternally lit lantern may be a visual reminder of magic Orientalism, of Muslim geomancy, which, in the *Arabian Nights*, is the most widely employed means of discovering the unknown.

Oriental Scenarios in 'The Land East of the Sun and West of the Moon' and 'The Man Who Never Laughed Again': A Text World Analysis

An interesting example of schema *tuning* is provided by Morris's narrative poem entitled 'The Land East of the Sun and West of the Moon', in which an unknown stargazer dreams that a gold-clad stranger appears at the court of the Norwegian King Magnus, telling secrets unknown to the outer world. It represents the outer frame of narration in which John the Shepherd is granted a vision of a magical realm inhabited by swan-maidens. Inspired by the 'Forbidden Chamber' cycle, and in particular by 'The Adventures of Hasan of Basrah', in which a man destroys his chances of an idyllic relationship with a bird-woman because of his curiosity, 'The Land East of the Sun and West of the Moon' is imbued with Oriental imagery. This is also confirmed by Peter Caracciolo, who maintains that 'the manner in which the material is worked by Morris as a nocturnal tale within a tale, oneiric and fragmented, suggests its Scandinavian origins are complemented by the analogue in the *Nights*' (Caracciolo 1988: 32).

From a cognitive perspective, Morris modifies the variable terms of 'The Adventures of Hasan of Basrah' but the basic relational structures among characters remain unchanged. Morris's tuning involves the evolution of old Oriental schemas into new ones by adding a few more terms. In particular, Morris's swan-maiden is an evolution of the Oriental bird-lady featured in 'The Adventures of Hasan of Basrah'. Endowed with 'unimagined loveliness' ('The Land East of the Sun and West of the Moon', l. 338), 'heavenly voice' (l. 333) and 'delicate round limbs' (l. 382), Morris's swan-maiden recalls the Oriental bird-lady in her sensual nakedness, 'a snow-white thing' (l. 406), which appears to be patterned on the bird-lady's naked limbs and is described as 'goodly rounded [. . .] like a bowl of silver or crystal' ('The Adventures of Hasan of Basrah', 189).

Both metamorphic women are able to drive their male observers mad with love, making them suffer the deepest physical pains. The symptoms of love sickness are clearly evident: if John the Shepherd is tortured by 'longings sweet / Piercing his heart' ('The Land East of the Sun and West of the Moon', ll. 215–16) and feels a fire burning within his throat ('He longed for with such strong desire, / That his heart sickened, and quick-fire / Within his parched throat seemed to burn', ll. 341–3), then Hasan suffers from insomnia and lack of appetite, resulting in 'sleeplessness delirious [. . .] and excess of love-longing' ('The Adventures of Hasan of Basrah', 175).

The prototypical Arabian love story does nothing but project the conceptual metaphor LOVE IS PAIN. Not only is the Oriental love depicted here associated with other concepts such as DESIRE, PASSION, NOSTALGIA and SICKNESS, but also there is a rich conceptual structure around the concept of this Oriental love. It is possible to apply the cognitive notion of scenario,[20] consisting of sequences of action concepts that are to be performed in recurrent situations with a particular goal. The most recurrent scenario in the *Arabian Nights* is the so-called palace garden scenario. Such a scenario provides a complex store of information for the characters who are about to enter a garden, so that they may have expectations about the situation in which they may be involved.

Both Hasan and John experience DESIRE AS SUFFERANCE, as exemplified by sentences such as '[Hasan] stood watching her, forgetting meat and drink' and 'longings sweet / piercing [John's] heart'. All this emotional distress occurs in the palace garden, a love scenario that places Hasan and John in a goal-oriented movement towards gardens. Both protagonists' motion events, involving motions towards the palace garden, are related to the sole purpose of erotic love.

From this perspective, the love scenario can be described in terms of motivation and result. Hasan and John *want* to enter the gardens, *get* to enter the gardens and *keep* close to the gardens because of their desire, passion and need for their bird-ladies. Figure 3.4, based

WANT / GET / KEEP BECAUSE OF	WANT / GET / KEEP BECAUSE OF
DESIRE = HUNGER	DESIRE/HUNGER = '[Hasan's] eyes sunken for lack of food and for much weeping by reason of his love and longing' 'As cold cup and warm fingers came / Into [John's] hand, the while his eyes / A look in hers must needs surprise / That made him flush'
PASSION = NATURAL FORCE	PHYSICAL FORCE = '[Hasan] drowned in the sea of his solitude' '[John's] heart sickened, and quick-fire / Within his parched throat seemed to burn'
NEED = ILLNESS	ILLNESS = 'Nor for [Hasan] was there any rest: he neither ate, drank, nor slept' 'Then did [John] fear to draw his breath / Lest he should find the hand of Death / Was showing him vain images'

Figure 3.4 Causation in love stories: 'The Adventures of Hasan of Basrah' and 'The Land East of the Sun and West of the Moon'.

on Zoltán Kövecses's theory of emotion concepts, illustrates the causation in Oriental love stories: motivation and negative results.

If it is true that falling in love is a cultural construct, then the object of love in both the *Arabian Nights* and *The Earthly Paradise* is conceptualised by means of a variety of conceptual metaphors related to romantic love. The first metaphor projected in both 'The Adventures of Hasan of Basrah' and 'The Land East of the Sun and West of the Moon' is the idea that love is a need, and that one of our most important needs is food. Therefore, it is not surprising that we see the object of love in terms of appetising food. The absence or lack of this object results in a condition of distress, restlessness and sickness, as in the case of Hasan, whose longing for the beautiful bird-woman makes him forget meat and drink. Likewise, the cup of wine offered by the fair damsel whose fingers touch John's hands produces an exciting effect in his mind, making him flush all of a sudden. In Kövecses's words, 'the fact that we conceptualise THE OBJECT OF LOVE as APPETISING FOOD does not only link love with needs but also with liking and sexual desire' (1986: 68).

The aforementioned metaphor brings into focus other aspects of love that include passivity, lack of control and pleasure. In both descriptions of Hasan's and John's longing for their damsels, LOVE IS A NATURAL FORCE and consequently the two protagonists – the first drowned in a sea of solitude and the second almost killed by the fire burning in his throat – correspond to the persons in love. Hasan and John play passive roles with respect to this force, since they can do nothing but be overwhelmed by water and burned by fire. To put it in more simplified terms, love is a force that is independent of us but which can affect us without our active participation.

One last metaphorical aspect of love is exemplified by its intensity and insanity. Oriental love appears to be conceptualised as having the highest degree of both of these. Intensity is commonly referred to a scale that represents the degree of depth and affect of love, while insanity is the uncontrolled nature of the effects of desire. If Hasan experiences his emotions with intensity, despairing at the lady's absence and thereby becoming completely sleepless and unable to rest, eat or drink, then John, whose desire is equated with a quick fire, is afraid that the vision of the swan-lady is just a sensory illusion ('vain images'). All the evidence suggests that the uncontrolled nature of the state of insanity is extended to both protagonists and that the conceptualisation of EMOTIONAL PAIN AS

PHYSICAL PAIN is again a very general conceptual metaphor in the Oriental notion of love.

The same metaphorical expression of love seems to be projected in Morris's *The Water of the Wondrous Isles* (1897), a prose romance whose female protagonist is pointedly named Birdalone. Even though Birdalone is not able to metamorphose into a bird like the damsel of surpassing beauty in the Arabian tale, her name metaphorically establishes a connection with her Oriental double. As the spiritual daughter of Habundia, the wood mother endowed with shape-shifting power, Birdalone appears to recall the Oriental bird-lady, daughter of one of the most powerful kings of the *jinn*.

Furthermore, and even more importantly, both heroines love to swim naked in the forest and garden pools, and coincidentally remain naked, both in and out the water, by choice. As for the bird-lady, Birdalone's beauty drives men mad with love, troubling knights, squires and merchants. Not only does she seduce the black knight, a wild, fierce man who kidnaps her and is not able to restrain his feelings,[21] but also she becomes an object of desire for the red knight, the tyrant and oppressor of the story, who finally captures her: 'Thou art my thrall and my having, since I had thus doomed it no few days ago; and thou art now in my hands for me to do with as I will' (Morris 1971: 198). Like Hasan, suffering the pains of love for the bird-lady, the black knight is caught in a state of constant craving, trying to keep the animal part[22] of his desire inside: that is, to control his emotions. According to the rules of romantic love, Hasan and the black knight lose control over love, whose intensity goes beyond the limit.

Alongside the sensuous aspect of 'The Adventures of Hasan of Basrah' that attracted Morris so deeply, there is the Oriental narrative device of the forbidden, which can be found in 'The Land East of the Sun and West of the Moon'. Like the Arabian tale in which Hasan is warned not to open a certain door, the lure of the forbidden dynamic determines the Morrisian hero's destiny as one who transgresses Oriental norms by summoning the swan-maiden in a twilight garden. Caught in a moment of discomfort, John starts crying out all his fear, misery and pain, thereby breaking the promise to conceal his longing: namely, the promise of letting 'no least word slip / Of such a longing past [his] lip' ('The Land East of the Sun and West of the Moon', ll. 1074–5).

This violation, or 'anomaly' as Pier Paolo Pasolini would call it (qtd in Paul Willemen 1977: 74), characterises not only Morris's narrative poem but also every tale in the *Arabian Nights*, beginning with the appearance of a destiny that manifests itself through an anomaly. Thus, a chain of anomalies is set up, which then tends to lead back to normality. From this perspective, John will be banished from the land east of the sun and west of the moon for calling the forbidden name, doomed to sink back into what Pasolini calls 'the somnolence of daily life' (74).

From a cognitive perspective, the issues that explain almost any story of the forbidden form a causal chain that is the basis for the reader's interest. As an almost narrative and argumentative text, 'The Adventures of Hasan of Basrah' presents a series of events that are causally related to each other. Moreover, the drive behind the causally related events is the goal of one of the participants in the series of events, which leads to a number of actions taken to achieve the goal. The forbidden scenario is characterised by the causal relationship between the scenes that lie at the basis of the forbidden scenario and the aforementioned causation/motivation table of desire. The causal links in the Arabian story are couched in terms of general conditions and effects, using the 'if . . . then . . .' formula of the forbidden: if you violate the rule, then you will be punished.

It is this causal coherence relation that also characterises Morris's narrative poem, whose association with the East, and especially with the *Arabian Nights*, is eminently revealed in the astronomic coordinates of the title – east of the sun and west of the moon – that set the story in a utopian dreamland, an in-between dimension whose Oriental sun and moon, in Charles M. Doughty's words, 'made [Morris] Arab' (Doughty 2010: 56).

Similar to 'The Land East of the Sun and West of the Moon', the second November tale of *The Earthly Paradise*, entitled 'The Man Who Never Laughed Again', restructures the Oriental schema of another successful marvel tale, 'The Fifth Wezeer's Tale' ('The Man Who Never Laughed Again for the Rest of His Life').[23] As explained by Jassim Ali, Morris faithfully reproduced the mood of this Arabic story but at the same time accentuated the 'pathos and romantic agony' (Ali 1981: 53) of the hero, who is renamed Bahram. The latter is taken from the aforementioned story, 'The Adventures of Hasan of Basrah', featuring the Persian magician Bahram the Guebre, who hates Muslims with an exceeding hatred and destroys all who fall into his power. Morris's fascination with such a character may be ascribed to Bahram's acquaintance with the art of alchemy, aimed at turning copper into gold. It is probable that Morris, the founder of the Arts and Crafts movement, which promoted the aesthetic alchemy of beauty and function, sympathised with the malicious fire-worshipper.

Morris's version of Bahram, though, appears to be morally different from the original, 'a callow sensualist who is motivated to disobey the [. . .] prescription by idle curiosity and [. . .] greed' (Boos 1991: 135). On the contrary, Morris's Braham is a more admirable human being, driven by desperation and love, and hoping to regain his lost love. For this reason, as a result of entering the forbidden chamber and drinking from the magic cup, he will become 'the man who never shall laugh again'.

Despite this change in personality, this change of heart, Morris's Braham is conducted to a palace of marvellous beauty near the Indian Sea, a white house characterised by lovely gardens ('Across the plain they saw a watch-tower high, / That 'neath the moonlight, like an angry star, / Shone over a white palace, and thereby / Within white walls did black-treed gardens' [sic]; 'The Man Who Never Laughed Again', ll. 198–201) and a sparkling fountain ('between / The whispering glades the fountain leaped on high'; 'The Man Who Never Laughed Again', ll. 215–16), which recalls the high mansion with the belvedere in the Arab tale:

> a high mansion, with lofty angles, ample, with chambers facing one another, and saloons; and in each saloon was a fountain of water, and birds were warbling over it, and there were windows overlooking, on every side, a beautiful garden within the mansion. ('Abstract of the Story of the King and His Son and the Damsel and the Seven Wezeers', Lane 1853: 169)

Supposed to be a place of joy and delight, the Oriental palace is revealed as a locus of dangerous secrets, as summarised by Oleg Grabar in his study, *The Formation of Islamic Art*:

> the interior of the forbidding and forbidden palace consists of a labyrinth of separate elements secretly and mysteriously related to each other. Such a world of courts, pavilions, baths, strange doors, and fantastically elaborate decorations appears in the stories [. . .] of *The Thousand and One Nights*. (Grabar 1973: 173)

Almost an Oriental chronotope, the palace and its environs are world-builders of Eastern legends, traditions, rituals and intrigues, giving a material form to a medieval time in an Arab space. The Oriental intensity of this chronotope is particularly evident in the scene of the forbidden chamber, a leitmotif of the *Arabian Nights*, representing a threshold into another world of heavenly pleasures inhabited by a delightful lady, 'a damsel who was like the shining sun in the clear sky' ('Abstract of the Story of the King and His Son and the Damsel and the Seven Wezeers', Lane 1853: 172).

The beauty and loveliness of the damsel deeply ravished Morris, who, like Keats[24] and Tennyson,[25] devoted delicate and sensual lines to this 'talismanic lady' (Ali 1981: 52), ruler of an Amazon-like world that the protagonist, Bharam, enters after unlocking the door with a forbidden golden key. Written to prove the craft and malice of women, which is also the general title of its narrative cycle, the story of 'The Man Who Never Laughed Again for the Rest of His Life ' appealed immensely to Morris's imagination because of its dream-like story-telling device, which was central to medieval Arab fiction because, in Pasolini's words, 'one does not find truth in a single dream, but rather in many dreams.'[26] Once he is in the secret chamber, the protagonist's fate is sealed and the dream turns dramatically into a nightmare, as Bharam, who drinks the magic cup's contents and ignores the fearful warning ('Drink then, and take what thou hast fairly won, / For make no doubt that thine old life is done'; 'The Man Who Never Laughed Again for the Rest of His Life', ll. 1435–6), will be banished from those gardens of bliss and be condemned to roam feverishly. As with the medieval Islamic tradition in which dreams foreshadowed the future and made it happen, Morris employs dreams that turn out to be self-fulfilling prophecies, prefiguring the overwhelming fear of losing what is desirable.

Like Ruskin, Morris reproduces the text world of the *Arabian Nights* in order to create its richness and cognitive complexity in the minds of his readers. Morbidly fascinated with the densely textured real-life representation of the combination of text and context, Morris seems to reconstruct the Oriental text world with similar world-building elements (time, location, characters and objects) and function-advancing propositions (states, actions, events and processes), in relation to the objects and characters in the text world. Morris employs Oriental world-builders such as medieval time and setting, as specified by the locative preposition in the very first line of the narrative poem: 'A CITY was there nigh the Indian Sea' (l. 1). Other Oriental locations such as the palace and the garden are faithfully reproduced in order to describe an Oriental context that is inseparable from the Arabian text.

Likewise, Morris's characters and objects recall the Oriental variables of the Arabian tale, since Bharam, the mysterious damsel and the forbidden door are featured in both the Arabian tale and the narrative poem. Morris's text world, which is built by function-advancers ('He gat the golden key into his hand', l. 1348; 'from the chamber did he pass', l. 1355; 'Upon a little table nigh his hand, / Beheld a cup the work of cunning men / For many a long year vanished from the land', ll. 1404–6), is more than these simple predications, since all of these elements are enriched by the reader's ongoing knowledge of the Arabian tale.

And all the subworlds created in the *Arabian Nights* in the form of stories within stories, of dreams within dreams, must be considered variations in the texture of the world in focus, without leaving the current text world. Such 'deictic sub-worlds' (Stockwell 2002: 140), including shifts in time and location, flashbacks and any other departure from the current situation, are reproduced in Morris's version, thanks to the oneiric device, since Bharam's journey into the Oriental world and the shifts into other scenes ('deictic sub-worlds') are enacted 'by some fearful dream within a dream' ('The Man Who Never Laughed Again', l. 1499).

This is the fearful symmetry of *quadar* (fate) in the Muslim universe of the *Arabian Nights*, echoed in Ruskin's writings as well as in Morris's narrative poems, in which fate becomes a thoroughly literary affair. Ruskin's and Morris's capacity to tune and restructure Oriental schemas in order to make them functional in their writings is deeply rooted in their mind styles. In particular, their descriptions of Oriental marvels and low life project their peculiar world-views, a characteristic way of perceiving and making sense of the contextual Victorian world[27] that they persistently tried to ameliorate with the help of the imagination.

Notes

1. The Asiatic mode of production is the most disputed mode of production outlined in the works of Marx and Engels. The Asiatic mode claims that the ruling classes derive their power from the stratification of society into clans, tribes and ethnic groups.
2. A dish composed of meat, wheat flour and vinegar.
3. Small pancakes or other sweet pastries.
4. Dickens's imagination is imbued with stories of poverty and illusions of improving the people's poverty-stricken conditions. For an interesting reading of Dickens's illusions see Bronzini (2014).

5. Gandhi read Ruskin's *Unto This Last* on the twenty-four-hour journey from Johannesburg to Durban. On this topic see Brantlinger (1996: 466–85).
6. Ruskin first met Charles Eliot Norton in 1855. Norton was a Dante scholar, editor of the essayist Thomas Carlyle, art historian and Professor of the History of Art at Harvard from 1875 until 1898.
7. For an analysis of Ruskin's reception of Dickens's idea of progress see Michela Marroni (2009–10: 71–83).
8. See Kelvin (1996: 563).
9. Lucian was a Syrian satirist from classical antiquity, born in Samosata on the Euphrates in Eastern Anatolia (AD 120–90).
10. See Goatly (1997: 258–9).
11. See Kövecses (2000). For a cognitive analysis of metaphors of emotion see Kövecses (1990).
12. See Emmott (1997).
13. On this topic see Ebbatson (2013).
14. On cognitive maps and way-finding behaviour see Golledge (2010).
15. The South Kensington Museum was renamed the Victoria and Albert Museum in 1899, when Queen Victoria laid the foundation stone for new buildings along Exhibition Road and Cromwell Road.
16. G. E. Street (1824–81) was an English architect and architectural writer, whose designs were mainly in the High Victorian Gothic style.
17. See Morris (1910–15: XXII).
18. All quotations from 'The Adventures of Hasan of Basrah' are taken from the third volume of the Routledge edition (Mardrus 2005).
19. All quotations from Morris's narrative poems in *The Earthly Paradise* are taken from the edition by Reeves and Turner (1890).
20. The term scenario is employed by Sanford and Garrod (1981) to describe situation-specific knowledge used for interpreting a text.
21. 'I crave of thee, if there is any grain of mercy in thee, that thou wilt draw thy sword and thrust me through' (Morris 1971: 170); 'Lady, he said, I will ask this as a reward of the way-leader, to wit, that thou abide with me here in this dale, in all honour holden, till to-morrow morning; [. . .] and I, I shall have had one happy day at least, if never another. Canst thou grant me this? If thou canst not, we will depart in an hour' (171).
22. 'She looked on him a moment or two, and then stepped forward and stooped to him, and touched his shoulder and said: "Rise up, I bid thee, and be a man and not a wild beast"' (Morris 1971: 170).
23. 'The Man Who Never Laughed Again' is substantially the tale of the fifth Wezeer in the story of 'The King and his Son and the Damsel and the Seven Wezeers', as given in the twenty-first chapter of Lane's *Arabian Nights*.
24. In a letter to Fanny Brawne (July 1819), Keats mentions an Oriental tale in which melancholy men reach gardens of heavenly delights inhabited by a most enchanting Lady. See Rollins 1958: II, 130.

25. Tennyson's poem entitled 'By An Exile of Bassorah' (1827) may be indebted to the story of 'The Man Who Never Laughed Again' because of the hero's melancholy tone and his longing for an earthly paradise. For an intertextual analysis of Tennyson's and Morris's poems see Sasso (2011).
26. Epigraph to Pier Paolo Pasolini's film *Il fiore delle mille e una notte* (*Arabian Nights*, 1974).
27. On the Victorian world and its socio-cultural oppositions see Francesco Marroni (2010).

Consumers of Intoxicating Fruits and Elixirs: The Cognitive Grammar of Christina Rossetti's and Ford Madox Ford's Oriental Fairy Tales

The Poet of 'small-gemmedness': Christina Rossetti as a Pre-Raphaelite Orientalist

Christina Rossetti and Ford Madox Ford conceive Orientalism as closely associated with imperialism in their fondness for the Eastern commodities brought to Britain from every corner of the expanding British Empire. Silk, peacock feathers, blue china, Persian cats and carpets, as well as opium, were only a few of the imports that deeply touched Rossetti's and Ford's imagination, confirming what Said defined as 'the continuing imperial design to dominate Asia' (1977: 322).

Both Rossetti and Ford were consumers of Oriental goods, which were marketed in specialised department stores such as Liberty's East India House in Regent Street, Whiteley's, Debenham and Freebody, and Swan and Edgar. Notably, Rossetti, in her poem entitled 'A Birthday' (1861; in C. Rossetti 2008), wishes a 'dais of silk and down' (l. 9) all hung with Oriental decorations: vair, purple dyes, pomegranates, peacocks with a hundred eyes, and gold and silver grapes. But her interest in the East is also attested to as early as 1842, when she wrote a poem entitled *The Chinaman* as a school assignment on the subject of the Anglo-Chinese Opium War. Defined by W. M. Rossetti 'the first thing that Christina wrote in verse' (1904: 464), *The Chinaman* reveals her fascination with the Far East, where the men in her poetical description wear pigtails as signifiers of Chinese culture:

> [. . .] The faithless English have cut off my tail,
> And left me my sad fortunes to bewail.
> Now in the streets I can no more appear,
> For all the other men a pig-tail wear.'
> (W. M. Rossetti 1895: 79, ll. 13–16)

In this juvenile Oriental poem, Rossetti seems to be criticising imperialism and military aggression by giving prominence to metonymic expressions of ethnicity. Stylistically, the Chinaman becomes the focus of the narrative and is associated with certain verb forms ('have cut' and 'left me'), which project the conceptual metaphor IMPERIALISM IS VIOLENCE. Rossetti builds up an image schema of imperialism in her mind and shares that particular image schema with her readers in order to raise awareness of imperialism's crimes.

It is highly significant that Rossetti's first attempt at poetry is a poem on the Opium War, whose resonance in Britain is drawn from the diffusion of the opium-based laudanum used for recreational purposes and in health remedies. As described in Louise Foxcroft's *The Making of Addiction: The 'Use and Abuse' of Opium in Nineteenth-Century Britain* (2007), there were many Victorians who used laudanum as a painkiller (Elizabeth Barrett and Robert Browning, Dickens, George Eliot, Bram Stoker and many others) but Rossetti was particularly sensitive to the drug, since her brother Dante Gabriel was a laudanum addict and Lizzie Siddal, his beloved wife and muse, committed suicide by taking an overdose of laudanum in February 1862.

Likewise, Ford, whose fondness for luxury and interior design led him to decorate his many houses with Oriental materials, cultivated opium poppies at the Villa Paul on Cap Brun (Toulon), where he lived with the American painter Janice Biala. In his poem 'L'Oubli, temps de sécheresse', he asks Janice, 'Do you remember what stood where the peppers / and eggplant now stand? / Or the opium poppies with heads like feathery wheels?' (Ford 2003a: 153). Even though Ford is commonly known as a tobacco smoker, collector of innumerable pipes and owner of a special machine for cutting tobacco, he prefers to fictionalise scenes of drug consumption in works such as *The Brown Owl* (1892), *The Feather* (1892), *The Queen Who Flew* (1894) and *Zeppelin Nights* (1916). This opium mania may be ascribed to the fact that, as Martin Booth says, 'opium taking was as much a part of society as the drinking of alcohol or the smoking of tobacco. Indeed, opium was more widely available in 1870 than tobacco was in 1970' (Booth 1996: 63).

Many of Rossetti's and Ford's poems and stories are imbued with metaphors about the intoxication of divine ecstasy. Like consumers of *banj* (hashish) and opium, the banqueters featured in 'The Dead City', Laura, the princess wearing poppies, Queen Eldrida, Princess Ismara and the blind ploughman experience moments of hallucination that render them, in the imagination, the happiest of characters. The emphasis laid on intoxicating fruits and elixirs recalls the drugs that feature in the *Arabian Nights*, which are called on by the storyteller as forms of chloroform, available for the use of villains but also useful as a fictional convention. Opium, which was more expensive than hashish, was grown and consumed openly in Upper Egypt. According to Irwin, stories about hashish/opium eaters in the *Arabian Nights* 'tend to be simple, crudely constructed [. . .], aimed at an audience which had a taste for bawdy or even lavatorial humour' (2004: 154). Opium was a distinctly foreign drug that was commonly available in the British marketplace too during the Victorian period, and Rossetti and Ford could not have been insensible to the mounting public concern over its use and the imperialistic aspirations that embroiled Britain in the two Opium Wars.

Apart from their family connection (Ford Madox Ford was the grandson of Ford Madox Brown and a nephew of Rossetti), the relationship between the two is characterised by the deep admiration felt by Ford for Rossetti's poems. Not only did he believe that Rossetti was 'the most skilful artist in verse of the nineteenth century' (Ford 2002: 64) but also he envisioned her as a poet imbued with Orientalism. Notably, in his critical essay on Rossetti's collected poems, Ford metaphorically describes her as an Oriental mosaic, whose poetic qualities are equated with precious stones: 'In the case of Christina Rossetti, the image is that of a mosaic rather than of a fresco, since hitherto the tendency has been to regard her as the poet of what some one has called small-gemmedness' (Ford 2002: 15). By projecting the conceptual metaphor ROSSETTI IS A MOSAIC, Ford seems to emphasise her narrative art, made up from the assemblage of different stories. Almost like a Victorian Scheherazade, Rossetti seems to ravish Ford's mind, filling it up with Oriental image schemas. It is not by chance that Ford tends to depict Rossetti by using a particular Oriental image of her as a poet who 'lived her whole life behind a veil' (16), underlining her life as a recluse without any literary contacts.

Admittedly infatuated with the *Arabian Nights*, which she considered to be 'far above [her] praise' (W. M. Rossetti 1908: 57), as attested to in a letter of 18 July 1876 sent to her brother Dante

Gabriel, Rossetti nourished her mind with Arabian tales such as 'The Story of Zobeide', 'The Story of Sinbad the Sailor' and 'The Adventures of Hasan of Basrah'. Rossetti's indebtedness to the *Arabian Nights* is further confirmed by Muhsin Jassim Ali, who explains the influence of 'The Story of Zobeide' in the following terms:

> The book which charmed and delighted Christina Rossetti throughout her life yielded not only that abundance of details which formed the exotic background of her 'Goblin Market' and 'A Birthday', but also that sense of the fleetingness of life with which she was obsessed. (Ali 1981: 51)

According to Ali, Rossetti seems to project conceptual metaphors such as EAST IS EXOTICISM, EAST IS MAGIC and LIFE IS DESTINY. Evidence of Rossetti's interest in the *Arabian Nights* can be found in her more markedly Oriental works – namely, 'The Dead City' (1847), 'A Birthday' (1861), 'Goblin Market' (1862), 'The Prince's Progress' (1866) and 'Hero'[1] (1870) – whose language reveals the Oriental cognitive structures of her mind. If it is true, as Craig Hamilton says, that 'language is a window onto the human mind' (2003: 62), then Rossetti's poetical language reflects the Oriental structures of her mind. In essence, Rossetti's narrative, metaphorical, alliterative, metonymic and hyperbolic language invites the reader to adopt an Oriental perspective on her fairy-tale poems. It is my aim to investigate, from a cognitive grammar perspective, the direct link between the conceptual Oriental system and the grammatical system of Rossetti's poems.

Profiling and Foregrounding the Orientalism of 'The Dead City'

A paramount example of Rossetti's Orientalism is provided by 'The Dead City', originally entitled 'The City of Statues', in which profiling – that is, the relationship between two entities – pervades Rossetti's poetry. As already suggested by B. Ifor Evans (1933), 'The Dead City' is a rewriting of 'The Story of Zobeide', in which petrification seems to be the punishment for 'luxury and pride' (l. 163)[2] rather than for the worship of a false god, as explained in the Arabian tale.

Both 'The Story of Zobeide' and 'The Dead City' are characterised by the iconic nature of language, which is a rhetorical commonplace in cognitive grammar. Such iconicity is visible in the description of the petrified city, in which it is possible to profile figures in relation to grounds: that is to say, to profile petrified people in relation to a magnificent and luxurious setting.

Verbs like 'turned to stones' and 'petrified', employed in 'The Story of Zobeide' and 'The Dead City', profile two participants: the petrifier (God) and the petrified (inhabitants). As Adele Goldberg has pointed out, in verbs there are 'participant roles' (1995: 46), but despite the same two roles for both of these verbs, what the reader profiles in both stories is different. In 'The Story of Zobeide' we profile townsmen, merchants, guards and royal representatives (a queen and a prince), whereas in 'The Dead City' we profile banqueters, men, women, young and old.

The use of the verb 'petrify' by the anonymous eighteenth-century translator in 'The Story of Zobeide' suggests a more horrific and instant transformation of the worshippers of fire and of Nardoun, 'the ancient king of the giants who rebelled against God' ('The Story of Zobeide', 130). Rossetti's explicitation of the aforementioned verb into 'Lo, they all were turned to stone' ('The Dead City', l. 225) draws attention to a slower process of metamorphosis, which is enacted by eating 'fruits of every size and hue, / Juicy in their ripe perfection' (ll. 197–8). Being punished for the sin of pride, Rossetti's banqueters fall into a 'warm delicious rest' (l. 207), as opposed to the Persian inhabitants, who were changed in an instant into stone, 'every one in the same condition and posture they happened then to be in' ('The Story of Zobeide', 130).

In this view, the verbal choice can subtly alter the perspective taken towards an event based on which role is profiled. For example, in the transitive verbs 'petrified' (127), 'converted into black stones' (Lane 1853: 78) and 'turned to stone' ('The Dead City', l. 225), we profile the same participants – that is, God and the inhabitants – but Lane's choice of the verb 'converted into black stones' offers an important key to the experience of reading Rossetti's poem. All the evidence suggests that Rossetti used to read Lane's translation of the *Arabian Nights* rather than the eighteenth-century version, not only because her brothers were particularly keen on Lane's edition and its illustrations but also because of her linguistic choices, which foreground an alternative and Pre-Raphaelite way of conceiving the same metamorphic event. Verbally more similar to Lane's style, Rossetti's verse seems to simplify the verb 'convert' into its plainer and shorter synonym, 'turn'. For poetic effect and to respect the rhyme scheme (*aabba*), she also employs the singular form of the structured phrase 'turned to stone' in its clearly figurative and thus idiomatic use:

> The low whispering voice was gone,
> And I felt awed and alone.
> In my great astonishment
> To the feasters up I went —
> Lo, they all were turned to stone!   (ll. 221–5)

To Rossetti, 'turn' + 'to' + singular noun is a more poetic and idiomatic use rather than 'convert' + 'into' + adjective + plural noun. The latter phrasal construction appears to be the result of Lane's literal translation from Arabic, as exemplified by the adjective phrase 'black' qualifying a plural noun ('stones'). This stylistically deviant feature, which Peter Stockwell defines as an 'attractor' (Gavins and Steen 2003: 16), is employed in the first English translation of Galland's *Mille et une nuits* not to describe the inhabitants but rather to draw attention to the royal representatives, the king and queen of the doomed city, who are the most responsible for the irreligious conduct of their subjugated people:

> This voice was heard three years successively, but nobody was converted; so the last day of the year, at four o'clock in the morning, all the inhabitants in general were changed in an instant into stone, every one in the same condition and posture they happened then to be in. The king my father had the same fate, for he was metamorphosed into a black stone, as he is to be seen in this palace; and the queen my mother had the like destiny. ('The Story of Zobeide', 130)

Rossetti's poetic remediation of the Arabian tale seems to avoid mentioning the black stones ever-present in Lane's translation, opting instead for a more generic rendering of the metamorphic event whose prominence is conferred in the following stanzas. From line 226 to line 255, Rossetti's adjective phrases semantically profile the inhabitants who are turned to stone, giving them individuality and prominence. Each stanza is devoted to describing the petrification process in a more detailed and better-focused way. A series of adjectives preceding and following the nouns ('they all were statue-cold', l. 226; 'The hard fingers kept their hold', l. 230; 'With a forward look unweeting', l. 235; 'human hand stony and cold', l. 244; 'And no life-breath struggling up', l. 245) confer prominence on the human figures, who evolve specific psychological and personal traits. Stylistically, they are the focus of the narrative poem, associated with certain verbs of frozen action: a seated child casting a merry glance, a young man who bears an unwitting look, a fair, shy maiden playing with the ringlets of her hair, a man drinking wine from a golden cup, a mother and a child smiling at each other, a sleepy old man, and a strong man staring at a girl.

It is highly significant that Rossetti introduces the banquet scene, foregrounding different fruits in an Oriental profusion of odours and spices. Like the Queen's apartments in 'The Story of Zobeide', the tent where 'the splendid banquet laid' (l. 166) is the scenario in which we can discern important intertextual triggers in the written discourse. The riches and magnificence of both the room and the tent are made textually prominent in stylistic terms. Rossetti achieves foregrounding through a variety of devices, such as rhyme, alliteration, enumeration, metonomy and creative metaphors. All of these can be seen as tools to defamiliarise the subject matter, to estrange the reader from aspects of the ordinary world in order to present an Oriental world in a creative and newly figured way.

The attention of the reader is caught first of all by a variety of attractors: primarily, the luxury and richness of the decorations made of gold, gems, silver and emerald, recalling the golden throne, the steps enriched with emeralds and the Queen's bed embroidered with pearls in 'The Story of Zobeide'. But even more than that, the most striking organising element of Rossetti's poem is enumeration, a rhetorical figure used for listing myriad fruits, echoing the hyperbolic descriptions of fruits in the *Arabian Nights* and foregrounding the Oriental allure of the poem.

> In green emerald baskets were
> Sun-red apples, streaked, and fair;
> Here the nectarine and peach
> And ripe plums lay, and on each
> The bloom rested every where.
>
> Grapes were hanging overhead,
> Purple, pale, and ruby-red;
> And in panniers all around
> Yellow melons shone, fresh found,
> With the dew upon them spread.   190

> And the apricot and pear
> And the pulpy fig were there;
> Cherries and dark mulberries,
> Bunch currants, strawberries,
> And the lemon wan and fair.
>
> And unnumbered others too,
> Fruits of every size and hue,
> Juicy in their ripe perfection,
> Cool beneath the cool reflection
>   Of the curtains' skyey blue.   200

Enumeration of the fruits in Rossetti's poem becomes what cognitive linguists call the *dominant*, a formal feature of the text around which the description is dynamically organised. Enumeration of fruits acquires prominence, thanks to Rossetti's alliterative patterns ('Yellow melons shone, fresh found', l. 189; 'And the apricot and pear / And the pulpy fig were there', ll. 191–2; 'Cherries and dark mulberries / Bunch currants, strawberries', ll. 193–4) and to her use of adjectives following the nouns ('Sun-red apples, streaked, and fair', l. 182; 'Purple, pale, and ruby-red', l. 186; 'And the lemon wan and fair', l. 195), which suggest that fruits are the most salient figures of the story.

Rossetti also seems to project the conceptual metaphor FRUITS ARE DOOM, since the description of the banquet recalls 'The Story of the Three Calenders, Sons of Kings; and of the Five Ladies of Bagdad', in which Zobeide's sister, Safie, is helped by a porter to carry all the delicious fruits home for a grand feast ('The lady [. . .] bought several sorts of apples, apricots, peaches, quinces, lemons, citrons, oranges, myrtles, sweet basil, lilies, jessamine, and some other sorts of flowers and plants that smell well'; 'The Story of the Three Calenders, Sons of Kings; and of the Five Ladies of Bagdad', 66). Like the porter in 'The Story of the Three Calenders, Sons of Kings; and of the Five Ladies of Bagdad', Rossetti's lyrical 'I' is seduced by the abundance of all these odorous, ripe fruits, unaware of the perils of luxury. If the porter's curiosity[3] about the ladies of Baghdad leads him almost to his death, then Rossetti's protagonist, who is invited by an uncanny breeze to enter the dead city, risks being turned to stone at the end of the poem. Surrounded by seven black slaves with scimitars in their hands, the porter obeys Zobeide's command to tell his own story in order to be spared. Likewise, Rossetti's character, the sole living being among the statues of the dead staring at her, recalls the breeze's warning – 'Touch not these, but pass them by' ('The Dead City', l. 129) – and saves her life with the power of her resolution: 'Full of fear I bent my head, / Shutting out each stony guest' (ll. 262–3).

Goblin Market and the Temptations of the East: Drugs, Antidotes and Elixirs in Christina Rossetti's Oriental Subworlds

If Rossetti describes the Oriental abundance of fruits in 'The Dead City', suggesting the idea of their poisonous and deadly nature, then she overtly associates fruits with intoxicating drugs leading to death in 'Goblin Market': 'Their fruits like honey to the throat / But poison in the blood' (ll. 554–5). Seen as a parable of sisterhood and salvation, 'Goblin Market' projects its story on to other stories in parabolic fashion, entailing Oriental mental patterns. From this perspective, 'Goblin Market' appears to be a blended space relying heavily on the *Arabian Nights* and in particular on the stories of the three sisters of Baghdad. Rossetti lifts characters, plots, settings and themes out of their original Oriental environment and places them into her new blended space, whose poetic structure allows new insights and new understandings of the elements of the input space to appear.

A primary input source is probably constituted by the abundance of fruits in the poem (apples, quinces, lemons, oranges, cherries, melons, raspberries, peaches, mulberries, cranberries, crab-apples, dewberries, pineapples, blackberries, apricots, strawberries, pomegranates, dates, pears, greengages, damsons, bilberries, gooseberries, barberries, figs and citrons), which refers loosely to the aforementioned fruits bought by Zobeide's oldest sister, Safie, at a fruit shop in 'The Story of the Three Calenders, Sons of Kings; and of the Five Ladies of Bagdad'.[4] A second domain might be the Oriental knowledge of markets as male-owned, as exemplified by 'The Story of Amine', in which Zobeide's second sister visits a malicious silk merchant who demands for his wares only the payment of a kiss. A third domain could be the Eastern knowledge of drug-taking and the consumption of hashish or opium, which, according to Irwin, were used in the recipes of occultists as ingredients in medicines, poisons, aphrodisiacs or even special cakes or decoctions. There are numerous Arabian tales mentioning poisonous food and wine but it is probable that Rossetti found 'The Fourth Voyage of Sinbad the Sailor' particularly appealing because of the survivors of a shipwreck who save their lives by eating fruits. Paradoxically, they are then obliged to eat poisonous herbs by the cannibals who inhabit the island.

The three aforementioned domains combine to structure a poetic story projecting the conceptual metaphor LIFE IS A MARKET. Such is the power of their vividness that, when projected and blended, they might trigger intertextual echoes of other Arabian tales. For example, the word 'market' may evoke 'The Story of Anime', which, as I have already shown in Chapter 1, so deeply touched Dante Gabriel's imagination. As in her brother's illustrations of Anime, Christina seems to reduplicate the violent aggression of the silk merchant who disfigured Anime's face by biting her cheek 'till the blood came' ('The Story of Anime', 135). In Rossetti's view, Oriental merchants become zoomorphic goblins who induce Laura to exchange their forbidden fruits for a lock of her golden hair:

> 'You have much gold upon your head,'
> They answered all together:
> 'Buy from us with a golden curl.'   125
> She clipped a precious golden lock,
> She dropped a tear more rare than pearl,
> Then sucked their fruit globes fair or red:

These lines nicely exemplify the Oriental violence of goblins, who deprive Laura of 'a part of her female identity' (Bloom 2005: 48): that is to say, one of the most taboo parts of the Oriental female body. Like Amine, who is convinced to lift her veil to let the merchant kiss her cheek, Laura is induced to cut off one of her golden locks, as if to trade her femininity for Oriental goods. An Oriental market world is created by the merchant and Anime, as well as by the goblins and Laura, whose discourse worlds involve two categories of participants: the tempter and the sinner. In the 'deictic sub-worlds' (Stockwell 2002: 140) created by their direct speech interactions, Anime and Laura are offered a pact with the devil. The following speech acts provide clear evidence of discourse worlds involving evil merchants and naive female victims:

> I will not sell it for gold or money, but I will make her a present of it, if she will give me leave to kiss her cheek. ('The Story of Anime', 135)

> 'You have much gold upon your head,'
> They answered all together:
> 'Buy from us with a golden curl.'   (ll. 123–5)

Both merchants handle the dimension of possibility and probability using a conditional construction of the prototypical form 'if . . . then . . .', as well as imperative predicates containing shifts in character and objects evoking a whole new world of possibility. In this context, the function-advancing propositions ('if she will give me leave to kiss her cheek'; 'buy from us') are aimed at requesting an exchange of bodily and fetishistic pleasures.

According to Fillmore (1982, 1985), the frame for 'buying and selling', involving participants such as buyer, seller, merchandise and price, is characterised by a rich set of inferences pertaining to ownership, commitments and exchange. But if a sentence like 'Buy from us with a golden curl' occurs in the discourse, and if the goblins, Laura and gold identify elements a, b and c in a mental space, then those elements will be mapped on to the appropriate slots in the Oriental 'buying and selling' frame (Figure 4.1).

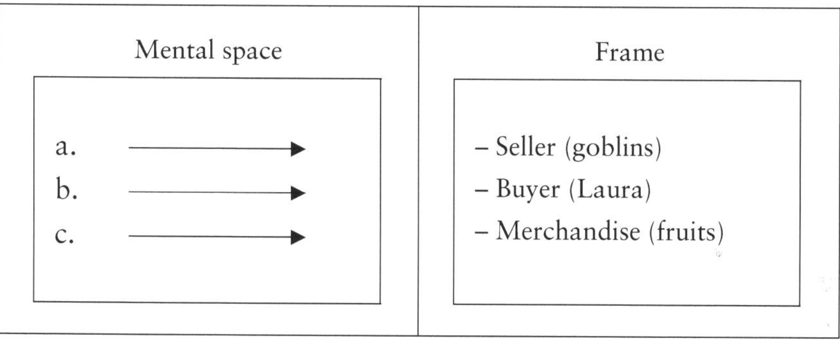

Figure 4.1 The 'buying and selling' frame in 'Goblin Market'.

The mapping between space and frame is straightforward and the roles identified are set up as elements connected to idealised cognitive models, providing a possible mechanism for the operation of metaphor in language. Rossetti seems to project the Oriental metaphor MERCHANTS ARE CORRUPTORS, which is central to the *Arabian Nights*, and offers several other metaphors that are subcategories of this concept. From this perspective, the primary metaphor MERCHANTS ARE CORRUPTORS entails that Oriental merchants (goblins) are evil creatures selling illegal goods whose consumption leads to damnation.

If Laura is obliged to sell her golden lock, becoming addicted to the exotic forbidden fruits, then Lizzie is literally assaulted by the goblins. In search of a remedy for her sister's dependence on the juice that is 'clearer than water' ('Goblin Market', l. 131), Lizzie first faces the verbal seduction of the monstrous merchants and then, after her refusal to feast with them, is attacked by the 'queer' (l. 94), 'sly' (l. 96) and mischievous creatures. Recalling Amine, who is bitten by the merchant and whipped by her husband's slaves, Lizzie risks being killed by the goblins. In verbs like 'trod', 'hustled', 'elbowed', 'jostled' and 'clawed', we profile the aggressors and the victim, evoking a feeble kind of violence, whereas in 'tore her gown', 'soiled her stocking', 'twitched her hair out' and 'stamped upon her tender feet' we profile an overt form of violence that reaches its climax in 'squeezed their fruits / Against her mouth to make her eat' (ll. 406–7). The latter is punishment for not feasting with the goblins and echoes the group violence almost undergone by Amine, whose sentence is described in the following terms:

> Pull her out of bed, said he, and lay her in the middle of the floor. The slaves obeyed his orders, one holding me by the head, another by the feet; he commanded the third to fetch him a scymitar, and when he had brought it, Strike, said he, cut her in two in the middle, and then throw her into the Tigris to feed the fishes. This is the punishment I give to those to whom I have given my heart, if they falsify their promise. When he saw that the slave made no haste to obey his orders, Why do not you strike? said he, who is it that holds you? what are you waiting for? slaves: Pull her out of bed, said he, and lay her in the middle of the floor. ('The Story of Anime', 137)

In 'The Story of Amine' we profile a form of bloody violence against women, as exemplified by verbs such as 'holding me by the head, another by the feet', 'cut her in two in the middle' and 'throw her into the Tigris'. Amine's punishment for disobeying her husband draws attention to the brutality of the Oriental law of retaliation, as opposed to the eerie, unpredictable violence of fairy tales. Filtered through Rossetti's Western imagination, Prince Amin's black slaves are turned into zoomorphic goblins and the deadly scimitar becomes a poisonous fruit whose watery juice leads to death. The shift from a subject–verb construction in lines 399–402 to a verb–object construction in lines 403–7 confirms the crescendo of violence in Rossetti's poem, whose syntax seems to profile the grammatical subject (Lizzie), who is able to resist temptations and violence like Princess Amine.

> They trod and hustled her,
> Elbowed and jostled her,
> Clawed with their nails,
> Barking, mewing, hissing, mocking . . .   (ll. 399–402)

> Tore her gown and soiled her stocking,
> Twitched her hair out by the roots,
> Stamped upon her tender feet,
> Held her hands and squeezed their fruits
> Against her mouth to make her eat.   (ll. 403–7)

If Amine's life is saved by the intervention of her old nurse, who reminds the Prince that 'who kills shall be killed' ('The Story of Amine', 137), then Lizzie, thanks to her stubbornness, which is equated with the temperament of a horse ('One may lead a horse to water, / Twenty cannot make him drink', 'Goblin Market', ll. 422–3), is able to rescue herself and take her sister the miraculous juice. No signs of violence appear on Lizzie's body, apart from the juice running down her face as a result of the goblins' attempt to force-feed her. More similar to Sinbad the Sailor in her smartness of action and in refusing to eat the poisonous food, Lizzie is able to rescue herself and turn the deadly juice into an elixir of life. After sucking the juice from Lizzie's face, Laura regains her light and her 'gleaming locks showed not one thread of grey' (l. 540).

From this perspective, it is worthwhile mentioning the blending between Lizzie's function-advancing propositions and the function-advancers that propel the narrative in 'The Fourth Voyage of Sinbad the Sailor'. Rossetti seems to rely heavily on Sinbad's adventures, which, as stated by Thomas Keightley, author of *The Fairy Mythology*,[5] were inspired by the events that befall Ulysses. As a devoted reader of Homer's *Odyssey*, and deeply influenced by her brother Dante Gabriel, who illustrated both Ulysses' adventures and Sinbad's voyages, Rossetti describes Lizzie as a Sinbad-like character. Unlike their companions, both Sinbad and Lizzie, suspecting some trick or evil, do not accept food from strangers – the blacks and the goblins – whose intentions are anything but friendly.

Sinbad and Lizzie witness the physical transformation of their beloved companions, caused by the poisonous herbs and fruits, and when faced with those forcing drugs on them they are able to escape without being pursued. The following excerpt from 'The Fourth Voyage of Sinbad the Sailor' clarifies the similarities with Rossetti's text world, whose world-building elements constitute the background against which the foreground events take place:

> I, and five of my comrades, were carried to one place; they made us sit down immediately, and gave us a certain herb, which they made signs to us to eat. [. . .] But I, suspecting some trick, would not so much as taste it, which happened well for me; for in a little time after, I perceived my

companions had lost their senses, and that, when they spoke to me, they knew not what they said.

The blacks filled us afterwards with rice, prepared with oil of cocoas; and my comrades, who had lost their reason, eat of it greedily. I eat of it also; but very sparingly. The blacks gave us that herb at first, on purpose to deprive us of our senses, that we might not be aware of the sad destiny prepared for us; and they gave us rice on purpose to fatten us: for, being cannibals, their design was to eat us as soon as we grew fat. They did accordingly eat my comrades, who were not sensible of their condition: but my senses being entire, you may easily guess, gentlemen, that, instead of growing fat, as the rest did, I grew leaner every day. The fear of death, under which I laboured, turned all my food into poison. I fell into a languishing distemper, which proved my safety; for the blacks, having killed and eat up my companions, seeing me to be withered, lean, and sick, deferred my death till another time. ('The Fourth Voyage of Sinbad the Sailor', 158)

All noun phrases specifying characters (Sinbad, mariners and black cannibals) and objects (food: poisonous herbs, rice and oil of cocoas) recall the world-builders of Rossetti's poem (Laura, Lizzie, the goblins and goblin fruits). Apart from different locative adverbs ('to an island' versus 'among the brookside rushes'), temporal adverbs and adverbial clauses from which place and time are recoverable, the text world of 'Goblin Market' resembles the text world of 'The Fourth Voyage of Sinbad the Sailor' in its similar, albeit modified, world-building elements and function-advancers. As in the Arab tale, almost every predication in 'Goblin Market' is a vertical action predication referring to material actions or events. All the actions performed by Lizzie and the goblins draw attention to the actionality of the action through goal-advancing functions related to poisonous food scenes. Figure 4.2 illustrates Rossetti's repatterning of Oriental function-advancers.

However, text world theory offers a means of exploring the details of the differences between an Oriental text and an Orientalised text written by a Western female poet. At the level of function-advancers, the huge difference between 'The Fourth Voyage of Sinbad the Sailor' and 'Goblin Market' is largely accounted for by the omission of a goal-advancing proposition in the Arab tale: namely, the rescue of his companions. If Sinbad witnesses the death of his mariners by poison without being able to help them, then Lizzie ventures into the goblins' glen to rescue her sister from an inevitable drug-induced death.

Function-advancing propositions in 'The Fourth Voyage of Sinbad the Sailor'	*Function-advancing propositions* in 'Goblin Market'
Blacks → 'they made us sit down immediately, and gave us a certain herb, which they made signs to us to eat'	Goblins → 'take a seat with us, / Honour and eat with us'
Sinbad → 'But I, suspecting some trick, would not so much as taste it'	Lizzie → 'If you will not sell me any / of your fruits though much and many, / Give me back my silver penny'
Sinbad's companions → 'my companions had lost their senses'	Lizzie's sister → 'Laura turned as cold as stone'; 'she never caught again the goblin cry'; 'her hair grew thin and grey'
Sinbad → 'Therefore, being sure that they could not come time enough to pursue me, I went on till night.'	Lizzie → 'she ran and ran / as if she feared some goblin man [. . .] / But not one goblin skurried after.'

Figure 4.2 Function-advancing propositions in 'The Fourth Voyage of Sinbad the Sailor' and 'Goblin Market'.

Cognitive Deixis and Orientalism in 'The Prince's Progress'

Another poem projecting the temptations of the East is 'The Prince's Progress', whose prototypical allegory activates the conceptual metaphor LIFE IS A JOURNEY. Like Laura in 'Goblin Market', the female protagonist is endowed 'With gold-dust on her hair' ('The Prince's Progress', l. 498) and experiences the symptoms of drug addiction as she waits in vain for her bridegroom's arrival. If Laura has visions of goblin fruits 'as a traveller sees / False waves in desert drouth' ('Goblin Market', ll. 289–90), then the Princess bride loses her perception of time, falling into a trance-like condition ('the bride she sleepeth, waketh, sleepeth'; 'The Prince's Progress', l. 4) while waiting for her Prince, who, unlike Lizzie, is not able to resist temptations. From this perspective, Rossetti's sleeping Princess, whose hair grows grey ('Till silvery hairs showed in her locks', l. 513), recalling the symptoms and signs of Laura's drug addiction ('But when the moon waxed bright / Her hair grew thin and grey'; 'Goblin Market', ll. 276–7), appears to be addicted to love and opium. More similar to Jeanie in 'Goblin Market', who eventually dies because of eating the goblins' fruits and wearing their flowers, Rossetti's Princess is always depicted with red and white poppies growing at her feet and crowning her royal head. Such an insistence on the image of poppies, commonly known as the principal source of opium, activates metaphorical concepts mapping between cognitive models. The following lines project the embedded metaphor OPIUM IS DEATH, aimed at representing Rossetti's world, in which Dante Gabriel and his wife Lizzie consumed laudanum on a daily basis:

> 'Red and white poppies grow at her feet,
> The blood-red wait for sweet summer heat,
> Wrapped in bud-coats hairy and neat;
>   But the white buds swell, one day they will burst,
> Will open their death-cups drowsy and sweet –
>   Which will open the first?'   (ll. 31–6)

The metaphorical patterns of these lines are so strong and wide that the reader can even understand Rossetti's philosophical view of life itself as being founded on a set of metaphorical representations mapping from flowers to many targets (POPPIES have been mapped with LOVE, LIFE, DEATH, WAITING and DESTINY). Rossetti's poppy metaphor is an expressive and poetic one that tends to have low clarity, since it is not obvious which features are being mapped, but a high degree of richness through the many relations that are carried in the mapping from the source domain to the target domain. Identified with the poppies, the Princess is waiting to know her destiny according to the colour of the poppies that she will wear at the end of the poem. By projecting the conceptual metaphors RED POPPIES ARE LIFE and WHITE POPPIES ARE DEATH, Rossetti not only describes the Princess's dualistic world of life and death but also communicates the uncertainty of the bride's destiny. Due to the impediments and obstacles to reaching his intended bride, the Prince arrives too late – 'too late for love, too late for joy' (l. 475) – and finds the Princess lying on her deathbed wearing white poppies in her locks.

Here, the shadow of Arabian tales becomes available to the reader, who may find links and connections with 'The Story of Amine' and 'The Adventures of Hasan of Basrah' when there are shifts in relational and spatial deixis. This means that when the poem shifts its deictic centre[6] to a different spatial location or even to the deixis of another character, the proximity of Rossetti's poem to the Arabian originator becomes salient. In particular, the first spatial shift enacted by movement predicates ('Forth he set in the breezy morn, / Crossing green field of nodding corn', ll. 49–50) projects the deictic centre to another character, a milkmaid who sells some milk to the thirsty Prince. Recalling the Oriental 'buying and selling' frame of 'The Story of Amine', according to which the merchant is allowed to kiss Amine in exchange for the goods sold, the fee fixed by the milkmaid appears to carry forward a similar stance. Lines like '"You may give the full moon to me; / Or else sit under this apple-tree / Here for one idle day by my side"' (ll. 80–2) identify a buyer, a seller, merchandise and price: that is, elements that are mapped in the 'buying and selling' frame. Instead of an immediate payment of gold, the Prince is asked to talk to the maid in the shade of the apple tree, symbol of the human fall.

Other spatial shifts project the viewpoint of the Prince in the desert – 'A lifeless land, a loveless land, / Without lair or nest on either hand: / Only scorpions jerked in the sand' (ll. 133–5) – and then project another embedded deictic centre to the cavern of an alchemist that the Prince finds while wandering in the untrodden and labyrinthine land. We can follow the Prince in different places through expressions locating the deictic centre in other sites, including the spatial adverbs 'here/there' and 'out'; the locatives 'above earth's molten centre' and 'out it flashed from a yawn-mouthed cave'; the demonstrative 'this way'; and the verbs of motion 'Up rose the Prince', 'going forth', 'off he set' and 'groping his way'.

Once in the cavern, the shift in deixis is perceptual and activated by expressions concerning the perceptive participants (the Prince and the alchemist), as exemplified by definite references such as 'an old, old mortal' (l. 178), 'with grimy fingers' (l. 182), 'a nose all bony and hooked' (l. 183) and 'his blinking eyes' (l. 185). In this section of the poem, literary voices are introduced through presentative structures and noun phrases in order to mention the perceptual voices of both the Prince and the alchemist frequently. From this perspective, deictic shifts occur up and down the virtual plane of the perceptual deictic field. When the narrator is describing the alchemist and his cave, the poem shifts its deictic centre down to the deictic centre of the Prince, who asks for shelter for the night. Then, there is a quick shift up to the narrative voice describing the sorcerer's reaction ('The old voice whistled as through a leak', l. 194), followed by a 'push'[7] into the deictic centre of the alchemist, who proposes a bargain to the exhausted Prince: '"Work for wage is a bargain fit"' (l. 196). By preserving his perceptual deixis, the narrator introduces characters that are accessible only through him. Pops and pushes are balanced throughout Rossetti's poem, but in this particular section the narrative pushes and pops from the deictic centres of the narrator, the Prince and the alchemist. The following lines surround this major deictic shift in narrative, from the narrator to the alchemist:

> The head turned not to hear him speak;
> The old voice whistled as through a leak
> (Out it came in a quavering squeak):
>   'Work for wage is a bargain fit:
> If there's aught of mine that you seek
>   You must work for it.
> 'Buried alive from light and air
> This year is the hundredth year,   200
> I feed my fire with a sleepless care,
>   Watching my potion wane or wax:
> Elixir of Life is simmering there,
>   And but one thing lacks.
>
> 'If you're fain to lodge here with me,
> Take that pair of bellows you see –
> Too heavy for my old hands they be –
>   Take the bellows and puff and puff:
> When the steam curls rosy and free
>   The broth's boiled enough.   210
>
> 'Then take your choice of all I have;
> I will give you life if you crave.
> Already I'm mildewed for the grave,
>   So first myself I must drink my fill:
> But all the rest may be yours, to save
>   Whomever you will.'

From these lines it is clear how Rossetti recreates and extends the text world of 'The Adventures of Hasan of Basrah' through the transposition of the Arabian plot into a different text world. As I have already shown in Chapter 3, the figure of Barham, the Persian fire worshipper in 'The Adventures of Hasan of Basrah', touched Morris's imagination deeply. Thus, Rossetti's projection of the Arabian themes and characters into a new blended space seems to confirm the Pre-Raphaelites' fascination with the Oriental mysteries of alchemy. In both the Arabian tale and 'The Prince's Progress' we find a similar action-chain pattern characterised by an agent (Barham/the alchemist) acting as the head of an action chain (preparing the potion), which moves through several stages including an instrument (Hasan/the Prince) to arrive at the tail of the action chain with the patient[8] (the elixir). These Oriental contexts are explicitly named in the poem:

> lines 196–216 bargaining
> lines 217–23 apprenticing
> lines 224–48 potion making

While there are many other aspects to the poem, it is essential to focus on the participant roles and patterns in the action chains. The first action chain represents a dynamic predication of a bargaining process that recalls Barham deceiving Hasan: '"Work for wage is a bargain fit"' (l. 196). Not only does Barham promise to turn brass into gold but also he offers to teach Hasan the mysteries of his science if he agrees to help him find the ingredient lacking from the potion: 'That high and pointed mountain [. . .] is Cloud Mountain and there I find the necessary elements for my elixir. If you will let yourself be led to its top, I swear by Light and Fire that you will not regret it' ('The Adventures of Hasan of Basrah', 167). Likewise, Rossetti's alchemist is the active agent who proposes an exchange to the Prince, the patient who is the receiver of the act of bargaining: the old man will agree to lodge the Prince only if the latter becomes his apprentice. In the second range of lines, however, the Prince is still the patient in the process, even though he is in subject position 'First he piled on resinous wood, / Next plied the bellows in hopeful mood' ('The Prince's Progress', ll. 218–19). All the magician's instructions are followed by the Prince, who is asked to take a pair of heavy bellows and to pile on wood in the same way that Hasan accomplishes his apprentice tasks: 'Hasan placed the pieces in the crucible, worked at the fire and blew upon the metal with his air cane until the metal melted' ('The Adventures of Hasan of Basrah', 163).

In the last lines, the magician plays a passive role in the process, which semantically diminishes him. Line 237, 'Death snapped the old worn-out tool', transforms the role of the former agent (the alchemist) into the patient similarly to 'The Adventures of Hasan of Basrah', in which the patient, Hasan, becomes the agent: 'With the quickness of light he hurled himself on the sorcerer and, snatching the drum from his hands, pushed him towards the edge of the mountain' ('The Adventures of Hasan of Basrah', 168). Despite a few minor differences, the action chains in 'The Prince's Progress' have to be tracked in the same dynamic sequence as in the Arabian tale. In cognitive terms, the active processes involving the changes in the relationship between agent, patient and instrument are 'sequentially scanned' (Stockwell 2002: 66) and not 'summarily scanned' (66) as a static configuration. As Stockwell clarifies, the difference between a summary and a sequential scanning has been likened to examining a still photograph and watching a film. This dynamism characterises Rossetti's poem, projecting the conceptual metaphor THE ELIXIR OF LIFE IS DEATH, since, despite its vivifying power, the potion defined as 'draught of life' ('The Prince's Progress', l. 257) leads inevitably to death: both the alchemist and the bride die because of the phial of life, and the Prince almost drowns in a deep river while clutching the phial in his hand.

Ford Madox Ford's Oriental Impressions: The Cognitive Grammar of *The Brown Owl*

As an impressionist storyteller, aiming at showing things rather than telling them, Ford found the *Arabian Nights* particularly fascinating for their crafty storytelling and incredible marvels. In *The March of Literature* (1939), he traces back the Eastern origins of the art of telling stories, seen as a practice well rooted in the Oriental meeting place *par excellence*, the bazaar. The following excerpt exemplifies Ford's interest in the East:

> The practice, indeed, of telling long stories, centered round one individual hero and the narration occupying several days or nights is one singularly widespread, enduring and ancient. Still in the bazaars of the whole East the practice continues, little crowds sitting round a narrator who continues to tell for day after day the adventures of some prince and a peri or some sheikh and a genie. (1994: 492)

As with Rossetti, Oriental bazaars are of the utmost importance to Ford, who envisions a world of marvels and adventures inhabited by archetypical Oriental figures such as Sinbad and Ali Baba. He defines 'Sinbad the Sailor' and 'Ali Baba and the Forty Thieves' as 'type-stories [which] have persisted since the Egyptian legendary days' (1994: 491). These emblematic characters and their characteristics are seen by Ford as significant beyond the specifics of their Oriental worlds. In this view, 'Sinbad the Sailor' becomes the emblem of seafaring and sea adventures, projecting the conceptual metaphor LIFE IS A JOURNEY. Similarly, 'Ali Baba and the Forty Thieves' is emblematic of stealing and the good fortune activating the conceptual metaphor LIFE IS A TREASURE. Both Sinbad and Ali Baba appear to be the architects of their fortunes and misfortunes because, in Irwin's words, they 'have no character, no inner depth and no psychological consistency. They are what they do, or, rather, they are what fate [. . .] makes them do' (Irwin 2004: 197).

These Oriental emblems can be metaphorically mapped back on to Ford's specific narratives, on to *The Brown Owl* (1892), *The Feather* (1892) and *The Queen Who Flew* (1894). Ford seems to be blending together parts of Oriental narratives and his biographical experiences, which are mapped to form a generic space and combined into a blended space. Ford's fairy tales thus become blends, whose conceptual contents take on a life of their own, revealing intertextual relations with the *Arabian Nights*. In particular, *The Brown Owl*, a fairy tale written to amuse Ford's sister Juliet, is a conceptual blend involving Oriental characters from disparate Arabian tales and holding together the imaginary and marvel domains of different stories. A case in point is King Intafernes, a powerful magician able to transform himself into an owl, a guardian animal for his exceedingly beautiful daughter, Princess Ismara, whose golden hair 'fell over her shoulders, like a shining waterfall falling in ripples to her waist' (*The Brown Owl*, 3).

Notably, metamorphosis into animals is a pervasive motif in the *Arabian Nights*, which is also indicative, according to Irwin, of Buddhist and Hindu ideas on reincarnation. There are many Arabian tales featuring men who turn into birds,[9] eagles[10] and owls[11]; it therefore seems probable that Ford was inspired by the Oriental element of metamorphosis as envisioned in the *Arabian Nights*. It is highly significant that King Intafernes turns into an owl, symbol of wisdom in Western culture, and epitome of luxuries and riches in Hindu mythology. According to the latter, each god has his or her own *vahana*, or vehicle, and Goddess Lakshmi's *vahana* is the owl, also known as *uluka* in Sanskrit. From this perspective, various input spaces (such as the positive and negative meanings pertaining to the owl) are mapped from a generic space and combined into a blended space. Though considered to be an omen of death ('[Owls] bring scarlatina, and they always carry the influenza epidemic', *The Brown*

Owl, 13), Ford's metamorphosed owl is a magic helper who protects Princess Ismara and saves her life: 'The touch of the Owl seemed to have driven away her grief, and she felt quite light and joyful in the beautiful sunshine' (19).

There are several source domains that are blended in the character of King Intafernes, whose name is of Greek origin[12] and whose kingdom, inhabited by a multitude of magicians, recalls the City of the Magicians in 'The Story of Prince Amgrad, and a Lady of the City of the Magicians'. We can then discern a second set of triggers that are located at a relational level: that is, the relational aspect of the participants within the text, in terms of how they are socially related to each other. In the fairy-tale scenario, Princess Ismara and the owl are socially anchored in relation to each other. Interestingly, the bath scene, in which Ismara washes herself in cold water in the presence of the owl before being crowned, seems to recall Scheherazade bathing in the *hammam* in preparation for her wedding. Cleansing in preparation for a new beginning appears to be a rite of passage for both Ismara and Scheherazade, and marks the evolution of their new social position: respectively, queen and queen bride. But it is the presence of the owl and the Princess's attitude that project Oriental deictic expressions evocative of Scheherazade's *hammam*-bath scene. Exactly like Scheherazade and her attendants, Ismara and the owl establish a relational deixis within an Oriental scenario in which the public bathing ritual is a means of washing away the old life in preparation for the new. Ismara's words, expressions and attitudes display all of these facets of Oriental deixis. Before her ritual bathing and purification, Ismara addresses the following words to her metamorphosed attendant: '"Come, my cherished Owl, sit there on the crown on the top of the looking-glass frame and wait while I wash my hands and face and make myself tidy"' (*The Brown Owl*, 20). All the rituals performed by Ismara are imbued with Oriental references, as exemplified by her combing her hair and encircling her head with jewels ('she put on her gold circlet as a sign of her rank', 21), similarly to Scheherazade and her sister, who decorate themselves with 'jewels of price' ('The Tale of Scheherazade Concluded', 651).

Even more than that, though, Ismara achieves cognitive prominence in a Scheherazade-like manner, as the small but prominent items belonging to her (eyes, hair and jewels) in the visual field receive attention and focus, thereby becoming the figure in the ground. Thanks to her bodily beauty and luminous apparel, Ismara becomes a prominent figure through the details of her attractive physical appearance, which are better focused and seem to be brighter and more appealing than the rest of the field. If Scheherazade's face outshines the brilliant flambeaux of wax in the gold candelabra, then the intensity of Ismara's luminous image reflected in the mirror almost blinds the owl, who shuts his eyes because 'the light was too strong for him' (*The Brown Owl*, 21).

Ismara's bath scene is characterised by Oriental visual determinants of prominence (eyes, hair and jewels), involving a process of renewing attention to create the relations between figure and ground. As suggested by Stockwell, 'reading a literary text is a dynamic experience' (2002: 18), characterised by different facets of attention that, in this case, are particularly useful in considering Oriental references.

Likewise, Merrymineral, the evil Chancellor of the kingdom, seems to recall Aladdin's African magician in his many acts of deceit, which project the conceptual metaphor ORIENTAL MAGIC IS DECEPTION. Supposed to be a faithful and pious figure, Merrymineral initially seems to be an 'acting participant' (Stockwell 2002: 64) serving a kingdom of magicians. Of note is his rhetorical question about being a servant to his master: '"To such a master and to such a mistress how could I but be faithful?"' (*The Brown Owl*, 4). But even more than that, it is Merrymineral's compassionate and empathic attitude toward the orphan Princess that activates an action-chain pattern evocative of Aladdin's African magician. Like the latter, Merrymineral, after deceiving the young Princess, soon reveals his mean intentions: that is, to usurp her power and ultimately kill her. All active processes involving the dynamic changes in Merrymineral's personality can be sequentially scanned in order to demonstrate the Oriental semantic role played by Ford's character in the cognitive model underlying sentences that are based on role archetypes. As suggested by Stockwell, patients are participants receiving the energy of a predicate, which, unlike nominals and stative modifiers, are not summarily scanned as objects but are sequentially scanned in the action chain. There is an Oriental cognitive impact in the sentences uttered by Merrymineral. Compare, for example:

'I came,' he moaned, 'to console you for your great loss. I too,' he continued in a voice choked with sobs, 'I too am an orphan.' (25)
    (patient 'you', as part of a sequentially scanned process)

'You jackanapes,' he screamed at the unfortunate page; 'you ape, you boar, you cow, you clumsy monkey, I'll be revenged on you.' (29)
    (patient 'you' again, sequentially scanned in the action chain)

In the first example, Merrymineral is a *mover*, since he physically moves to another location with the aim of consoling the orphan Princess, exactly like the African magician who 'went up to [Aladdin] and taking him aside from his comrades, said to him, Child, [. . .] I am your uncle' ('The Story of Aladdin, or, the Wonderful Lamp', 652). As a relief for his affliction, caused by his brother's death, the African magician embraces Aladdin,[13] who was orphaned so early, and tries to find some comfort and relief in the arms of his nephew. But the second example reveals the true nature of Merrymineral, who, provoked by the Princess's pages, soon expresses his intentions of revenge. Both magical *agents*, Merrymineral and the African magician cause things to happen by uttering magical words meant to hurt Ismara and Aladdin, playing passive roles as themes in the process, a process that semantically diminishes them in both cases.

If Merrymineral threatens Ismara and her pages with revenge by uttering offensive epithets such as 'jackanapes', 'ape', 'boar', 'cow' and 'clumsy monkey', which are able to turn them into animals, then the African magician pronounces two magical words in order to close off the underground cave with Aladdin in it. The following extract reveals the magician's true nature and his use of magic for evil purposes:

> Give me the lamp first, replied the magician; it will be troublesome to you. Indeed, uncle, answered Aladdin, I cannot now; it is not troublesome to me; but I will as soon as I am up. The African magician, provoked at this obstinate refusal of the lad, grew into a terrible passion, and threw a little of his perfume into the fire, which he had taken care to keep in; and no sooner pronounced two magical words, but the stone moved into its place, and the earth closed again, in the same manner as it had opened at the arrival of the magician and Aladdin. ('The Story of Aladdin, or, the Wonderful Lamp', 659)

The selected extracts from 'The Story of Aladdin, or, the Wonderful Lamp' and *The Brown Owl* consist of a similar action-chain pattern (*showing up*, *deceiving*, *consoling* and *revenging*), representing a dynamic predication of a cognitive process according to which magicians are active agents whose magical speech acts give them prominence in the action chain. But there is a difference, of course, between the predications. Merrymineral's illocutionary act 'I'll be revenged on you' introduces his wicked nature, drawing in the domain knowledge of cruel intentions, while the African magician is an *experiencer*: 'throw his perfume into the fire' and 'pronounce magical words'. Though there are differences of predications in the action-chain scheme (threaten to revenge versus revenge), both magicians appear to be artful deceivers employing magic for evil purposes.

Restructuring and Tuning Oriental Schemas in *The Feather*

Conceptually dependent on the *Arabian Nights*, Ford's *The Feather* contains language and a selection of words that appear to be influenced by the sets of ideas projected in the stories of Sinbad the Sailor. With a frontispiece on glazed paper by Ford Madox Brown representing Princess Ernalie carried across the mountains by Jupiter's Eagle, *The Feather* seems to pay homage to 'The Second Voyage of Sinbad the Sailor', in which the hero escapes from an island by tying himself to a giant eagle's leg. Like Sinbad, Ernalie is visually and linguistically associated with a monstrous bird, a hyperbolically marvellous creature belonging to phenomena 'which are supernatural only by virtue of their dimensions' (Todorov 1975: 54). By looking at Brown's illustration the reader will link elements together and see figures that are derived from previously read Arabian tales. The visual Oriental frame of the illustration, along with the Oriental conceptual structures drawn from memory to assist in understanding utterances, may suggest what to expect from Ford's fairy tale. Oriental scripts are found in *The Feather* consisting of Oriental slots that are assumed to pertain in an Arabian situation: props, participants, entry conditions, results and sequence of events. According to schema theory, Princess Ernalie's story seems to apply so-called 'tuning': that is to say, a kind of evolution of Oriental schemas that is able to modify facts or relations within the schema. For readers who have only a passing familiarity with the story of Sinbad the Sailor, its schema typically has slots such as ships, jewels and diamonds (props); mariners, merchants and monsters (participants); desert islands, caves and valleys of diamonds (entry conditions); avoidance of death and treasure enrichment (results); and journeys, combats against monsters and stratagems to save his life (sequence of events).

This type of schema is refreshed and expanded in *The Feather*, where new facts are added to the existing Oriental schema, enlarging its scope and explanatory range. Ford's literary Oriental schema is treated in a different way because, when compared with the organising principles of Sinbad's world schema, it is possible to measure the divergence from the reader's expectations of text and language schemas. On a scale of informativity,[14] both 'The Second Voyage of Sinbad the Sailor' and *The Feather* are characterised by impossible or highly unlikely things showing a high degree of deviation from reality: that is, a third-order informativity. But compared with 'The Second Voyage of Sinbad the Sailor', *The Feather* is a more feminist view of the conceptual metaphor LIFE IS A JOURNEY. All the headers that instantiate the Oriental script – that is to say, all the references to Sinbad's adventures, to the actions leading to the realisation of the Arabian script, as well as to the setting in which it usually applies – invoke a feminist schema, as exemplified by Princess Ernalie's journey. The following extract describes how the eagle seized Ernalie and later let her down on a rock:

> It was only an eagle, not a boggles; but it was on the look-out for food, and the sun shining on the Princess's hair had caught its eyes, and in spite of the cries of the nurse it swooped down, and, seizing the Princess in its claws, began to carry her off. [. . .]
> Meanwhile the eagle continued flying straight towards the sun, which was getting lower and lower, so that by the time they reached the mountains it was dark altogether. But the eagle didn't seem at all afraid of the darkness, and just went on flying as if nothing had happened, until suddenly it let the Princess down on a rock – at least, that was what it seemed to her to be. Not knowing what else to do, she sat where the eagle had let her fall, for she remembered something about the precipice three miles deep, and she did not at all wish to tumble down that. (*The Feather*, 7–8)

Such instrumental and locale headers as 'the eagle seized the Princess in its claws, and began to carry her off' and 'the eagle let the Princess down on a rock' seem to evoke the schemas related to the story of Sinbad the Sailor, who, unlike Ernalie, was voluntarily carried by an eagle to the valley of diamonds.

> As I perceived her coming, I crept close to the egg, so that I had before me one of the legs of the bird, that was as big as the trunk of a tree; I tied myself strongly to it with the cloth that went round my turban, in hopes that when the roc[15] flew away next morning, she would carry me with her out of this desert island. [. . .] The place where it left me was a very deep valley, encompassed on all sides with mountains so high that they seemed to reach above the clouds, and so full of steep rocks, that there was no possibility to get out of the valley. ('The Second Voyage of Sinbad the Sailor', 148)

By modifying some facts and relations within the Arabian schema, Ford restructures the story of Sinbad the Sailor, whose props (diamonds) are substituted by the feather of invisibility that belonged to one of Jupiter's eagles. The latter was banished from Mount Olympus for accusing the god of giving its brother eagle more than its share of food. It is highly significant that food is also the prop in the schema scenario of Sinbad the Sailor. In order to escape the valley of diamonds, which is haunted by a great number of serpents, Sinbad covers himself up with a large piece of meat in order to lure the eagle, which eventually carries him to its nest on the top of the rocks. 'The Second Voyage of Sinbad the Sailor' projects the conceptual metaphor FOOD IS LIFE because Sinbad is able to escape from the valley thanks to the pieces of meat left by the merchants as baits used to lure the eagles. On the contrary, Ford uses the conceptual metaphor FOOD IS DEATH in *The Feather*, since Jupiter's eagle is banished from Mount Olympus for complaining about its portions of food. Once on earth, the Olympian creature is killed by a man who shoots an arrow into the centre of its 'mass of tumbled feathers' (*The Feather*, 11).

The Elixir of Life/Death: Oriental Patterns and Variables in *The Queen Who Flew*

Also founded on similar metaphorical representations, *The Queen Who Flew* refreshes the Oriental schema of Sinbad the Sailor and enlarges the scope of the existing schema of 'The Adventures of Hasan of Basrah'. Like the stories of Sinbad and Hasan, *The Queen Who Flew* is characterised by a particularly high degree of deviation from our sense of reality. Such impossible things as flying over the valleys and drinking the elixir of immortality invoke the Oriental schemas of the *Arabian Nights*. The story of Eldrida, Queen of the Narrowlands and all the isles, flying away from her corrupt kingdom with the help of a talking bat who reveals to her the secrets of a magical flower, seems to revise the marvellous schema of 'The Second Voyage of Sinbad the Sailor'. The typical slots of this story – eagle, treasure and flying – are revisited by Ford, who turns a giant eagle into a small talking bat. Oriental membership elements and relations are recast, but if in 'The Second Voyage of Sinbad the Sailor' the eagle is a vehicle for flying, then in *The Queen Who Flew* the talking bat reveals the secret to activate the flight sorcery: 'Put the flower somewhere about you, and then go off. Only be careful not to knock against things' (*The Queen Who Flew*, 20).

Both non-prototypical flying animals (the roc and the small talking bat) are fatally attracted by raw meat. It is not by chance that Sinbad and Eldrida offer the roc and the bat pieces of raw meat in order to obtain their liberty. As already mentioned, Sinbad's stratagem to save himself is based on the pieces of raw meat spread all over the valley in order to attract the roc, which eventually seizes them for feeding its young eaglets. Likewise, albeit with an overt *do ut des* approach, Queen Eldrida persuades the bat to tell her the secret of the wind-flower by offering him some raw meat: 'Well, I'll tell you if you'll bring me a nice piece of raw meat, and a little red flannel for my rheumatism' (*The Queen Who Flew*, 8). Thanks to this instrumental header ('Eldrida offered the bat some raw meat'), which is a means towards realisation of the script, it is possible to understand how Ford restructures the Arabian schema of 'The Second Voyage of Sinbad the Sailor' by enlarging its scope and modifying some props. From this perspective, *The Queen Who Flew* projects the Oriental conceptual metaphors FLYING IS ESCAPING and FLYING IS SURVIVING, as inspired by the adventures of Sinbad the Sailor.

At the same time, however, such anomalies as the elixir of life and the infusion of wind-flowers that is able to cure blindness can be downgraded backwards into the memory of another Arabian tale like 'The Adventures of Hasan of Basrah'. Like Rossetti's Prince in 'The Prince's Progress', who desperately tries to save his intended bride with the elixir of life, Queen Eldrida aims to cure the blindness of her beloved ploughman with an infusion of dried wind-flowers, the same wind-flowers encircling her gold–brown hair and activating the flight sorcery. The instructions for preparing the magical infusion are explained in the following dialogue:

> And the Queen replied, 'Don't be stupid. Oh, and tell me how one can cure blindness with wind-flowers.'
> The bat said, 'Do you know how to make tea?'
> 'Of course I do,' the Queen answered.
> 'Well, you make an infusion of dried windflowers just like tea, and then you give it to the young scamp to drink.' (*The Queen Who Flew*, 104)

As a Pre-Raphaelite sympathiser, Ford creates a new schema by generalising an old one. Notably, for the Pre-Raphaelites, drinking a cup of tea was, in Weintraub's words, 'a heart relished luxury' (1978: 32), a health-giving and addictive practice that, in Ford's imagination, becomes a magical remedy for blindness. In this case, he would pattern the tea schema on the infusion schema, but with certain variables much more tightly specified. Compared to the elixir of life, the infusion of wind-flowers is a result of what Rumelhart and Norman call *patterned schema generation* (1978: 46), according to which new schemas can be patterned on old ones. Ford seems to restructure and refine the Oriental schema representing 'The Adventures of Hasan of Basrah', showing the interrelationship between Hasan and the Persian alchemist called Bahram from a new feminist perspective. As Timothy Weiss maintains, 'Ford was fascinated by the idea of woman; her image is a powerful creative force in his psyche' (1984: 33). Thus, Ford forms the concept of 'the elixir of life' by substituting Hasan with Eldrida and replacing the fire-worshipper with 'the famous witch who has the well of the Elixir of Life' (*The Queen Who Flew*, 64). Through the adjustment of a few variables, 'the curative infusion' schema can be created by patterning it on the Oriental 'elixir of life' schema, modifying it in just the way the elixir schema differs from the infusion schema.

Paradoxically, the elixir of life prepared by both Bahram and the witch leads to death, while the infusion of wind-flowers made by Eldrida has the power to cure. After boiling the only remaining wind-flowers, Eldrida pours the golden, straw-coloured infusion into a drinking horn and takes it to her beloved ploughman:

> She put the horn into his hand, and said, 'Drink this.'
> 'Why, what is it ?' she asked.
> 'It is what I went to fetch,' she said; 'drink it and see.'
> The light was shining on his face as he raised it to his mouth and drank it off, and suddenly came into his eyes a look of great joy.
> 'Why,' he said, 'I can see' and in a moment he had thrown his arms round her and drew her tightly to him.
> 'I love you more than all the world!' he said 'Do you love me?'
> She seemed to have forgotten all about the elixir, for instead of saying, 'Don't be ridiculous' she just said, 'Yes, I love you very much.'
> (*The Queen Who Flew*, 116–17)

In her journey across the kingdom, Eldrida comes to understand that the elixir of life is the elixir of love, since anyone who drinks the water from the well of immortality falls desperately in love with her. She receives various marriage proposals before she meets the blind ploughman: one from Lord Blackjowl, the Regent of the kingdom, one from the cruel and ugly King Mark, and one from the gentleman demon, who wants to bargain her soul away, as well as one from the Prince in shepherd's clothes, and one from the tailor, who is ready to kill his witch-wife. All these suitors have drunk the elixir of life or at least have asked for the elixir from Mrs Hexer, the horrible witch who lives with a black cat in a hollow among the sand dunes.

Mrs Hexer seems to blend two Oriental magic schemas, whose different variables are constrained. With her well containing the elixir of life, she recalls Bahram, the alchemist who is able to produce the elixir that transmutes brass into gold. But in transforming a multitude of people, including the Prince/shepherd who proposes to Eldrida, into geese, Mrs Hexer is similar to Queen Labe,[16] the most prototypical sorceress in the *Arabian Nights*, a Circe-like character who turns all her lovers into animals by feeding them with poisoned food. Figure 4.3 illustrates the conceptual blending that creates not just a new mental space but also a new type of Orientalism in Ford's fairy tale.

As the figure shows, information from the generic space of Oriental sorcerers includes evil, deception and death. The generic background informs the construction of both Bahram's story and

Generic space
Oriental sorcerers
Evil, deception and death

Specific source	General target
Arabian Nights 'The Adventures of Hasan of Basrah' Bahram is a terrible magician, able to produce the elixir of life, who asks Hasan to find the necessary ingredients for his elixir on Cloud Mountain; he eventually dies by *falling* from a high rock 'The Story of Beder, Prince of Persia, and Giahaure, Princess of Samandal' Queen Labe is an evil sorceress, ruler of the Enchanted City, who turns her lovers into animals by feeding them with poisoned food	Oriental sorcerers are evil magicians who prepare elixirs of life as well as poisoned food and potions

Blend
Ford's Mrs Hexer is like Bahram and Queen Labe
A class member is the prototype

Figure 4.3 Conceptual blending network for Ford's Mrs Hexer.

Queen Labe's story, which is vital for conceptualising the blend of the general with the specific. Ford's witch appears to be a member of the Oriental sorcerers category, within which Bahram and Queen Labe are the prototypes. Properties and elements of both generic space and specific space are combined together in the blended space, where new Oriental relations become apparent.

Of particular interest is Ford's description of the witch's hut, which is rich in tonal effects and ambient features, evoking Oriental stories. The ambience of the following literary passage can be explored systematically within cognitive linguistics:

> And there, in a hollow among the sand-dunes, stood a funny little black erection, such as you might see upon a beach.
>
> So the Queen alighted and walked towards the house. In front of the door a cat was sitting – a black cat. But not a magnificent creature with a glossy coat that sits on the rug in front of the drawing-room fire and only drinks cream, deeming mice too vulgar. This was a long-limbed, little creature, that looked half-starved and seemed as if its proper occupation would be stealing along, very lanky and grim in the moonlight, over the dunes to catch rabbits. (*The Queen Who Flew*, 45)

This passage reveals Ford's impressionist style, which is based mainly on the psychology of the viewer/reader. There are a great number of evaluative elements that foreground the subjectivity of the narrative voice and encourage the reader towards a *subjective construal*[17]: a foregrounding of multi-adjective phrases such as 'funny little black erection' and 'long-limbed, little creature', a conscious use of expressions of implication such as 'and seemed as if', and a deployment of litotes as a form of verbal irony to describe the witch's black cat ('not a magnificent creature with a glossy coat that sits on the rug in front of the drawing-room fire'). The latter is the prominent figure of Ford's description, whose evaluative lexis serves to focus readerly attention on the specific Oriental features of the world in view. Far from being a Persian cat, which Ford regarded as the quintessential embodiment of elegance,[18] Mrs Hexer's black cat is depicted as 'lanky and grim', chasing rabbits among the dunes. Just like the cat described in the poem 'The Cat of the House', who attests his origins with pride ('I, born of a race of strange things / of deserts, great temples, great kings, / in the hot sands where the nightingale never sings!', Ford 2003a: 128), the black cat soon reveals his hyperbolic marvellous nature. Mrs Hexer's black cat is endowed with the power to change his size in order to devour his prey easily. This transformation is perceived anxiously by Eldrida, who witnesses the magical growth of the animal, the latter reaching the size of a lion. In a crescendo of hyperbolic expressions, the narrator is able to encourage the reader to see through Eldrida's eyes and feel as if he/she is experiencing the presented world directly. The following selected chunks of sentences determine the ambience of the scene, which is characterised by what linguists call *lexical priming*:

1. 'Your cat doesn't seem to be very sociable,' she said to the old woman. (*The Queen Who Flew*, 48)
2. The cat began to grow visibly. (49)
3. The cat was growing larger and larger, till the Queen grew positively afraid. (49)
4. The great cat rubbed against her skirt and licked its jaws. It was about the size of a lion now. (50)

All the evidence suggests that atmospheric fear is induced by the lexical priming of words, collocations and clause constructions that are aimed at visualising the slow transformation of the animal from a skinny cat to a large lion. Such a 'marvellous growth' schema seems to be patterned on another Arabian marvellous growth schema that can be found in 'The Story of Noureddin Ali, and Bedreddin Hassan'. In this story, a black cat who grows as big as a buffalo appears to a humpback in order to deliver to him a mysterious message. As a magical helper to an evil genius, the black cat featuring in the *Arabian Nights* appears to be the old schema on which a new black cat schema can be patterned by modifying some of the variable components (a genie is replaced by a witch and the expression of equality 'to grow as big as a buffalo' is turned into 'to grow as a lion').

The pervasive influence of the *Arabian Nights* on Ford's writings is also attested to by *Zeppelin Nights – A London Entertainment* (1916), written in collaboration with Violet Hunt during the war years. Apparently more similar in style to Boccaccio's *Decameron*, the Zeppelin stories are nevertheless imbued with exotic and Oriental references. Like Scheherazade, a group of intellectuals afraid of dying under the German bombs that Ford metaphorically calls 'Zeppelins', find refuge in a 'cellar *garni*' and pass the time by reading aloud a series of sketches dealing with historical world events spanning the period from the year 490 BC to the coronation of King George V. Candour Viola (alias Violet Hunt) and Serapion Hunter (alias Ford

Madox Ford) organise these reading sessions in their dwellings in order to exorcise the fear of 'the German Night Hag' (Ford 1916: 1), and above all to keep 'civilisation going beneath the shades' (8). More similar to historians rather than storytellers, the Violas (the authors gathering at Candour's house) and the Hunters (the guests at Serapion's house) employ projection and blending in their parabolic stories in order to fight against the mental paralysis induced by the fear of death.

This cognitive process of parable is particularly evident in the first story, entitled 'No Heroes', which projects Oriental conceptual metaphors such as LIFE IS A BATTLE and LIFE IS A MARKET. The story of Ramen, an Etruscan slave to Euripides, a gardener from Athens, selling figs at the market and waiting for news from the Battle of Marathon, is a parable of fear that projects Ramen's mental state on to Serapion's mind. The battle, which took place on 29 September in 490 BC, represents the first Persian invasion of Greece during the Greco-Persian Wars, which ended in the eventual Greek triumph. From this perspective, 'No Heroes' helps Serapion to make sense of the battle that he is fighting against the Zeppelins, projecting such positive concepts as HOPE and FREEDOM. Through parabolic projection and conceptual blending, Ford suggests that Londoners, like the Athenians, can defeat the more numerous and powerful Germans/ Persians.

But even more than that, Ford blends together all Arabian schemas – marketplace, treasure, liquor and slavery – restructuring them and replacing some variables to offer a new impressionist version of Orientalism. Ford seems to create a grammar of Oriental ambience, even though the scene is set in Athens. Despite an impressionistic description of the broad and open marketplace with its acropolis, white edifices and statues, Ford creates a Greek marketplace schema by patterning it on the Arabian marketplace schema. Within this schema, Ramen, the malevolent slave selling figs, is a figure who moves across the ground, either spatially or qualitatively, as he evolves and collects traits for his apparent psychological development. His movements are stylistically represented through verbs of motion ('he had brought with him', 17; 'the unsold figs that he would have to bear', 18) and through locative expressions using prepositions ('in the market-place', 20; 'upon the steps', 21; 'from the distant street', 22; 'into the vacant market-place', 22) that are understood as image schemas. Probably due to his inability to sell figs at the marketplace and to the upcoming invasion of the Persians,

Ramen, who recalls all the evil merchants analysed so far (Rossetti's goblins, the merchant who disfigures Anime, and Ali Baba's forty thieves), plans to steal a hidden treasure and lead the Persians to it in order to be rewarded.

To conclude, the image schemas that Ford uses for conceptualising the East not only are structured on a large number of tales from the *Arabian Nights* that function as patterns of understanding the Oriental world, but also are dependent on Rossetti's influence. As Grover Smith has summarised, Rossetti and Ford 'were both ritualists of sorts and both seekers' (1986: 293), building up image schemas in their minds that they tended to share with the community in which they lived. If Rossetti conceived poetry as discovery, then Ford aimed at promoting 'the comprehension of one kind of mind by another' (2012: 55), thereby Orientalising their writings with powerful visual images evoking the temptations of the East.

Notes

1. 'Hero' is the story of a girl, metamorphosed into a diamond, who encounters a tribe of semi-barbarous fishermen trading diamonds and opals. Probably inspired by the Koh-i-noor diamond exhibited at the Great Exhibition of 1851, 'Hero' is a feminist parable dealing with imperialism and commodity culture. See Burlinson (1998) and Harrison (1988).
2. All quotations from Christina Rossetti's poems, unless otherwise indicated, are taken from the Oxford World's Classics edition (2008).
3. The rule that the ladies of Baghdad impose as the condition for their hospitality is that the porter and the other guests do not ask any questions about the mysterious things happening in their house, but when the porter sees Zobeide whipping two dogs ritualistically, he starts making enquiries.
4. For an analysis of 'Goblin Market' and the importance of fruits from a translation perspective see Marroni (2012).
5. Among the books read by Christina Rossetti was Thomas Keightley's *The Fairy Mythology* (1828). For a study of Rossetti's literary contacts see Costantini (2000).
6. The deictic categories in speech are founded on the so-called deictic centre or zero-point: the speaker, place and time of utterance.
7. Shifting the deictic centre down is, in Stockwell's words, a 'push' (2002: 47), a term borrowed from computer science. By contrast, moving up a level is a 'pop' back to the narrative level.
8. In cognitive linguistics, the participant in an utterance who receives the energy of a predicate is the *patient*.

9. In the story of 'Julnar the Sea-Born and her Son King Badr Basim', the sorceress Queen Labe, a Circe-like character, uses a drug to transform her former lovers into birds.

10. The Princess depicted in 'The Story of the Envious Man, and of Him that He Envied' turns herself into a serpent and fights a scorpion, which takes the shape of an eagle.

11. In 'The Story of Beder, Prince of Persia, and Giahaure, Princess of Samandal', Labe, outraged at Beder's treachery, transforms him into an owl.

12. Notably, Intafernes appears in *The Nine Books of the History of Herodotus* as one of the slayers of the magician.

13. In *The Good Soldier*, Ford mentions Princess Badrulbadour, Aladdin's beloved, featured in 'The Story of Aladdin, or, the Wonderful Lamp': 'She remembered someone's love for the Princess Badrulbadour' (2003b: 206).

14. The degree of deviation from our sense of reality can be measured on a scale of informativity.

15. The roc, or *rukh*, is a fowl of monstrous size capable of carrying in its talons heavy creatures such as elephants.

16. Queen Labe tries to turn her lover (Beder) into an animal by preparing a poisoned cake that he luckily does not eat.

17. Langacker's notion of *subjective construal* corresponds with tonal effects produced by the quality of the narrative or authorial voice. On this topic see Harrison, Nuttall, Stockwell and Yuan (2014).

18. In *Parade's End*, Ford compares Mlle de Bailly to a white Persian cat, 'luxuriating, sticking out a tentative pawful of expanding claws' (1963: 60). On cats in Ford's life see Saunders (2012).

Appendix

The following appendix is intended as a supplement to the critical text, in order to provide the reader with significant examples from the primary texts being discussed.

D. G. Rossetti, *Aladdin, or The Wonderful Lamp* (2008: 26–7)

D. G. Rossetti's *Aladdin, or The Wonderful Lamp* is a play-picture appearing in the holograph manuscript entitled 'The Slave' (1835). By turning a narrative text into a play, Rossetti remediates the tale of the *Arabian Nights* in order to achieve immediacy of presentation. The scene is characterised by various sketches interconnected with the Oriental schemas of the *Arabian Nights* and representing warriors wielding swords, a bird flying by a tree and a stylised crown. The list of characters playing roles in the *Arabian Nights* is highly significant, since they attest to Rossetti's fondness for theatre. He assigns the roles of Aladdin and the African magician to great performers such as John Philip Kemble and Edmund Kean. Kemble was an English actor, born into a theatrical family, who enjoyed success on the stage playing Shakespearean characters along with his sister Sarah Siddons, the best-known tragedienne of the eighteenth century. Edmund Kean, whose life Rossetti deeply admired, thanks to F. W. Hawkins's published biography (1869), was considered one of the greatest Shakespearean actors of the nineteenth century, able to restore authenticity to the Bard's works. Cognitively speaking, Rossetti's *Aladdin, or The Wonderful Lamp* recreates and extends the same Oriental world of the *Arabian Nights* into a theatrical piece that lifts characters, plots, settings and themes out of their original texts and places them in a new blended space.

Sultana. Mrs Siddons.
Aladdin. – Mr. Kemble.
Sultan. Mrs Cobham.
African Magician. Mr Kean
Princess Badroulboudour. Mrs Kemble
Aladdin's Mother. Mrs. Bland.
Grand Vizier. Mr. King.
African Magician's Brother. Mr. Hart.
Genius of the Lamp. Mr. Fiers
Genius of the Ring. Mr. Johnson.
Fatima. Mrs. Powell.
Grand Vizier's Son. Mr. Elton
Officers, Eunuchs, Guards, Slaves, Servants, Jewellers,
Heralds, Soldiers, Grooms, Genii, Attendants,
Cupbearers, Musicians &c. &c. &c. &c.

Act 1ˢᵗ. Scene 1ˢᵗ.

Enter African Magician & Aladdin.

Al. Where will you lead me?
Mag. Into a bea[u]tiful garden, where all sorts of fruits grow. Al. Is't this?
Mag. Nay, it is not. Al. What is't then?
Mag. A much more beautiful garden than this.

D. G. Rossetti, 'Cassandra' (1999: 251)

Cassandra (1861) and *Helen of Troy* (1863) are double works of art remediating Turkish Orientalism through a tuning approach. The first sonnet of *Cassandra* is an example of cognitive prominence and image schemas aimed at rendering the powerful image of Cassandra prophesying among her kindred, as Hector leaves them for his last battle. Rossetti executed the drawing in 1860 and finished it late that year, expressing his intent to develop the subject into a painting, but he never did. The ekphrastic sonnets were composed in 1869 and sent to his printer in mid-September. They show Rossetti's interest in conceptual dooms as represented linguistically and in paint in this double work of art.

> Rend, rend thine hair, Cassandra: he will go.
> Yea, rend thy garments, wring thine hands, and cry
> From Troy still towered to the unreddened sky.
> See, all but she that bore thee mock thy woe: –

He most whom that fair woman arms, with show   5
Of wrath on her bent brows; for in this place
This hour thou bad'st all men in Helen's face
The ravished ravishing prize of Death to know.

What eyes, what ears hath sweet Andromache,
Save for her Hector's form and step; as tear   10
On tear make salt the warm last kiss he gave?
He goes. Cassandra's words beat heavily
Like crows above his crest, and at his ear
Ring hollow in the shield that shall not save.

D. G. Rossetti, 'Troy Town' (1999: 257–9)

Written in the Summer of 1869, 'Troy Town' is a ballad that blends together historical and mythological materials. There were numerous revisions to the poem after it was typeset, such as the elimination of an epigraph attributed to Herodotus. Focusing on the conceptual metaphor LOVE IS DESTRUCTION, the ballad is imbued with visions of doom related to the Victorian era. The painting *Helen of Troy* (1863), representing a full-face study of Helen, and the drawing *Troy Town* (1870), remediating the first three stanzas of the ballad, are to be seen as part of Rossetti's syncretic approach to Oriental mythology. From a remediating point of view, the ballad is both a faulty ekphrastic remediation of the painting *Helen of Troy* and the source domain on which the drawing *Troy Town* relies. The following are the stanzas of the ballad that appear to be remediated in the black-chalk drawing envisioning Helen as the figure kneeling to the left of Venus' altar. To the right, Venus and Cupid watch from behind a curtain, Venus offering Helen a double cup moulded on her own breasts.

Heavenborn Helen, Sparta's queen,
   (*O Troy Town!*)
Had two breasts of heavenly sheen,
The sun and moon of the heart's desire:
All Love's lordship lay between.   5
   (*O Troy's down,*
   Tall Troy's on fire!)

Helen knelt at Venus' shrine,
   (*O Troy Town!*)
Saying, 'A little gift is mine,   10
A little gift for a heart's desire.

Hear me speak and make me a sign!
    (*O Troy's down,*
    Tall Troy's on fire!)

'Look, I bring thee a carven cup;   15
    (*O Troy Town!*)
See it here as I hold it up, –
Shaped it is to the heart's desire,
Fit to fill when the gods would sup.
    (*O Troy's down,*   20
    Tall Troy's on fire!)

'It was moulded like my breast;
    (*O Troy Town!*)
He that sees it may not rest,
Rest at all for his heart's desire.   25
O give ear to my heart's behest!
    (*O Troy's down,*
    Tall Troy's on fire!)

'See my breast, how like it is;
    (*O Troy Town!*)   30
See it bare for the air to kiss!
Is the cup to thy heart's desire?
O for the breast, O make it his!
    (*O Troy's down,*
    Tall Troy's on fire!)   35

'Yea, for my bosom here I sue;
    (*O Troy Town!*)
Thou must give it where 'tis due,
Give it there to the heart's desire.
Whom do I give my bosom to?   40
    (*O Troy's down,*
    Tall Troy's on fire!)

'Each twin breast is an apple sweet.
    (*O Troy Town!*)
Once an apple stirred the beat   45
Of thy heart with the heart's desire: —
Say, who brought it then to thy feet?
    (*O Troy's down,*
    Tall Troy's on fire!)

'They that claimed it then were three: 50
    (*O Troy Town!*)
For thy sake two hearts did he

Make forlorn of the heart's desire.
Do for him as he did for thee!
      (*O Troy's down,*   55
      Tall Troy's on fire!)

'Mine are apples grown to the south,
      (*O Troy Town!*)
Grown to taste in the days of drouth,
Taste and waste to the heart's desire: 60
Mine are apples meet for his mouth.'
      (*O Troy's down,*
      Tall Troy's on fire!)

Venus looked on Helen's gift,
      (*O Troy Town!*)   65
Looked and smiled with subtle drift,
Saw the work of her heart's desire: —
'There thou kneel'st for Love to lift!'
      (O Troy's down,
      Tall Troy's on fire!)   70

Venus looked in Helen's face,
      (*O Troy Town!*)
Knew far off an hour and place,
And fire lit from the heart's desire;
Laughed and said, 'Thy gift hath grace!'   75
      (*O Troy's down,*
      Tall Troy's on fire!)

Cupid looked on Helen's breast,
      (*O Troy Town!*)
Saw the heart within its nest,   80
Saw the flame of the heart's desire, –
Marked his arrow's burning crest.
      (*O Troy's down,*
      Tall Troy's on fire!)

Cupid took another dart,   85
      (*O Troy Town!*)
Fledged it for another heart,
Winged the shaft with the heart's desire,
Drew the string and said, 'Depart!'
      (*O Troy's down,*   90
      Tall Troy's on fire!)

Paris turned upon his bed,
      (*O Troy Town!*)

Turned upon his bed and said,
Dead at heart with the heart's desire, –   95
'Oh to clasp her golden head!'
    (*O Troy's down,*
     Tall Troy's on fire!)

D. G. Rossetti, 'Mary's Girlhood (For a Picture)' (1999: 7)

'Mary's Girlhood (For a Picture)' (1848–9) is comprised of two sonnets that accompany and comment on Rossetti's painting entitled *The
Girlhood of Mary Virgin* (1849). This triple work of art (one painting
and two sonnets) is the first of the series envisioning a kind of biblical
Orientalism according to a logic of remediation that blends together
biblical and medieval schemas. Aimed at revolutionising the aesthetic
and conceptual canons of art, *The Girlhood of Mary Virgin* and its sonnets are characterised by many forms of cognitive deviations from the
expected representation of the Virgin. By foregrounding medieval and
Christian details, Rossetti projects the conceptual metaphor ANNUN-
CIATION IS INNOVATION, in both religious and artistic terms. The first
sonnet was written on 21 November 1848, while the second was not
composed until Rossetti had completed the painting in March 1849.

    Mary's Girlhood (For a Picture)

    I
This is that blessed Mary, pre-elect
God's Virgin. Gone is a great while, and she
Was young in Nazareth of Galilee.
Her kin she cherished with devout respect:
Her gifts were simpleness of intellect
And supreme patience. From her mother's knee
Faithful and hopeful; wise in charity;
Strong in grave peace; in duty circumspect.
So held she through her girlhood; as it were
An angel-watered lily, that near God   10
Grows, and is quiet. Till one dawn, at home,
She woke in her white bed, and had no fear
At all, – yet wept till sunshine, and felt awed;
Because the fulness of the time was come.

    II
These are the symbols. On that cloth of red
I' the centre, is the Tripoint: perfect each
Except the second of its points, to teach
That Christ is not yet born. The books (whose head

Is golden Charity, as Paul hath said)
Those virtues are wherein the soul is rich:
Therefore on them the lily standeth, which
Is Innocence, being interpreted.
The seven-thorned briar and the palm seven-leaved
Are her great sorrows and her great reward.   10
Until the time be full, the Holy One
Abides without. She soon shall have achieved
Her perfect purity: yea, God the Lord
Shall soon vouchsafe His Son to be her Son.

D. G. Rossetti, 'Astarte Syriaca (For a Picture)' (1999: 415)

Rossetti wrote an ekphrastic sonnet for the picture entitled *Astarte Syriaca* in 1877. Intended to be the representation of the Syrian Venus Al Husa, *Astarte Syriaca* is a double work of art characterised by a high degree of deviation from Oriental schemas. By blending Christian and Islamic symbols, Rossetti restructures old schemas in order to create a new vision of Oriental sensuality projecting the conceptual metaphor LOVE IS A MYSTERY. As suggested by Jerome McGann (2008), the sonnet opens with an allusion to the Book of Revelation (12: 1), in which there is a description of a 'woman clothed with the sun'. Rossetti seems to revise this characterisation by creating a new blended goddess (Syrian–Babylonian) who is able to combine sun and moon, divine and demonic orders. All instrumentalities of Oriental magic are also mentioned in the sonnet ('Amulet, talisman, and oracle', l. 13), foregrounding a complex and variegated vision of Orientalism in which different cults coexist.

MYSTERY: lo! betwixt the sun and moon
Astarte of the Syrians: Venus Queen
Ere Aphrodite was. In silver sheen
Her twofold girdle clasps the infinite boon
Of bliss whereof the heaven and earth commune: 5
And from her neck's inclining flower-stem lean
Love-freighted lips and absolute eyes that wean
The pulse of hearts to the spheres' dominant tune.

Torch-bearing, her sweet ministers compel
All thrones of light beyond the sky and sea   10
The witnesses of Beauty's face to be:
That face, of Love's all-penetrative spell
Amulet, talisman, and oracle, –
Betwixt the sun and moon a mystery.

Algernon Swinburne, 'To Sir Richard F. Burton (On His Translation of "The Arabian Nights")' (1904: III, 258)

First published in *The Athenaeum* on 6 February 1886, Swinburne's 'To Sir Richard F. Burton (On His Translation of "The Arabian Nights")' is a tribute to Burton's uncensored version. Compared to Edward William Lane's informative translation, Burton's approach is more personal, revealing the Oriental customs and traditions related to sex. As a form of foreignising translation, Burton's *Arabian Nights* deeply affected Swinburne's imagination, which was attracted by a form of corporeal Orientalism. Attesting to the superiority of Burton's translation, Swinburne also aims at exalting the superiority of the East, with the help of visual conceptual metaphors that give prominence to the Eastern world.

> Westward the sun sinks, grave and glad; but far
> Eastward, with laughter and tempestuous tears,
> Cloud, rain, and splendour as of orient spears,
> Keen as the sea's thrill toward a kindling star,
> The sundawn breaks the barren twilight's bar
> And fires the mist and slays it. Years on years
> Vanish, but he that hearkens eastward hears
> Bright music from the world where shadows are.
>
> Where shadows are not shadows. Hand in hand
> A man's word bids them rise and smile and stand   10
> And triumph. All that glorious orient glows
> Defiant of the dusk. Our twilight land
> Trembles; but all the heaven is all one rose,
> Whence laughing love dissolves her frosts and snows.

Algernon Swinburne, 'On the Death of Richard Burton' (1904: VI, 199–201)

The death of Richard Burton occurred on 19 October 1890, deeply shocking Swinburne, who promptly composed these elegiac verses celebrating his beloved friend. Formally and thematically imbued with Orientalism, the poem is comprised of a series of quatrains following the Rubáiyát stanza (*aaba*) with minor changes in the rhyming scheme. Swinburne's Orientalism is formally exposed, since the *Rubáiyát* collection of poems by the Persian poet Omar Khayyám is the quintessential expression of Oriental poetry. Other Pre-Raphaelite artists and authors admired the *Rubáiyát*, but Swinburne was the only one who

employed the Oriental stanza to celebrate Burton's sensual Orientalism. From a cognitive point of view, the poem continually shifts its
deictic centre in order to give the whole picture of Burton's grandeur.
There are many conceptual metaphors projected in the poem that are
aimed at exalting Burton as a unique figure in the Victorian scenario.

> Night or light is it now, wherein
> Sleeps, shut out from the wild world's din,
> Wakes, alive with a life more clear,
> One who found not on earth his kin?
>
> Sleep were sweet for awhile, were dear
> Surely to souls that were heartless here,
> Souls that faltered and flagged and fell,
> Soft of spirit and faint of cheer.
>
> A living soul that had strength to quell
> Hope the spectre and fear the spell,   10
> Clear-eyed, content with a scorn sublime
> And a faith superb, can it fare not well?
>
> Life, the shadow of wide-winged time,
> Cast from the wings that change as they climb,
> Life may vanish in death, and seem
> Less than the promise of last year's prime.
>
> But not for us is the past a dream
> Wherefrom, as light from a clouded stream,
> Faith fades and shivers and ebbs away,
> Faint as the moon if the sundawn gleam.   20
>
> Faith, whose eyes in the low last ray
> Watch the fire that renews the day,
> Faith which lives in the living past,
> Rock-rooted, swerves not as weeds that sway.
>
> As trees that stand in the storm-wind fast
> She stands, unsmitten of death's keen blast,
> With strong remembrance of sunbright spring
> Alive at heart to the lifeless last.
>
> Night, she knows, may in no wise cling
> To a soul that sinks not and droops not wing,   30
> A sun that sets not in death's false night
> Whose kingdom finds him not thrall but king.

Souls there are that for soul's affright
Bow down and cower in the sun's glad sight,
Clothed round with faith that is one with fear,
And dark with doubt of the live world's light.

But him we hailed from afar or near
As boldest born of the bravest here
And loved as brightest of souls that eyed
Life, time, and death with unchangeful cheer,   40

A wider soul than the world was wide,
Whose praise made love of him one with pride,
What part has death or has time in him,
Who rode life's lists as a god might ride?

While England sees not her old praise dim,
While still her stars through the world's night swim,
A fame outshining her Raleigh's fame,
A light that lightens her loud sea's rim,

Shall shine and sound as her sons proclaim
The pride that kindles at Burton's name.   50
And joy shall exalt their pride to be
The same in birth if in soul the same.
But we that yearn for a friend's face – we
Who lack the light that on earth was he –
Mourn, though the light be a quenchless flame
That shines as dawn on a tideless sea.

Algernon Swinburne, 'The Masque of Queen Bersabe' (1904: 221; 235–6)

Swinburne's miracle play is the story of Queen Bersabe, the wife of Uriah, whom King David caused to be murdered in order that he could marry her. Queen Bersabe is the object of desire for a multitude of men, who are hypnotised by her 'goodly body bare' (l. 394). This adulterous queen activates the process of desire through the exhibition of her flowing hair in a bath scene that recalls the sensuality of Scheherazade while taking a Turkish bath (*hammam*). Bersabe's naked body is the main focus of the scene, foregrounding sensuous images imbued with Orientalism. Cognitively speaking, Bersabe and Scheherazade are trajectors, tracing a path that leads to their male observers. There are numerous visual and verbal trajectors in Swinburne's poem, over-emphasising Bersabe's Oriental sensuality. By naming and describing other temptresses (Herodias, Cleopatra and Messalina), as well as other Oriental female figures (Aholibah, Abihail, Azubah, Aholah, Ahinoam, Atarah and so on), Swinburne assigns the primacy of Oriental seductress to Bersabe. In the catalogue of Oriental-sounding names denoting Oriental female characters, Bersabe appears to be the most Oriental figure of them all. In line with the Pre-Raphaelite revival of archaisms, Swinburne's language appears to be imbued with Oriental names and words, creating a scenario that recalls the atmospheres of the *Arabian Nights*.

> King David
> Knights mine, all that be in hall,
> I have a counsel to you all,
> Because of this thing God lets fall
> Among us for a sign.
> For some days hence as I did eat
> From kingly dishes my good meat,
> There flew a bird between my feet
> As red as any wine.
> This bird had a long bill of red
> And a gold ring above his head;   10
> Long time he sat and nothing said,
> Put softly down his neck and fed
> From the gilt patens fine:
> And as I marvelled, at the last
> He shut his two keen eyën fast
> And suddenly woxe big and brast
> Ere one should tell to nine.
> [. . .]
> Nathless he had great joy to see
> The long hair of this Bersabe
> Fall round her lap and round her knee
> Even to her small soft feet, that be
> Shod now with crimson royally
> And covered with clean gold.
> Likewise great joy he had to kiss   100
> Her throat, where now the scarlet is
> Against her little chin, I wis,
> That then was but cold.
> No scarlet then her kirtle had
> And little gold about it sprad;
> But her red mouth was always glad
> To kiss, albeit the eyes were sad
> With love they had to hold.

[. . .]
King David
Certes his mouth is wried and black,
Full little pence be in his sack;
This devil hath him by the back,
It is no boot to lie.

Nathan
Sitteth now still and learn of me;
A little while and ye shall see
The face of God's strength presently.
All queens made as this Bersabe,
All that were fair and foul ye be,   130
Come hither; it am I.
Et hìc omnes cantabunt.

[. . .]
King David

[. . .]
For the fair green weather's heat,
And for the smell of leavés sweet,
It is no marvel, well ye weet,
A man to waxen amorous.
This I say now by my case
That spied forth of that royal place;
There I saw in no great space   390
Mine own sweet, both body and face,
Under the fresh boughs.
In a water that was there
She wesshe her goodly body bare
And dried it with her owen hair:
Both her arms and her knees fair,
Both bosom and brows;
Both shoulders and eke thighs
Tho she wesshe upon this wise;
Ever she sighed with little sighs,   400
And ever she gave God thank.

Yea, God wot I can well see yet
Both her breast and her sides all wet
And her long hair withouten let
Spread sideways like a drawing net;
Full dear bought and full far fet
Was that sweet thing there y-set;

It were a hard thing to forget
How both lips and eyen met,
Breast and breath sank.   410
So goodly a sight as there she was,
Lying looking on her glass
By wan water in green grass,
Yet saw never man.
So soft and great she was and bright
With all her body waxen white,
I woxe nigh blind to see the light
Shed out of it to left and right;
This bitter sin from that sweet sight
Between us twain began.   420

Nathan
Now, sir, be merry anon,
For ye shall have a full wise son,
Goodly and great of flesh and bone;
There shall no king be such an one,
I swear by Godis rood.
Therefore, lord, be merry here,
And go to meat withouten fear,
And hear a mass with goodly cheer;
For to all folk ye shall be dear,
And all folk of your blood.   430
Et tunc dicant Laudamus.

Aubrey Beardsley, *Under the Hill* (1921: 13–20)

Under the Hill is an unfinished erotic novel based on the legend of
Tannhäuser. Its first parts came out in *The Savoy* and were later published in book form by Leonard Smithers (1896). The inhabitants of
the Hill of Venus appear to indulge in sensual practices that recall
the eroticism of the *Arabian Nights*. The arts of bathing, dressing
and make-up are characterised by Oriental references or, cognitively
speaking, by Oriental world-building elements and function-advancing
propositions, constructing an Oriental text world of erotic sensuality.
In particular, the toilet of Helen/Venus is based on the same world-
builders (time, location and characters) as 'The Tale of Scheherazade
Concluded', thereby sharing the same cult of bodily beauty that, in
accordance with Eastern customs, was celebrated before suppertime.
According to his logic of distortion, Beardsley's restructuring of Oriental schemas intends to pervert the *hammam* scenes in the *Arabian
Nights* and blend together Western and Eastern cultures. The following

excerpt is taken from the second chapter of *Under the Hill* and exemplifies the Oriental rituals aimed at embellishing the female figure.

Chapter II

'Of the Manner in Which Venus Was Coiffed and Prepared for Supper'

Before a toilet that shone like the altar of Notre Dame des Victoires, Venus was seated in a little dressing-gown of black and heliotrope. The coiffeur Cosmé was caring for her scented chevelure, and with tiny silver tongs, warm from the caresses of the flame, made delicious intelligent curls that fell as lightly as a breath about her forehead and over her eyebrows, and clustered like tendrils round her neck. Her three favourite girls, Pappelarde, Blanchemains and Loreyne, waited immediately upon her with perfume and powder in delicate flacons and frail cassolettes, and held in porcelain jars the ravishing paints prepared by Chateline for those cheeks and lips that had grown a little pale with anguish of exile. Her three favourite boys, Claude, Clair and Sarrasine, stood amorously about with salver, fan and napkin. Millamant held a slight tray of slippers, Minette some tender gloves, La Popelinière – mistress of the robes – was ready with a frock of yellow and yellow. La Zambellina bore the jewels, Florizel some flowers, Amadour a box of various pins, and Vadius a box of sweets. Her doves, ever in attendance, walked about the room that was panelled with the gallant paintings of Jean Baptiste Dorat, and some dwarfs and doubtful creatures sat here and there lolling out their tongues, pinching each other, and behaving oddly enough. Sometimes Venus gave them little smiles.

As the toilet was in progress, Priapusa, the fat manicure and fardeuse, strode in and seated herself by the side of the dressing-table, greeting Venus with an intimate nod. She wore a gown of white watered silk with gold lace trimmings and a velvet necklet of false vermilion. Her hair hung in bandeaux over her ears, passing into a huge chignon at the back of her head, and the hat, wide-brimmed and hung with a valance of pink muslin, was floral with red roses.

Priapusa's voice was full of salacious unction; she had terrible little gestures with the hands, strange movements with the shoulders, a short respiration that made surprising wrinkles in her bodice, a corrupt skin, large horny eyes, a parrot's nose, a small loose mouth, great flaccid cheeks, and chin after chin. She was a wise person, and Venus loved her more than any of her servants, and had a hundred pet names for her, such as Dear Toad, Pretty Pol, Cock-robin, Dearest Lip, Touchstone, Little Cough-drop, Bijou, Buttons, Dear Heart, Dick-dock, Mrs. Manly, Little Nipper, Cochon-de-lait, Naughty-naughty, Blessèd Thing, and Trump.

The talk that passed between Priapusa and her mistress was of that excellent kind that passes between old friends, a perfect understanding giving to scraps of phrases their full meaning, and to the merest reference a point. Naturally Tannhäuser, the newcomer, was discussed a little. Venus had not seen him yet, and asked a score of questions on his account that were delightfully to the point.

Priapusa told the story of his arrival, his curious wandering in the gardens, and calm satisfaction with all he saw there, his impromptu affection for a slender girl upon the first terrace, of the crowd of frocks that gathered round and pelted him with roses, of the graceful way he defended himself with his mask, and of the queer reverence he made to the God of all gardens, kissing that deity with a pilgrim's devotion. Just now Tannhäuser was at the baths, and was creating a favourable impression.

The report and the coiffing were completed at the same moment. 'Cosmé,' said Venus, 'you have been quite sweet and quite brilliant. You have surpassed yourself tonight.' 'Madam flatters me,' replied the antique old thing, with a girlish giggle under his black satin mask. 'Gad, Madam; sometimes I believe I have no talent in the world, but tonight I must confess to a touch of the vain mood.' It would pain me horribly to tell you about the painting of her face; suffice it that the sorrowful work was accomplished frankly, magnificently, and without a shadow of deception. Venus slipped away the dressing-gown, and rose before the mirror in a flutter of frilled things. She was adorably tall and slender. Her neck and shoulders were wonderfully drawn, and the little malicious breasts were full of the irritation of loveliness that can never be entirely comprehended, or ever enjoyed to the utmost. Her arms and hands were loosely, but delicately articulated, and her legs were divinely long. From the hip to the knee, twenty-two inches; from the knee to the heel, twenty-two inches, as befitted a Goddess.

I should like to speak more particularly about her, for generalities are not of the slightest service in a description. But I am afraid that an enforced silence here and there would leave such numerous gaps in the picture that it had better not be begun at all than left unfinished.

Priapusa grew quite lyric over the dear little person, and pecked at her arms with kisses.

'Dear Tongue, you must really behave yourself,' said Venus, and called Millamant to bring her the slippers. The tray was freighted with the most exquisite and shapely pantoufles, sufficient to make Cluny a place of naught. There were shoes of grey and black and brown suède, of white silk and rose satin, and velvet and sarcenet; there were some of sea-green sewn with cherry blossoms, some of red with willow branches, and some of grey with bright-winged birds. There were heels of silver, of ivory and of gilt; there were buckles of very precious stones set in most strange and esoteric devices; there were ribands tied and twisted into cunning forms; there were buttons so beautiful that the buttonholes might have no pleasure till they closed upon them; there were soles of delicate leathers scented with maréchale, and linings of soft stuffs scented with the juice of July flowers. But Venus, finding none of them to her mind, called for a discarded pair of blood-red maroquine, diapered with pearls. They looked very distinguished over her white silk stockings.

As the tray was being carried away, the capricious Florizel snatched as usual a slipper from it, and fitted the foot over his penis, and made the necessary movements. That was Florizel's little caprice. Meantime, La Popelinière stepped forward with the frock.

'I shan't wear one tonight,' said Venus. Then she slipped on her gloves.

When the toilet was at an end all her doves clustered round her feet, loving to frôler her ankles with their plumes, and the dwarfs clapped their hands, and put their fingers between their lips and whistled. Never before had Venus been so radiant and compelling. Spiridion, in the corner, looked up from his game of Spellicans and trembled. Claude and Clair, pale with pleasure, stroked and touched her with their delicate hands, and wrinkled her stockings with their nervous lips, and smoothed them with their thin fingers; and Sarrasine undid her garters and kissed them inside and put them on again, pressing her thighs with his mouth. The dwarfs grew very daring, I can tell you. There was almost a mêlée. They illustrated pages 72 and 73 of Delvau's Dictionary. In the middle of it all, Pranzmungel announced that supper was ready upon the fifth terrace. 'Ah!' cried Venus, 'I'm famished!'

Aubrey Beardsley, 'The Ballad of a Barber' (1921: 49–50)

Beardsley's poem first appeared in the July 1896 issue of *The Savoy*. The idea of the demon barber may have come from Sweeney Todd, appearing in *The String of Pearls: A Romance*, a fictional story first published as a penny dreadful serial from 1846 to 1847. The main antagonist of the story is Sweeney Todd, 'the demon barber of Fleet Street', who here makes his literary debut. With its treacherous and violent themes, the ballad evokes the schemas of 'The Story of the Barber's Fourth Brother', in which a butcher sells the meat of humans rather than that of sheep. If the protagonist of the ballad seems to recall a malevolent sorcerer from the *Arabian Nights* performing a magical ritual, then the illustration for the poem appears to be blending together Christian and Muslim symbols. In the poem, Orientalism lurks behind the conceptual metaphors projected, and the visual and verbal prominence given to Oriental details. Numerology assumes great importance in the verbal rituals uttered and performed by the demon barber, whose magic has much in common with Oriental occultism.

Here is the tale of Carrousel,
The barber of Meridian Street,
He cut, and coiffed, and shaved so well,
That all the world was at his feet.

The King, the Queen, and all the Court,   5
To no one else would trust their hair,
And reigning belles of every sort
Owed their successes to his care.

With carriage and with cabriolet
Daily Meridian Street was blocked,   10
Like bees about a bright bouquet
The beaux about his doorway nocked.

Such was his art he could with ease
Curl wit into the dullest face;
Or to a goddess of old Greece   15
Add a new wonder and a grace.

All powders, paints, and subtle dyes,
And costliest scents that men distil,
And rare pomades, forgot their price
And marvelled at his splendid skill.   20

The curling irons in his hand
Almost grew quick enough to speak,
The razor was a magic wand
That understood the softest cheek.

Yet with no pride his heart was moved;   25
He was so modest in his ways!
His daily task was all he loved,
And now and then a little praise.

An equal care he would bestow
On problems simple or complex;   30
And nobody had seen him show
A preference for either sex.

How came it then one summer day,
Coiffing the daughter of the King,
He lengthened out the least delay   35
And loitered in his hairdressing?

The Princess was a pretty child,
Thirteen years old, or thereabout.
She was as joyous and as wild
As spring flowers when the sun is out.   40

Her gold hair fell down to her feet
And hung about her pretty eyes;
She was as lyrical and sweet
As one of Schubert's melodies.

Three times the barber curled a lock,   45
And thrice he straightened it again;
And twice the irons scorched her frock,
And twice he stumbled in her train.

His fingers lost their cunning quite,
His ivory combs obeyed no more;   50
Something or other dimmed his sight,
And moved mysteriously the floor.

He leant upon the toilet table,
His fingers fumbled in his breast;
He felt as foolish as a fable,   55
And feeble as a pointless jest.

He snatched a bottle of Cologne,
And broke the neck between his hands;
He felt as if he was alone,
And mighty as a king's commands.   60

The Princess gave a little scream,
Carrousel's cut was sharp and deep;
He left her softly as a dream
That leaves a sleeper to his sleep.

He left the room on pointed feet;   65
Smiling that things had gone so well.
They hanged him in Meridian Street.
You pray in vain for Carrousel.

John Ruskin, 'The Valley of Diamonds' (1908a: 11–13)

'The Valley of Diamonds' is the first lecture of *Ethics of the Dust*.
It takes the form of a play, which focuses mainly on the process of
storytelling. Defined as one of the most experimental lectures of

the collection, it derives its fanciful language and metaphors from 'Sinbad the Sailor'. Rich in moral lessons connected with Sinbad's valley of diamonds, Ruskin's lecture restructures the existing tale, whose Oriental schemas are modified for Victorian didactic purposes. If, in Sinbad's story, diamonds help the hero to bestow large sums of money on the poor, in Ruskin's lecture diamonds are seen as causes of corruption throughout imperial history. Florrie, Isabel, May, Lily and Sibyl are completely ravished by the Lecturer's story, which blends together fancy and imagination, playing with Oriental words and metaphors mapped on to the source story of 'Sinbad the Sailor'.

Lecture I

'The Valley of Diamonds'

A very idle talk, by the dining-room fire, after raisin-and-almond time
Old Lecturer; Florrie, Isabel, May, Lily, and Sibyl.
Old Lecturer (L.). Come here, Isabel, and tell me what the make-believe was, this afternoon.
Isabel (*arranging herself very primly on the footstool*).
Such a dreadful one! Florrie and I were lost in the Valley of Diamonds.
L. What! Sindbad's, which nobody could get out of?
Isabel. Yes; but Florrie and I got out of it.
L. So I see. At least, I see you did; but are you sure Florrie did?
Isabel. Quite sure.
Florrie (*putting her head round from behind* L.'s *sofa-cushion*). Quite sure. (*Disappears again.*)
L. I think I could be made to feel surer about it.
(Florrie *reappears, gives* L. *a kiss, and again exit.*)
L. I suppose it's all right; but how did you manage it?
Isabel. Well, you know, the eagle that took up Sindbad was very large – very, very large – the largest of all the eagles.
L. How large were the others?
Isabel. I don't quite know – they were so far off. But this one was, oh, so big! and it had great wings, as wide as – twice over the ceiling. So, when it was picking up Sindbad, Florrie and I thought it wouldn't know if we got on its back too: so I got up first, and then I pulled up Florrie, and we put our arms round its neck, and away it flew.
L. But why did you want to get out of the valley? and why haven't you brought me some diamonds?
Isabel. It was because of the serpents. I couldn't pick up even the least little bit of a diamond, I was so frightened.
L. You should not have minded the serpents.

Isabel. Oh, but suppose they had minded me?

L. We all of us mind you a little too much, Isabel, I'm afraid.

Isabel. No – no – no, indeed.

L. I tell you what, Isabel – I don't believe either Sindbad, or Florrie, or you, ever were in the Valley of Diamonds.

Isabel. You naughty! when I tell you we were!

L. Because you say you were frightened at the serpents.

Isabel. And wouldn't you have been?

L. Not at those serpents. Nobody who really goes into the valley is ever frightened at them – they are so beautiful.

Isabel (*suddenly serious*). But there's no real Valley of Diamonds, is there?

L. Yes, Isabel; very real indeed.

Florrie (*reappearing*). Oh, where? Tell me about it.

L. I cannot tell you a great deal about it; only I know it is very different from Sindbad's. In his valley, there was only a diamond lying here and there; but, in the real valley, there are diamonds covering the grass in showers every morning, instead of dew: and there are clusters of trees, which look like lilac trees; but, in spring, all their blossoms are of amethyst.

Florrie. But there can't be any serpents there, then?

L. Why not?

Florrie. Because they don't come into such beautiful places.

L. I never said it was a beautiful place.

Florrie. What! not with diamonds strewed about it like dew?

L. That's according to your fancy, Florrie. For myself, I like dew better.

Isabel. Oh, but the dew won't stay; it all dries!

L. Yes; and it would be much nicer if the diamonds dried too, for the people in the valley have to sweep them off the grass, in heaps, whenever they want to walk on it; and then the heaps glitter so, they hurt one's eyes.

Florrie. Now you're just playing, you know.

L. So are you, you know.

Florrie. Yes, but you mustn't play.

L. That's very hard, Florrie; why mustn't I, if you may?

Florrie. Oh, I may, because I'm little, but you mustn't, because you're – (*hesitates for a delicate expression of magnitude*).

L. (*rudely taking the first that comes*). Because I'm big? No; that's not the way of it at all, Florrie. Because you're little, you should have very little play; and because I'm big I should have a great deal.

Isabel *and* Florrie (*both*). No – no – no – no. That isn't it at all. (Isabel *sola, quoting Miss Ingelow*).

'The lambs play always – they know no better.' (*Putting her head very much on one side.*) Ah, now – please – please – tell us true; we want to know.

L. But why do you want me to tell you true, any more than the man who wrote the 'Arabian Nights'?

Isabel. Because – because we like to know about real things; and you can tell us, and we can't ask the man who wrote the stories.

L. What do you call real things?

Isabel. Now, you know! Things that really are.

L. Whether you can see them or not?

Isabel. Yes, if somebody else saw them.

L. But if nobody has ever seen them?

John Ruskin, *The King of the Golden River* (1860: 53–4; 58–9; 66–7)

The King of the Golden River or The Black Brothers: A Legend of Stiria was originally written in 1841 for the twelve-year-old Effie Gray, whom Ruskin later married, and then published in book form in 1851 with twenty-two illustrations by Richard Doyle. Acclaimed as a Victorian fairy tale, the book was a great success and went to three editions within a year of publication. Apart from the influence of Western fairy tales (by the Grimm brothers), there is evidence to suggest that Ruskin's fairy tale is patterned on the Arabian tale 'The Story of Two Sisters Who Envied Their Younger Sister', the Cinderella-like story of Princess Parisad, whose golden water is endowed with transformative and magical powers. This Oriental story of oppression and reward deeply affected Ruskin's imagination to the point that he purchased Rossetti's drawing, *Golden Water*, representing Princess Parisad holding the black barrel containing the magical golden water. Cognitively speaking, Ruskin's fairy tale develops a new schema on the basis of the Oriental one, modifying its scripts, schemas, image-schemas, conceptual metaphors, deixis and so on. It is also significant that the forbidden dynamics characterise both the Arabian tale and Ruskin's fairy tale. By violating magical rules, the protagonists of both stories are turned into black stones as a punishment for their transgression. But Ruskin's Western version of Oriental magic is imbued with Victorian patriarchal values because the male protagonist, Gluck, lacks any compassion for his brothers, unlike the source story in which the parable of the forbidden ensures a happy ending for Parisad and her brothers.

At this instant a faint cry fell on his ear. He turned, and saw a gray-haired old man extended on the rocks. His eyes were sunk, his features deadly pale, and gathered into an expression of despair. 'Water!' he stretched his arms to Hans, and cried feebly, 'Water! I am dying'.

'I have none,' replied Hans; 'thou hast had thy share of life.' He strode over the prostrate body, and darted on. And a flash of blue lightning rose out of the East, shaped like a sword; it shook thrice over the whole heaven, and left it dark with one heavy, impenetrable shade. The sun was setting; it plunged towards the horizon like a red-hot ball.

The roar of the Golden River rose on Hans's ear. He stood at the brink of the chasm through which it ran. Its waves were filled with the red glory of the sunset: they shook their crests like tongues of fire, and flashes of bloody light gleamed along their foam. Their sound came mightier and mightier on his senses; his brain grew giddy with the pro-longed thunder. Shuddering, he drew the flask from his girdle, and hurled it into the centre of the torrent. As he did so, an icy chill shot through his limbs; he staggered, shrieked, and fell. The waters closed over his cry. And the moaning of the river rose wildly into the night, as it gushed over The Black Stone.

[. . .]

Then Schwartz climbed for another hour, and again his thirst returned; and as he lifted his flask to his lips, he thought he saw his brother Hans lying exhausted on the path before him, and, as he gazed, the figure stretched its arms to him, and cried for water. 'Ha, ha,' laughed Schwartz, 'are you there? remember the prison bars, my boy. Water, indeed! do you suppose I carried it all the way up here for you?' And he strode over the figure; yet, as he passed, he thought he saw a strange expression of mockery about its lips.

And, when he had gone a few yards farther, he looked back; but the figure was not there.

And a sudden horror came over Schwartz, he knew not why; but the thirst for gold prevailed over his fear, and he rushed on. And the bank of black cloud rose to the zenith, and out of it came bursts of spiry light-ning, and waves of darkness seemed to heave and float between their flashes, over the whole heavens. And the sky where the sun was setting was all level, and like a lake of blood; and a strong wind came out of that sky, tearing its crimson clouds into fragments, and scattering them far into the darkness. And when Schwartz stood by the brink of the Golden River, its waves were black, like thunder clouds, but their foam was like fire; and the roar of the waters below, and the thunder above met, as he cast the flask into the stream. And, as he did so, the lightning glared in his eyes, and the earth gave way beneath him, and the waters closed over his cry.

And the moaning of the river rose wildly into the night, as it gushed over the Two Black Stones.

[. . .]

And Gluck climbed to the brink of the Golden River, and its waves were as clear as crystal, and as brilliant as the sun. And when he cast the three drops of dew into the stream, there opened where they fell, a small circular whirlpool, into which the waters descended with a musical noise. Gluck stood watching it for some time, very much disappointed, because not only the river was not turned into gold, but its waters seemed much diminished in quantity. Yet he obeyed his friend the dwarf and descended the other side of the mountains, towards the Treasure Valley; and, as he went, he thought he heard the noise of water working its way under the ground. And, when he came in sight of the Treasure Valley, behold, a river, like the Golden River, was springing from a new cleft of the rocks above it, and was flowing in innumerable streams among the dry heaps of red sand.

And as Gluck gazed, fresh grass sprang beside the new streams, and creeping plants grew, and climbed among the moistening soil. Young flowers opened suddenly along the river sides, as stars leap out when twilight is deepening, and thickets of myrtle, and tendrils of vine, cast lengthening shadows over the valley as they grew. And thus the Treasure Valley became a garden again, and the inheritance, which had been lost by cruelty, was regained by love.

William Morris, 'The Writing on the Image', in *The Earthly Paradise* (2001: 464–71)

'The Writing on the Image' is a tale from the month of May about sorcery, treasures and failure. The protagonist is a scholar who, after discovering great marvels, dies miserably. This parable of death, despite its Faustian theme, appears to be patterned on 'The Story of Aladdin, or, the Wonderful Lamp'. Similar to Aladdin's African magician, the scholar seems to be blending all the variables related to sorcery in the story of Aladdin. By adding new facts and details to the existing schema of 'The Story of Aladdin, or, the Wonderful Lamp', enlarging its scope and explanatory range, 'The Writing on the Image' modifies the Oriental schema, albeit preserving the lure of the forbidden. Like the African magician, the scholar is a powerful sorcerer whose aim is to steal a jewel from an underground vault. There is no reference in Morris's tale to the figure of Aladdin and the treachery schema but the action-chain pattern is almost the same since, after entering a cave and seizing a wonderful green stone, the sorcerer is sealed up in the cave. The variables of the Oriental schema are changed in Morris's tale, as the sorcerer steals a wonderful green stone rather than the wonderful lamp, but the latter is ever-present in the description. Aladdin's lamp is turned into one that illuminates the great hall without a burning flame.

May
ARGUMENT.

How on an Image that stood anciently in Rome were written certain words, which none understood, until a Scholar, coming there, knew their meaning, and thereby discovered great marvels, but withal died miserably.

In half-forgotten days of old,
As by our fathers we were told,
Within the town of Rome there stood
An image cut of cornel wood,
And on the upraised hand of it   5
Men might behold these letters writ –
'PERCUTE HIC:' which is to say,
In that tongue that we speak to-day,
'*Strike here!*' nor yet did any know
The cause why this was written so.   10

    Thus in the middle of the square,
In the hot sun and summer air,
The snow-drift and the driving rain,
That image stood, with little pain,
For twice a hundred years and ten;   15
While many a band of striving men
Were driven betwixt woe and mirth
Swiftly across the weary earth,
From nothing unto dark nothing:
And many an Emperor and King,   20
Passing with glory or with shame,
Left little record of his name,
And no remembrance of the face
Once watched with awe for gifts or grace.
Fear little, then, I counsel you,   25
What any son of man can do;
Because a log of wood will last
While many a life of man goes past,
And all is over in short space.

    Now so it chanced that to this place   30
There came a man of Sicily,
Who when the image he did see,
Knew full well who, in days of yore,
Had set it there; for much strange lore,
In Egypt and in Babylon,   35
This man with painful toil had won;

And many secret things could do;
So verily full well he knew
That master of all sorcery
Who wrought the thing in days gone by,   40
And doubted not that some great spell
It guarded, but could nowise tell
What it might be. So, day by day,
Still would he loiter on the way,
And watch the image carefully,   45
Well mocked of many a passer-by.
And on a day he stood and gazed
Upon the slender finger, raised
Against a doubtful cloudy sky,
Nigh noontide; and thought, 'Certainly   50
The master who made thee so fair
By wondrous art, had not stopped there,
But made thee speak, had he not thought
That thereby evil might be brought
Upon his spell.' But as he spoke,   55
From out a cloud the noon sun broke
With watery light, and shadows cold
Then did the Scholar well behold
How, from that finger carved to tell
Those words, a short black shadow fell   60
Upon a certain spot of ground,
And thereon, looking all around
And seeing none heeding, went straightway
Whereas the finger's shadow lay,
And with his knife about the place   65
A little circle did he trace;
Then home he turned with throbbing head,
And forthright gat him to his bed,
And slept until the night was late
And few men stirred from gate to gate.   70
So when at midnight he did wake,
Pickaxe and shovel did he take,
And, going to that now silent square,
He found the mark his knife made there,
And quietly with many a stroke   75
The pavement of the place he broke:
And so, the stones being set apart,
He 'gan to dig with beating heart,
And from the hole in haste he cast
The marl and gravel; till at last,   80
Full shoulder high, his arms were jarred,

For suddenly his spade struck hard
With clang against some metal thing:
And soon he found a brazen ring,
All green with rust, twisted, and great   85
As a man's wrist, set in a plate
Of copper, wrought all curiously
With words unknown though plain to see,
Spite of the rust; and flowering trees,
And beasts, and wicked images,   90
Whereat he shuddered: for he knew
What ill things he might come to do,
If he should still take part with these
And that Great Master strive to please.
But small time had he then to stand   95
And think, so straight he set his hand
Unto the ring, but where he thought
That by main strength it must be brought
From out its place, to! easily
It came away, and let him see   100
A winding staircase wrought of stone,
Wherethrough the new-come wind did moan.
Then thought he, 'If I come alive
From out this place well shall I thrive,
For I may look here certainly   105
The treasures of a king to see,
A mightier man than men are now.
So in few days what man shall know
The needy Scholar, seeing me
Great in the place where great men be,   110
The richest man in all the land?
Beside the best then shall I stand,
And some unheard-of palace have;
And if my soul I may not save
In heaven, yet here in all men's eyes   115
Will I make some sweet paradise,
With marble cloisters, and with trees
And bubbling wells, and fantasies,
And things all men deem strange and rare,
And crowds of women kind and fair,   120
That I may see, if so I please,
Laid on the flowers, or mid the trees
With half-clad bodies wandering.
There, dwelling happier than the king.
What lovely days may yet be mine!   125
How shall I live with love and wine,

And music, till I come to die!
And then – Who knoweth certainly
What haps to us when we are dead?
Truly I think by likelihead   130
Nought haps to us of good or bad;
Therefore on earth will I be glad
A short space, free from hope or fear;
And fearless will I enter here
And meet my fate, whatso it be.'   135

   Now on his back a bag had he,
To bear what treasure he might win,
And therewith now did he begin
To go adown the winding stair;
And found the walls all painted fair   140
With images of many a thing,
Warrior and priest, and queen and king,
But nothing knew what they might be.
Which things full clearly could he see,
For lamps were hung up here and there   145
Of strange device, but wrought right fair,
And pleasant savour came from them.
At last a curtain, on whose hem
Unknown words in red gold were writ,
He reached, and softly raising it   150
Stepped back, for now did he behold
A goodly hall hung round with gold,
And at the upper end could see
Sitting, a glorious company:
Therefore he trembled, thinking well   155
They were no men, but fiends of hell.
But while he waited, trembling sore,
And doubtful of his late-learned lore,
A cold blast of the outer air
Blew out the lamps upon the stair   160
And all was dark behind him; then
Did he fear less to face those men
Than, turning round, to leave them there
While he went groping up the stair.
Yea, since he heard no cry or call   165
Or any speech from them at all,
He doubted they were images
Set there some dying king to please
By that Great Master of the art;
Therefore at last with stouter heart   170
He raised the cloth and entered in

In hope that happy life to win,
And drawing nigher did behold
That these were bodies dead and cold
Attired in full royal guise,   175
And wrought by art in such a wise
That living they all seemed to be,
Whose very eyes he well could see,
That now beheld not foul or fair,
Shining as though alive they were.   180
And midmost of that company
An ancient king that man could see,
A mighty man, whose beard of grey
A foot over his gold gown lay;
And next beside him sat his queen   185
Who in a flowery gown of green
And golden mantle well was clad,
And on her neck a collar had
Too heavy for her dainty breast;
Her loins by such a belt were prest   190
That whoso in his treasury
Held that alone, a king might be.
On either side of these, a lord
Stood heedfully before the board,
And in their hands held bread and wine   195
For service; behind these did shine
The armour of the guards, and then
The well-attired serving-men,
The minstrels clad in raiment meet;
And over against the royal seat   200
Was hung a lamp, although no flame
Was burning there, but there was set
Within its open golden fret
A huge carbuncle, red and bright;
Wherefrom there shone forth such a light   205
That great hall was as clear by it,
As though by wax it had been lit,
As some great church at Easter-tide.
Now set a little way aside,
Six paces from the dais stood   210
An image made of brass and wood,
In likeness of a full armed knight
Who pointed 'gainst the ruddy light
A huge shaft ready in a bow.
Pondering how he could come to know   215
What all these marvellous matters meant,
About the hall the scholar went,

Trembling, though nothing moved as yet;
And for awhile did he forget
The longings that had brought him there   220
In wondering at these marvels fair;
And still for fear he doubted much
One jewel of their robes to touch.

William Morris, 'The Land East of the Sun and West of the Moon', in *The Earthly Paradise* (2001: 43–9)

'The Land East of the Sun and West of the Moon' is a tale that appears in the Autumn section and has a unique series of multiple inner frames. The central story focuses on a fairy swan-maiden who is able to drive men mad with love. Originally inspired by Scandinavian accounts of swan-maidens, popularised through such works as Benjamin Thorpe's *Yule-Tide Stories* (1853) and George Webbe Dasent's *Popular Tales from the Norse* (1859), Morris's 'The Land East of the Sun and West of the Moon' is a narrative poem imbued with Orientalism. In particular, it seems to restructure the Oriental figure of the bird-lady featured in 'The Adventures of Hasan of Basrah'. Both stories project the conceptual metaphor LOVE IS PAIN, as John and Hasan suffer physical pains of love while waiting to meet the swan-maiden and the bird-lady. The word-builders (time, location and characters) are the same and Morris appears to be the only Victorian to use the Scandinavian story directly.

Then, though his watch was but begun,
E'en at that tide, as well he knew,
O'er John a drowsiness there drew,   280
And nothing seemed so good as sleep,
And sweet dreams o'er his eyes 'gan creep
That made him smile, then wake again
In terror that his watch was vain;
But in the midst of one of these   285
He started up, for through the trees
A mighty rushing sound he heard,
As of the wings of many a bird;
And, stark awake, with beating heart,
He put the hawthorn twigs apart,   290
And yet saw no more wondrous thing
Than seven white swans, who on wide wing
Went circling round, till one by one

They dropped the dewy grass upon.
He smiled thereat, and thought to shout   295
And scare them off; but yet a doubt
Clung to him, as he gazed on those,
And in the brake he held him close,
And watched them bridle there, and preen
Their snowy feathers well beseen;   300
So near they were, that he a stone
Might have cast o'er the furthest one
With his left hand, as there he lay.

   Apace came on the summer day,
Though the sun lingered, and more near   305
The swans drew, and began to peer
About in strange wise, and John deemed,
In after days, he must have dreamed
Again, if for the shortest space;
For a cloud seemed to dull the place   310
And silence of the birds there was;
And when he next looked o'er the grass,
Six swan-skins lay anigh his hand,
And nearby on the grass did stand
Seven white-skinned damsels, wrought so fair   315
That John must sit and tremble there,
And flush blood-red, and cast his eyes
Down on the ground in shamefast wise,
Then look again with longings sweet
Piercing his heart; because their feet   320
Moved through the long grey-seeded grass
But some two yards from where he was.

   A while in gentle wise they went,
Among the ripe long grass that bent
Before their beauty; then there ran   325
A thrill through him as they began,
In musical sweet speech and low,
To talk a tongue he did not know;
But when at last one spake alone,
It was to him as he had known   330
That heavenly voice for many years,
His heart swelled, till through rising tears
He saw them now, nor would that voice
Suffer his hot heart to rejoice,
In all that erst his eyes did bless   335
With unimagined loveliness:

Because her face, that yet had been
Alone among those girls unseen,
He longed for with such strong desire,
That his heart sickened, and quick-fire   340
Within his parched throat seemed to burn.

   A while she stood and did not turn,
While still the music of her voice
Made the birds' song seem tuneless noise;
And she alone of all did stand,   345
Holding within her down-drooped hand
The swan-skin – like a pink-tinged rose
Plucked from amidst a July close,
And laid on January snow,
Her fingers on the plumes did show: 350
A rosy flame of inner love
Seemed glowing through her; she did move
Lightly at whiles, or the soft wind
Played in her hair no coif did bind.
Then did he fear to draw his breath   355
Lest he should find the hand of Death
Was showing him vain images;
Then did he deem the morning breeze
Blew from the flowery fields of heaven,
Such fragrance to the morn was given.   360

   And now across the long dawn's grey
The climbing sun's first level ray,
Long hoped, yet sudden when it came,
Over the trembling grass did flame
And made the world alive once more;   365
And therewithal a pause came o'er
The earth and heaven, because she turned,
And with such longing his heart burned
That there he thought he needs must die,
And, breathless, opened mouth to cry.   370
And yet how soft and kind she seemed;
What a sweet helpful smile there gleamed
Over the perfect loveliness
That now his feeble eyes did bless!
   Now fell the swan-skin from her hand,   375
And silent all a space did stand,
And then again she turned away,
And seemed some whispered word to say
Unto her fellows; and therewith

Their delicate round limbs and lithe   380
Began to sway in measured time
Unto a sweet-voiced outland rhyme
As they cleft through the morning air
Hither and thither: fresh and fair
Beyond all words indeed were these,   385
Yet unto him but images
Well wrought, fair coloured: while she moved
Amid them all, a thing beloved
By earth and heaven: could she be   390
Made for his sole felicity? –
Yet if she were not, earth and heaven
Belike for nought to men were given
But to torment his weary heart.
He put the thorny twigs apart   395
A little more to gaze his fill;
And as he gazed a thought of ill
Shot through him: close unto his hand,
Nigher than where she erst did stand,
Nigher than where her unkissed feet   400
Had kissed the clover-blossoms sweet,
The snowy swan-skin lay cast down.
His heart thought, 'She will get her gon
E'en as she came, unless I take
This snow-white thing for her sweet sake;   405
Then whether death or life shall be,
She needs must speak one word to me
Before I die.'
And therewithal
His hand upon the skin did fall   410
Almost without his will, while yet
His eyes upon her form were set.
He drew it to him, and there lay
Until the first dance died away,
And from amid the rest thereof   415
Another sprang, whose rhythm did move
Light foot, long hair, and supple limb,
As the wind moves the poplars slim;
Then as the wind dies out again,
Like to the end of summer rain   420
Amid their leaves, and quivering now
No more their June-clad heads they bow,
So sank the rippling song and sweet,
And gently upon level feet
They swayed, and circle-wise did stand   425

Each scarcely touching each with hand,
Until at last all motion ceased.

    Still as the dewy shade decreased,
Panting John lay, and did not move,
Sunk in the wonder of his love,   430
Though fear weighed on him; for he knew
That short his time of pleasance grew
Though none had told him.
Now the one
His heart was set on spake alone,   435
And therewith hand and arm down-dropped,
Their scarce-heard murmuring wholly stopped,
And softly in long line they passed
Unto the thorn-brake, she the last.
Then unto agony arose
John's fear, as once again all close   440
She was to him. The wind ran by
The notched green leaves, the sun was high,
Dappling the grass whereon he lay:
Fresh, fair, and cheery was the day,
And nought like guile or wizardry   445
Could one have thought there was anigh,
Till, suddenly, did all things change,
E'en as his heart, and dim and strange
The old familiar world had grown,
That blithe and rough he erst had known,   450
And racked and mined time did seem.

    A sudden, sharp cry pierced his dream,
And then his cleared eyes could behold
His love, half-hid with hair of gold,   455
Her slim hands covering up her face,
Standing amid the grassy place,
Shaken with sobs, and round her woe,
With long caressing necks of snow
And ruffling plumes, the others stood'   460
Bird-like again. Chilled to the blood,
Yet close he lay and did not move,
Strengthening his heart with thoughts of love,
Wild as a morning dream. Withal
Some murmured word from her did fall,   465
Closer awhile the swans did press
Around her woeful loveliness,

As though a loth farewell they bade;
And she one fair hand softly laid
Upon their heads in wandering wise,   470
Nor drew the other from her eyes,
As one by one her body fair
They left, and rose into the air
With clangorous cries, and circled wide
Above her, till the blue did hide   475
Their soaring wings, and all were gone.

   As scarce she knew that she was lone,
She stood there for a little space,
One hand still covering up her face,
The other drooped down, half stretched out,   480
As if her lone heart yet did doubt
Somewhat was left her to caress.
Yet soon all sound of her distress
Was silent, though thought held her fast
And nought she moved; the field-mouse passed   485
Close to her feet, the dragon-fly,
A thin blue needle flickered by,
The bee whirled past her as the morn
Grew later, and strange thoughts were born
Within her. So she raised her head   490
At last, and, gazing round, she said:
'Is pitying love all dead on earth?
Is no heart left that holds of worth
Love that hands touch not, and that eyes
Behold not? Is none left so wise   495
As not to know the smart of bliss
That dieth out 'twixt kiss and kiss?'

William Morris, 'The Man Who Never Laughed Again', in *The Earthly Paradise* (2001: 172–3; 178–80; 214–15)

Morris's 'The Man Who Never Laughed Again' relies heavily on another identifiable Oriental text, the fifth Wezeer's account in the *Arabian Nights*, entitled 'The Man Who Never Laughed Again for the Rest of His Life'. As explained by Morris's daughter in the introduction to his collected works, Morris's tale is characterised by a different atmosphere that is 'particularly English' (Morris 1911, in 1910–15: V, xxv) with its lovely rural landscape. By transposing the

Oriental plot into a different English world, whose protagonist is not the incredibly cruel figure featured in the *Arabian Nights* but rather a generous and genuinely curious character, Morris seems to de-Orientalise the general schema of the source story. Though the general schema and its variables (the parable of the predestined; the forbidden door; the talismanic lady and so on) are preserved, some particular values are substituted according to the purpose for which the schema is being used by Morris. Probably inspired by his personal experiences, Morris's Bahram seems to share his own values of beauty, dignity and devotion, criticising all social futilities and illusions. Likewise, the proto-feminist world ruled by an Amazon-like woman is substituted with a Western medieval world whose melancholy and languid queen is anything but authoritative. From this perspective, Oriental schemas vary in the adequacy with which they account for any of Morris's Oriental-inspired tales.

OCTOBER
ARGUMENT.

A CERTAIN man, who from rich had become poor, having been taken by one of his former friends to a fair house, was shown strange things there, and dwelt there awhile among a company of doleful men; but these in the end dying, and he desiring above all things to know their story, so it happened that he at last learned it to his own cost.

A CITY was there nigh the Indian Sea,
As tells my tale, where folk for many an age
Had lived, perforce, such life as needs must be
Beneath the rule of priestly king and mage,
Bearing with patient hearts the summer's rage,   5
Yea, even bowing foolish heads in vain
Before the mighty sun, their life and bane.

Now ere the hottest of the summer came,
While yet the rose shed perfume on the earth,
And still the grass was green despite the flame   10
Of that land's sun – while folk gave up to mirth
A little of their life, so little worth,
And the rich man forgot his fears awhile
Beneath the soft eve's still recurring smile –

Mid those sweet days, when e'en the burning land   15
Knew somewhat of the green north's summer rest,
A stately house within the town did stand,

When the fresh morn was failing from its best,
Though the street's pavement still the shadow blessed
From whispering trees, that rose, thick-leaved and tall,   20
Above the well-built marble bounding-wall.

 Each side the door therein rose-garlands hung,
And through the doorway you might see within
The glittering robes of minstrel-men that sung,
And resting dancing-girls in raiment thin,   25
Because the master there did now begin
Another day of ease and revelry,
To make it harder yet for him to die.

 And toward the door, perfumed and garlanded,
The guests passed, clad in wonderful attire,   30
And this and that one through the archway led
Some girl, made languid by the rosy fire
Of that fair time; with love and sweet desire
The air seemed filled, and how could such folk see
In any eyes unspoken misery?   35

[. . .]

 Then as the boughs grew thinner overhead,
That glimmer widened into moonlit night,
And 'twixt the trees grown sparse their pathway led   185
Unto a wide bare plain, that 'neath that light
Against the black trunks showed all stark and white;
Then Bharam, more at ease thereat, began
His fellow's visage in that light to scan.

 No change was in his face, and if he knew   190
Who rode beside him, 'twas but as some hook
Within an engine knows what it must do,
His hand indeed from his friend's rein he took,
But never cast on him one slightest look;
Then, shuddering, Bharam 'gan to sing again   195
To make him turn, but spent his breath in vain.

 But when the trees were wholly past, afar
Across the plain they saw a watch-tower high,
That 'neath the moonlight, like an angry star,
Shone over a white palace, and thereby   200
Within white walls did black-treed gardens lie:
And Firuz smote his mule and hastened on
To where that distant sign of trouble shone.

And as they went, thereon did Bharam stare,
Nor turned his eyes at all unto the plain,   205
Nor heeded when from out her form the hare
Started beneath the mule's feet, and in vain
The owl called from the wood, for he drew rein
Within a little while before the gate,
Casting his soul into the hands of fate.   210

Then Firuz blew the horn, nor waited long
Ere the gate, opened by a man scarce seen,
Gave entry to a garden, where the song
Of May's brown bird had hardly left the green
Sweet-blossomed tree-tops lonely, and between   215
The whispering glades the fountain leaped on high,
And the rose waited till morn came, to die.

But when the first wave of that soft delight
Swept o'er the spendthrift's sense, he smiled and turned
Unto his guide throughout the wondrous night,   220
And while his heart with hope and wonder burned,
He said, 'Indeed a fair thing have I learned
With thee for master; yet is this the end?
Will they not now bring forth the bride, O friend?'

Drunk with the sweetness of that place he spoke,   225
And hoped to see the mask fall suddenly
From his friend's face, from whose thin lips there broke
A dreadful cry of helpless misery,
Scaring the birds from flowery bush and tree;
'O fool!' he said; 'say such things in the day,   230
When noise and light take memory more away!'

Bharam shrank back abashed, nor had a word
To say thereto, and 'twixt the trees they rode,
Noted of nothing but some wakeful bird,
Until they reached a fair and great abode   235
Whereon the red gold e'en in moonlight glowed.
There silently they lighted down before
Smooth marble stairs, and through the open door.

They entered a great, dimly-lighted hall;
Yet through the dimness well our man could see   240
How fair the hangings were that clad the wall,
And what a wealth of beast and flower and tree
Was spent wherever carving there might be,

And what a floor was 'neath his wearied feet,
Not made for men who call death rest and sweet.   245

   Now he, though fain to linger and to ask
What was the manner of their living there,
And what thenceforth should be his proper task,
And who his fellows were, did nowise dare
To meet that cry again that seemed to bare   250
A wretched life of every softening veil –
A dreadful prelude to a dreadful tale.

   So silently whereas the other led
He followed, and through corridors they passed,
Dim lit, but worthy of a king new wed,   255
Till to a chamber did they come at last,
O'er which a little light a taper cast,
And showed a fair bed by the window-side;
Therewith at last turned round the dreary guide,

   And said, 'O thou to whom night still is night   260
And day is day, bide here until the morn,
And take some little of that dear delight,
That we for many a long day have outworn.
Sleep, and forget awhile that thou wast born,
And on the morrow will I come to thee   265
To show thee what thy life with us must be.'

[. . .]

He rose within a while, and turned about
Unto the door, and said, 'Three days it is
Before she comes to take away all doubt
And wrap my soul again in utter bliss;   1400
I will depart, that she may smile at this,
Giving the pity and forgiveness due
Unto a heart whose feebleness she knew.

   Therewith he turned to go, but even then,
Upon a little table nigh his hand,   1405
Beheld a cup the work of cunning men
For many a long year vanished from the land,
And up against it did a tablet stand;
Whereon were gleaming letters writ in gold;
Then breathlessly these things did he behold;   1410

For never had his eyes beheld them erst,
And well he deemed the secret lay therein;
Trembling, he said, 'This cup may quench my thirst,
Fair rest from this strange tablet may I win,
And if I sin she will forgive my sin;   1415
Nay, rather since her word I disobey
In entering here, no heavier this will weigh.'

   Withal he took the tablet, and he read;
'O thou who, venturing much, hast gained so much,
Drink of this cup, and be remembered   1420
When all are gone whose feet the green earth touch:
Dull is the labouring world, nor holdeth such
As think and yet are happy; then be bold,
And things unthought of shall thine eyes behold!

   'Yea, thou must drink, for if thou drinkest not   1425
Nor soundest all the depths of this hid thing,
Think'st thou that these my words can be forgot,
How close soever thou to love mayst cling,
How much soever thou art still a king:
Drink then, and take what thou hast fairly won,   1430
For make no doubt that thine old life is done.'

   He took the cup and round about the bowl
Beheld strange figures carved, strange letters writ,
But mid the hurrying tumult of his soul,
He of their meaning then could make no whit,   1435
Though afterwards their smallest lines would flit
Before his eyes, in times that came to him
When many a greater matter had grown dim.

   So with closed eyes he drank, and once again,
While on his quivering lip the sweet draught hung,   1440
Did he think dimly of those mourning men
And saw them winding the dark trees among,
And in his ears their doleful wailing rung;
His love and all the glories of his home
E'en in that minute shadows had become.   1445

   E'en in that minute, though at first indeed
In one quick flash of pain unbearable,
His love, his queen, made bare of any weed,
Seemed standing there, as though some tale to tell
From opened lips; and then a dark veil fell   1450
O'er all things there, a chill and restless breeze
Seemed moaning through innumerable trees.

Christina Rossetti, 'The Dead City' (2008: 5–11)

Written in 1847, 'The Dead City' is a poem describing a visit to a city whose inhabitants have become statues. There are many interpretations of this poem (seen as a moral form of grotesque, a Gothic tale, an Inferno-like story and so on), whose petrified characters are mapped on to those turned to stone for worshipping a false god in 'The Story of Zobeide'. Rossetti's remediation of the Arabian tale is linguistically connected with an Oriental kind of foregrounding through a variety of devices, such as rhyme, alliteration, enumeration, metonomy and creative conceptual metaphors. The magnificent banquet that has been prepared, and the gold and silver vessels filled with rich and exotic fruits are the attractors of this scenario of death. By projecting the conceptual metaphor EXOTIC FRUITS ARE DOOM, Rossetti suggests that anything coming from the East is potentially dangerous.

> By that gate I entered lone
> A fair city of white stone;
> And a lovely light to see
> Dawned, and spread most gradually
> Till the air grew warm and shone.   90
>
> Thro' the splendid streets I strayed
> In that radiance without shade,
> Yet I heard no human sound;
> All was still and silent round
> As a city of the dead.
>
> All the doors were open wide;
> Lattices on every side
> In the wind swung to and fro;
> Wind that whispered very low;
> Go and see the end of pride.   100
>
> With a fixed determination
> Entered I each habitation,
> But they were all tenantless;
> All was utter loneliness,
> All was deathless desolation.
>
> In the noiseless market-place
> Was no care-worn busy face;
> There were none to buy or sell,
> None to listen or to tell,
> In this silent emptiness.   110

Thro' the city on I went
Full of awe and wonderment;
Still the light around me shone,
And I wandered on, still on,
In my great astonishment,

Till at length I reached a place
Where amid an ample space
Rose a palace for a king;
Golden was the turreting,
And of solid gold the base.   120

The great porch was ivory,
And the steps were ebony;
Diamond and chrysoprase
Set the pillars in a blaze,
Capitalled with jewelry.

None was there to bar my way –
And the breezes seemed to say:
Touch not these, but pass them by,
Pressing onwards: therefore I
Entered in and made no stay.   130

All around was desolate:
I went on; a silent state
Reigned in each deserted room,
And I hastened thro' the gloom
Till I reached an outer gate.

Soon a shady avenue
Blossom-perfumed, met my view.
Here and there the sun-beams fell
On pure founts, whose sudden swell
Up from marble basins flew.   140

Every tree was fresh and green;
Not a withered leaf was seen
Thro' the veil of flowers and fruit;
Strong and sapful were the root,
The top boughs, and all between.

Vines were climbing everywhere
Full of purple grapes and fair:
And far off I saw the corn
With its heavy head down borne,
By the odour-laden air.   150

Who shall strip the bending vine?
Who shall tread the press for wine?
Who shall bring the harvest in
When the pallid ears begin
In the sun to glow and shine?

On I went, alone, alone,
Till I saw a tent that shone
With each bright and lustrous hue;
It was trimmed with jewels too,
And with flowers; not one was gone.   160

Then the breezes whispered me:
Enter in, and look, and see
How for luxury and pride
A great multitude have died: –
And I entered tremblingly.

Lo, a splendid banquet laid
In the cool and pleasant shade.
Might tables, every thing
Of sweet Nature's furnishing
That was rich and rare, displayed;   170

And each strange and luscious cate
Practised Art makes delicate;
With a thousand fair devices
Full of odours and of spices;
And a warm voluptuous state.

All the vessels were of gold
Set with gems of worth untold.
In the midst a fountain rose
Of pure milk, whose rippling flows
In a silver basin rolled.   180

In a green emerald baskets were
Sun-red apples, streaked, and fair;
Here the nectarine and peach
And ripe plums lay, and on each
The bloom rested every where.

Grapes were hanging overhead,
Purple, pale, and ruby-red;
And in panniers all around
Yellow melons shone, fresh found,
With the dew upon them spread.   190

And the apricot and pear
And the pulpy fig were there;
Cherries and dark mulberries,
Bunch currants, strawberries,
And the lemon wan and fair.

And unnumbered others too,
Fruits of every size and hue,
Juicy in their ripe perfection,
Cool beneath the cool reflection
Of the curtains' skyey blue.   200

All the floor was strewn with flowers
Fresh from sunshine and from showers,
Roses, lilies, Jessamine;
And the ivy ran between
Like a thought in happy hours.

And this feast too lacked no guest
With its warm delicious rest;
With its couches softly sinking,
And its glow, not made for thinking,
But for careless joy at best.   210

Many banquetters were there,
Wrinkled age, the young, the fair;
In the splendid revelry
Flushing cheek and kindling eye
Told of gladness without care.

Yet no laughter rang around,
Yet they uttered forth no sound;
With the smile upon his face
Each sat moveless in his place,
Silently, as if spell-bound.   220

The low whispering voice was gone,
And I felt awed and alone.
In my great astonishment
To the feasters up I went –
Lo, they all were turned to stone.

Yea they all were statue-cold,
Men and women, young and old;

With the life-like look and smile
And the flush; and all the while
The hard fingers kept their hold.   230

Here a little child was sitting
With a merry glance, befitting
Happy age and heedless heart;
There a young man sat apart
With a forward look unweeting.

Nigh them was a maiden fair;
And the ringlets of her hair
Round her slender fingers twined;
And she blushed as she reclined,
Knowing that her love was there.   240

Here a dead man sat to sup,
In his hand a drinking cup;
Wine cup of the heavy gold,
Human hand stony and cold,
And no life-breath struggling up.

There a mother lay, and smiled
Down upon her infant child;
Happy child and happy mother
Laughing back to one another
With a gladness undefiled.   250

Here an old man slept, worn out
With the revelry and rout;
Here a strong man sat and gazed
On a girl, whose eyes unraised
No more wandered round about.

And none broke the stillness, none;
I was the sole living one.
And methought that silently
Many seemed to look on me
With strange steadfast eyes that shone.   260

Full of fear I would have fled;
Full of fear I bent my head,
Shutting out each stony guest: –
When I looked again the feast
And the tent had vanished.

> Yes, once more I stood alone
> Where the happy sunlight shone
> And a gentle wind was sighing,
> And the little birds were flying,
> And the dreariness was gone.   270
>
> All these things that I have said
> Awed me, and made me afraid.
> What was I that I should see
> So much hidden mystery?
> And I straightway knelt and prayed.

Christina Rossetti, 'Goblin Market' (2008: 105; 107–8; 114–16; 118–19)

Commonly known as Christina Rossetti's masterpiece, 'Goblin Market' is a puzzling text, rich in Oriental references that make it the most Eastern-inspired of her poems. As a parable of sisterhood, 'Goblin Market' seems to be mapped on to the stories of the three sisters of Baghdad (Anime, Safie and Zobeide) in the *Arabian Nights*. The Oriental 'buying and selling' frame is all-pervasive in the poem, involving such variables as buyer (Laura), seller (goblins), merchandise (fruits) and price (a lock of golden hair). By projecting the conceptual metaphor LIFE IS A MARKET, Rossetti recreates and extends the Oriental world inhabited by the sisters of Baghdad, a world of violence and survival. But Lizzie is the most Oriental character of the story, whose function-advancers that propel the narrative appear to be similar to those of 'The Fourth Voyage of Sinbad the Sailor'. From this perspective, Lizzie, the heroine and Christ-like figure, seems to have much in common with Sinbad in her attitude towards fruits. Like Sinbad, Lizzie resists the temptations of the East and witnesses the transformation of her beloved sister due to poisonous food. This Oriental interpretation may justify Rossetti's obsession with exotic fruits, which appear in the *Arabian Nights* as dangerous temptations. Last but not least, the goblins selling fruits to Lizzie and assaulting her with animal-like violence seem to recall the Oriental merchants in the *Arabian Nights*. See Chapter 4 in this book for a cognitive linguistic analysis of the Orientalism in 'Goblin Market'.

> Morning and evening
> Maids heard the goblins cry:
> 'Come buy our orchard fruits,
> Come buy, come buy:

Apples and quinces,
Lemons and oranges,
Plump unpecked cherries,
Melons and raspberries,
Bloom-down-cheeked peaches,
Swart-headed mulberries,   10
Wild free-born cranberries,
Crab-apples, dewberries,
Pine-apples, blackberries,
Apricots, strawberries; –
All ripe together
In summer weather, –
Morns that pass by,
Fair eves that fly;
Come buy, come buy:
Our grapes fresh from the vine,   20
Pomegranates full and fine,
Dates and sharp bullaces,
Rare pears and greengages,
Damsons and bilberries,
Taste them and try:
Currants and gooseberries,
Bright-fire-like barberries,
Figs to fill your mouth,
Citrons from the South,
Sweet to tongue and sound to eye;
Come buy, come buy.'

[. . .]

Backwards up the mossy glen
Turned and trooped the goblin men,
With their shrill repeated cry,
'Come buy, come buy.'   90
When they reached where Laura was
They stood stock still upon the moss,
Leering at each other,
Brother with queer brother;
Signalling each other,
Brother with sly brother.
One set his basket down,
One reared his plate;
One began to weave a crown
Of tendrils, leaves and rough nuts brown   100
(Men sell not such in any town);
One heaved the golden weight

Of dish and fruit to offer her:
'Come buy, come buy,' was still their cry.
Laura stared but did not stir,
Longed but had no money:
The whisk-tailed merchant bade her taste
In tones as smooth as honey,
The cat-faced purr'd,
The rat-paced spoke a word   110
Of welcome, and the snail-paced even was heard;
One parrot-voiced and jolly
Cried 'Pretty Goblin' still for 'Pretty Polly;' –
One whistled like a bird.

But sweet-tooth Laura spoke in haste:
'Good folk, I have no coin;
To take were to purloin:
I have no copper in my purse,
I have no silver either,
And all my gold is on the furze   120
That shakes in windy weather
Above the rusty heather.'
'You have much gold upon your head,'
They answered all together:
'Buy from us with a golden curl.'
She clipped a precious golden lock,
She dropped a tear more rare than pearl,
Then sucked their fruit globes fair or red:
Sweeter than honey from the rock,
Stronger than man-rejoicing wine,   130
Clearer than water flowed that juice;
She never tasted such before,
How should it cloy with length of use?
She sucked and sucked and sucked the more
Fruits which that unknown orchard bore;
She sucked until her lips were sore;
Then flung the emptied rinds away
But gathered up one kernel-stone,
And knew not was it night or day
As she turned home alone.   140

[. . .]

'Good folk,' said Lizzie,
Mindful of Jeanie:
'Give me much and many:' –
Held out her apron,

Tossed them her penny.
'Nay, take a seat with us,
Honour and eat with us,'
They answered grinning: 370
'Our feast is but beginning.
Night yet is early,
Warm and dew-pearly,
Wakeful and starry:
Such fruits as these
No man can carry;
Half their bloom would fly,
Half their dew would dry,
Half their flavour would pass by.
Sit down and feast with us,   380
Be welcome guest with us,
Cheer you and rest with us.' –
'Thank you,' said Lizzie: 'But one waits
At home alone for me:
So without further parleying,
If you will not sell me any
Of your fruits though much and many,
Give me back my silver penny
I tossed you for a fee.' –
They began to scratch their pates,   390
No longer wagging, purring,
But visibly demurring,
Grunting and snarling.
One called her proud,
Cross-grained, uncivil;
Their tones waxed loud,
Their looks were evil.
Lashing their tails
They trod and hustled her,
Elbowed and jostled her,   400
Clawed with their nails,
Barking, mewing, hissing, mocking,
Tore her gown and soiled her stocking,
Twitched her hair out by the roots,
Stamped upon her tender feet,
Held her hands and squeezed their fruits
Against her mouth to make her eat.

White and golden Lizzie stood,
Like a lily in a flood, –
Like a rock of blue-veined stone   410
Lashed by tides obstreperously, –

Like a beacon left alone
In a hoary roaring sea,
Sending up a golden fire, –
Like a fruit-crowned orange-tree
White with blossoms honey-sweet
Sore beset by wasp and bee, –
Like a royal virgin town
Topped with gilded dome and spire
Close beleaguered by a fleet   420
Mad to tug her standard down.

One may lead a horse to water,
Twenty cannot make him drink.
Though the goblins cuffed and caught her,
Coaxed and fought her,
Bullied and besought her,
Scratched her, pinched her black as ink,
Kicked and knocked her,
Mauled and mocked her,
Lizzie uttered not a word;   430
Would not open lip from lip
Lest they should cram a mouthful in:
But laughed in heart to feel the drip
Of juice that syrupped all her face,
And lodged in dimples of her chin,
And streaked her neck which quaked like curd.
At last the evil people
Worn out by her resistance
Flung back her penny, kicked their fruit
Along whichever road they took,   440
Not leaving root or stone or shoot;
Some writhed into the ground,
Some dived into the brook
With ring and ripple,
Some scudded on the gale without a sound,
Some vanished in the distance.

[. . .]
Life out of death.
That night long Lizzie watched by her,
Counted her pulse's flagging stir,
Felt for her breath,
Held water to her lips, and cooled her face
With tears and fanning leaves:
But when the first birds chirped about their eaves,   530
And early reapers plodded to the place

Of golden sheaves,
And dew-wet grass
Bowed in the morning winds so brisk to pass,
And new buds with new day
Opened of cup-like lilies on the stream,
Laura awoke as from a dream,
Laughed in the innocent old way,
Hugged Lizzie but not twice or thrice;
Her gleaming locks showed not one thread of grey,   540
Her breath was sweet as May
And light danced in her eyes.

Days, weeks, months, years,
Afterwards, when both were wives
With children of their own;
Their mother-hearts beset with fears,
Their lives bound up in tender lives;
Laura would call the little ones
And tell them of her early prime,
Those pleasant days long gone   550
Of not-returning time:
Would talk about the haunted glen,
The wicked, quaint fruit-merchant men,
Their fruits like honey to the throat
But poison in the blood;
(Men sell not such in any town:)
Would tell them how her sister stood
In deadly peril to do her good,
And win the fiery antidote:
Then joining hands to little hands   560
Would bid them cling together,
'For there is no friend like a sister
In calm or stormy weather;
To cheer one on the tedious way,
To fetch one if one goes astray,
To lift one if one totters down,
To strengthen whilst one stands.'

Christina Rossetti, 'The Prince's Progress' (2008: 161; 164–7)

'The Prince's Progress', conceived as a sequel to 'Goblin Market', is a long narrative poem that introduces Christina Rossetti's second volume of verse. Like 'Goblin Market', 'The Prince's Progress' concerns the false expectations of love, the story focusing on a princess awaiting the return of her tarrying prince. The fragmentary composition of the poem is attested to in Rossetti's correspondence with her brothers: lines 481–540 were written in October 1861 and published in 1863, while lines 1–480 were written in January 1865 and published together with the remaining lines in 1866. 'The Prince's Progress' seems to be patterned on two tales from the *Arabian Nights*: that is, 'The Story of Anime' and 'The Adventures of Hasan of Basrah'. An extensive use of shifts in relational and spatial deixis demonstrates Rossetti's restructuring of different Oriental schemas. Both the Oriental buying and selling schema and the elixir of life schema are restructured in Rossetti's poem, whose action-chain pattern (bargaining, apprenticing and potion-making) is patterned on 'The Adventures of Hasan of Basrah'. In the creation of her new schema, Rossetti replaces Oriental schemas with variables to produce a new, Pre-Raphaelite schema.

> 'By her head lilies and rosebuds grow;
> The lilies droop, will the rosebuds blow?
> The silver slim lilies hang the head low;
> Their stream is scanty, their sunshine rare;
> Let the sun blaze out, and let the stream flow,
> They will blossom and wax fair.   30
>
> 'Red and white poppies grow at her feet,
> The blood-red wait for sweet summer heat,
> Wrapped in bud-coats hairy and neat;
> But the white buds swell, one day they will burst,
> Will open their death-cups drowsy and sweet –
> Which will open the first?'
>
> Then a hundred sad voices lifted a wail,
> And a hundred glad voices piped on the gale:
> 'Time is short, life is short,' they took up the tale:
> 'Life is sweet, love is sweet, use to-day while you may;   40
> Love is sweet, and to-morrow may fail;
> Love is sweet, use to-day.'
>
> While the song swept by, beseeching and meek,
> Up rose the Prince with a flush on his cheek,
> Up he rose to stir and to seek,
> Going forth in the joy of his strength;
> Strong of limb if of purpose weak,
> Starting at length.

Forth he set in the breezy morn,
Crossing green fields of nodding corn,   50
As goodly a Prince as ever was born;
Carolling with the carolling lark; –
Sure his bride will be won and worn,
Ere fall of the dark.

[. . .]

A land of chasm and rent, a land
Of rugged blackness on either hand:
If water trickled its track was tanned
With an edge of rust to the chink;   130
If one stamped on stone or on sand
It returned a clink.

A lifeless land, a loveless land,
Without lair or nest on either hand:
Only scorpions jerked in the sand,
Black as black iron, or dusty pale;
From point to point sheer rock was manned
By scorpions in mail.

A land of neither life nor death,
Where no man buildeth or fashioneth,   140
Where none draws living or dying breath;
No man cometh or goeth there,
No man doeth, seeketh, saith,
In the stagnant air.

Some old volcanic upset must
Have rent the crust and blackened the crust;
Wrenched and ribbed it beneath its dust
Above earth's molten centre at seethe,
Heaved and heaped it by huge upthrust
Of fire beneath.   150

Untrodden before, untrodden since:
Tedious land for a social Prince;
Halting, he scanned the outs and ins,
Endless, labyrinthine, grim,
Of the solitude that made him wince,
Laying wait for him.

By bulging rock and gaping cleft,
Even of half mere daylight reft,
Rueful he peered to right and left,
Muttering in his altered mood: 160
'The fate is hard that weaves my weft,
Though my lot be good.'
Dim the changes of day to night,
Of night scarce dark to day not bright.
Still his road wound towards the right,
Still he went, and still he went,
Till one night he espied a light,
In his discontent.

Out it flashed from a yawn-mouthed cave,
Like a red-hot eye from a grave.   170
No man stood there of whom to crave
Rest for wayfarer plodding by:
Though the tenant were churl or knave
The Prince might try.

In he passed and tarried not,
Groping his way from spot to spot,
Towards where the cavern flare glowed hot: –
An old, old mortal, cramped and double,
Was peering into a seething-pot,
In a world of trouble.   180

The veriest atomy he looked,
With grimy fingers clutching and crooked,
Tight skin, a nose all bony and hooked,
And a shaking, sharp, suspicious way;
His blinking eyes had scarcely brooked
The light of day.

Stared the Prince, for the sight was new;
Stared, but asked without more ado:
'May a weary traveller lodge with you,
Old father, here in your lair?   190
In your country the inns seem few,
And scanty the fare.'

The head turned not to hear him speak;
The old voice whistled as through a leak
(Out it came in a quavering squeak):
'Work for wage is a bargain fit:

If there's aught of mine that you seek
You must work for it.

'Buried alive from light and air
This year is the hundredth year,   200
I feed my fire with a sleepless care,
Watching my potion wane or wax:
Elixir of Life is simmering there,
And but one thing lacks.

'If you're fain to lodge here with me,
Take that pair of bellows you see –
Too heavy for my old hands they be –
Take the bellows and puff and puff:
When the steam curls rosy and free
The broth's boiled enough.   210

'Then take your choice of all I have;
I will give you life if you crave.
Already I'm mildewed for the grave,
So first myself I must drink my fill:
But all the rest may be yours, to save
Whomever you will.'

'Done,' quoth the Prince, and the bargain stood.
First he piled on resinous wood,
Next plied the bellows in hopeful mood;
Thinking, 'My love and I will live.   220
If I tarry, why life is good,
And she may forgive.'

The pot began to bubble and boil;
The old man cast in essence and oil,
He stirred all up with a triple coil
Of gold and silver and iron wire,
Dredged in a pinch of virgin soil,
And fed the fire.

But still the steam curled watery white;
Night turned to day and day to night;   230
One thing lacked, by his feeble sight
Unseen, unguessed by his feeble mind:
Life might miss him, but Death the blight
Was sure to find.

So when the hundredth year was full
The thread was cut and finished the school.
Death snapped the old worn-out tool,
Snapped him short while he stood and stirred
(Though stiff he stood as a stiff-necked mule)
With never a word.   240

Thus at length the old crab was nipped.
The dead hand slipped, the dead finger dipped
In the broth as the dead man slipped, –
That same instant, a rosy red
Flushed the steam, and quivered and clipped
Round the dead old head.

The last ingredient was supplied
(Unless the dead man mistook or lied).
Up started the Prince, he cast aside
The bellows plied through the tedious trial,   250
Made sure that his host had died,
And filled a phial.

'One night's rest,' thought the Prince: 'This done,
Forth I start with the rising sun:
With the morrow I rise and run,
    Come what will of wind or of weather.
This draught of Life when my Bride is won
    We'll drink together.'

Ford Madox Ford, *The Brown Owl* (1892a: 1–4; 21–2; 25–6; 28–30)

The Brown Owl, Ford's first publication, appeared when he was only seventeen. Written for his sister Juliet, the medieval story is about Princess Ismara's transition from adolescence to adulthood. King Intafernes, the Princess's father, dies at the beginning of the story, leaving her with a brown owl as her sole aid. In this fairy tale, Ford seems to pattern his characters on Oriental ones by employing similar action-chain patterns. A case in point is Princess Ismara, whose toilet scene recalls Scheherazade bathing in the *hammam*. Likewise, Merrymineral, the evil Chancellor of the kingdom, appears to be a replica of Aladdin's African magician with his mischievous personality and, above all, with his use of magic for evil purposes. Merrymineral's language is of the utmost importance for tracing back his Oriental influence. His speech acts reveal his true evil nature – that of artful deceiver, activating the following action chain: *deceiving*, *consoling* and *revenging*. Ford seems to lift the characters of the *Arabian Nights* out of their original stories and place them into new blended spaces.

Once upon a time, a long while ago – in fact long before Egypt had risen to power and before Rome or Greece had ever been heard of – and that was some time before you were born, you know – there was a king who reigned over a very large and powerful kingdom.

Now this king was rather old, he had founded his kingdom himself, and he had reigned over it nine hundred and ninety-nine and a half years already. As I have said before, it was a very large kingdom, for it contained, among other things, the whole of the western half of the world. The rest of the world was divided into smaller kingdoms, and each kingdom was ruled over by separate princes, who, however, were none of them so old as Intafernes, as he was called.

Now King Intafernes was an exceedingly powerful magician – that was why he had remained so long on the throne; for you must know that in this country the people were divided into two classes – those who were magicians, and those who weren't. The magicians called themselves Aristocrats, and the others called themselves what they liked; also in this country, as in all other countries, the rich magicians had the upper hand over the rest, but still the others did not grumble, for they were not badly treated on the whole. Now of all the magicians in the country the King was the greatest, and no one approached him in magic power but the Chancellor, who was called Merrymineral, and he even was no match for the King.

Among other things King Intafernes had a daughter, who was exceedingly beautiful – as indeed all princesses are or ought to be. She had a very fair face, and a wealth of golden hair that fell over her shoulders, like a shining waterfall falling in ripples to her waist.

Now in the thousandth year of her father's reign the Princess was eighteen, and in that country she was already of age. Three days before her nineteenth birthday, however, her father fell sick and gradually weakened, until at last he had only strength left to lie in his royal bed. Still, however, he retained his faculties, and on the Princess's birthday he made all the magicians file before his bed and swear to be faithful for ever to the Princess. Last of all came the Chancellor, the pious Merrymineral, and as he took the oath the King looked at him with a loving glance and said:

'Ah! my dear Merrymineral, in truth there was no need for thee to have taken the oath, for it is thy nature to be faithful; and it being thy nature, thou couldst not but be faithful.'

To which the pious Merrymineral answered:

'To such a master and to such a mistress how could I but be faithful?' and to this noble sentiment the three hundred and forty-seven magicians could not help according unanimous applause.

When they were quiet again the King said:

'So be it, good Merrymineral, do thou always act up to thy words. But now leave, good men all, for I am near my end, and would fain spend my last moments with my daughter here.'

[. . .]

'Come, my cherished Owl, sit there on the crown on the top of the looking-glass frame and wait while I wash my hands and face and make myself tidy.'

The Owl did as he was told, and the Princess began to wash in cold water – a thing she had never done before – but she did not like to call to her ladies-in-waiting, lest they should see how red her eyes were. So she had to put up with the cold water, and very pleasant she found it, for it cleared the tear-mist out of her eyes and made her feel quite happy and cheerful again:

'And I have heard,' she thought to herself, 'that washing in cold water is matchless for the complexion.'

When she had finished washing she went and combed her hair before the glass. For she was a very artistic Princess, and liked looking at beautiful things, and so she liked sometimes to look at herself in the glass. Not that she was in the least conceited.

So she combed her hair with a gold comb, and when she had finished combing it, she put on her gold circlet as a sign of her rank, and then she said to the Owl, who had been sitting patiently on the looking-glass blinking at her as if he quite enjoyed himself:

'Now, cherished Owl, you may sit on my shoulder again.'

When the Owl was again in his place he blinked in the glass at his own reflection as if the light were too strong for him, and he shut his eyes and drew in his neck and lifted up one foot into his feathers, as if he felt quite happy and comfortable, and the Princess smiled at his happy look, for she seemed quite to have forgotten her sorrow in the company of the Owl.

[. . .]

The good Chancellor received her laughing reproach with his head bowed down. He heaved a deep sigh, and drew his pocket-handkerchief from his pocket and applied it to his eyes. As he drew it away the tears could be seen flowing fast down his withered cheeks.

'I came,' he moaned, 'to console you for your great loss. I too,' he continued in a voice choked with sobs, 'I too am an orphan.'

It seemed funny to the Princess to see him weeping thus, and she could hardly help laughing at him, but her grief soon came back.

'Poor Merrymineral,' she sighed, 'to you also it must be a sad blow, for you were always faithful and attached. But it was fated to happen thus, and you must really try and be comforted, for crying will not mend matters.'

The Chancellor began again:

'The beloved King your father'; but his sobs choked him, and he hid his face.

'The beloved King your father,' echoed a loud voice, exactly mimicking the tones of the Chancellor, but where the voice came from no one could tell.

The Chancellor started.

'Did you say that?' said the Princess.

'Not the second time,' answered Merrymineral.

'Who could it be?' said the Princess; 'for there is no one in the room except the cherished Owl; and you can't speak, can you, Owl dear?'

The Owl shook his head dismally.

[. . .]

'So he refuses to obey my orders,' said the Princess. 'He must be punished for this. However, now go and get a bucketful of water and pour it on him. Perhaps that will bring him to.'

Now when she said he was to be punished, she was only joking, but she said it very gravely, so that many people might have thought it was quite in earnest. Meanwhile the pages departed to fetch the water. They soon came back and brought a large pailful.

'You had better not throw it all over him,' said the Princess; 'just let it trickle over his face gently.'

So one of the pages began to do as he was told, but somehow either he had a sudden push, or, as he said afterwards, the Owl looked at him, and startled him – he let the pail go, and all the water and the pail too fell over the unlucky Chancellor. This really did bring him very much to – much too much to, in fact – for he sprang up in such a rage that the Princess really wished herself out of the room.

'You jackanapes,' he screamed at the unfortunate page;

'you ape, you boar, you cow, you clumsy monkey, I'll be revenged on you.'

But the Princess, who had gained courage while he was screaming, said:

'You will not be revenged on him.'

'But I shall,' he said.

'Indeed you will not,' said the Princess, 'for he did it by my orders.'

'Oh! he did it by your orders,' said the Chancellor;

'then I'll be revenged on you too,' and he began to move uncomfortably near to the Princess.

But the three pages threw themselves on him and tried to drag him back, but he turned suddenly on them.

'What,' he said scornfully, 'you try to stop me ye frogs! Ah! a good idea – by virtue of my magic power I command you to turn into water-rats then perhaps the Owl there will eat you up.'

No sooner said than done, and the three pages instantly became water-rats, squattering in the water that was still in a pool on the floor.

Somehow the Princess did not seem to be at all frightened at this; she was only very angry.

'I thought I told you not to hurt those pages.'

'Who cares what you say?'

'Dear me,' thought the Princess, 'he is getting excessively insolent – I shall have to be severe with him in a moment.'

Ford Madox Ford, *The Feather* (1892b: 4–9)

Ford's second fairy tale is entitled *The Feather*, referring to the feather of invisibility belonging to one of Jupiter's eagles. Both *The Brown Owl* and *The Feather* were written to amuse Ford's sister. The publisher of *The Feather* paid Ford only £10 but the book sold many thousands more copies than any other book he ever wrote. More clearly than *The Brown Owl*, *The Feather* is conceptually dependent on the *Arabian Nights* and, in particular, on 'The Second Voyage of Sinbad the Sailor', in which Sinbad escapes from an island by tying himself to a giant eagle's leg. Likewise, albeit with a very different intention, Princess Ernalie is seized by a giant eagle, which takes her to the mountain top. From a cognitive perspective, Ford restructures the story of Sinbad, whose schemas are modified in order to create an emergent structure that develops independently. By tuning the scripts of Sinbad's story, Ford refreshes and expands the existing Oriental schema.

But at that moment a black shadow came across the sun, and the swans, with a terrified 'honk, honk,' darted across the water to hide themselves in the reeds on the other side of the river, churning dark tracks in the purple of the sunlit water's glassy calmness.

'Oh dear! oh dear! it's a boggles, and it's coming this way,' cried the nurse.

'But what is a boggles, nurse?'

'Oh dear, it's coming! Come into the house and I'll tell you – come.'

'Not until you tell me what a boggles is.'

The nurse perforce gave in.

'A boggles is a thing with a hooked beak and a squeaky voice, with hair like snakes in corkscrews; and it haunts houses and carries off things; and when it once gets in it never leaves again – oh dear, it's on us! Oh-h-h!'

Her cries only made the thing see them sooner. It was only an eagle, not a boggles; but it was on the look-out for food, and the sun shining on the Princess's hair had caught its eyes, and in spite of the cries of the nurse it swooped down, and, seizing the Princess in its claws, began to carry her off. The nurse, however, held on to her valiantly, screaming all the while for help; but the eagle had the best of it after all, for it carried up, not only the Princess, but the nurse also.

The nurse held on to her charge for some seconds, but finding the attempt useless she let go her hold; and since it happened that at the moment they were over the river, she fell into it with a great splash, and was drifted on shore by the current.

Thus the Princess was carried off; and although the land far and wide was searched, no traces of her were discoverable. You may imagine for yourself what sorrow and rage the King indulged in. He turned the nurse off without warning, and even, in a paroxysm of rage, kicked one of his pages downstairs; nevertheless that did not bring back the Princess.

As a last resource he consulted a wise woman (ill-natured people called her a witch) who lived near the palace. But the witch could only say that the Princess would return some day, but she couldn't or wouldn't say when, even though the King threatened to burn her. So it was all of no use, and the King was, and remained, in despair. But, since his Majesty is not the important personage in the story, we may as well leave him and return to the Princess.

She, as you can think, was not particularly happy or comfortable, for the claws of the eagle pinched her, and besides, she was very frightened; for, you see, she didn't know that it wasn't a boggles, as the nurse had called it, and a boggles is a great deal worse than the worst eagle ever invented.

Meanwhile the eagle continued flying straight towards the sun, which was getting lower and lower, so that by the time they reached the mountains it was dark altogether. But the eagle didn't seem at all afraid of the darkness, and just went on flying as if nothing had happened, until suddenly it let the Princess down on a rock – at least, that was what it seemed to her to be. Not knowing what else to do, she sat where the eagle had let her fall, for she remembered something about the precipice three miles deep, and she did not at all wish to tumble down that.

She expected that the eagle would set to and make a meal off her at once. But somehow or other, either it had had enough to eat during the day, or else did not like to begin to have supper so late for fear of nightmare; at any rate, it abstained, and that was the most interesting matter to her. Everything was so quiet around that at last, in spite of herself, she fell asleep. She slept quite easily until daylight, although the hardness of the rock was certainly somewhat unpleasant. When she opened her eyes it was already light, and the sun at her back was darting black shadows of the jagged mountains on to the shimmering gray sea of mist that veiled the land below. Her first thought was naturally of the eagle, and she did not need to look very far for him, since he was washing himself in a little pool close by, keeping an eye on her the while.

As soon as he saw her move he gave himself a final shake, so that the water flew all around, sparkling in the sunlight; after which he came towards her by hops until he was quite close – rather too close, she thought. Nevertheless she did not move, having heard somewhere that, under the circumstances, that is the worst thing to do; she also remembered animals cannot stand being looked at steadily by the human eye, therefore she looked very steadfastly at the eyes of the eagle. But the remedy did not seem to work well in this case, for the glassy yellow eyes of the bird looked bad-tempered, and it winked angrily, seeming to say, 'Whom are you staring at?' And then it began to stretch out its bill towards her until it was within a few inches of her face.

Ford Madox Ford, *The Queen Who Flew* (1894: 1–3; 19–21; 45–50)

The Queen Who Flew is Ford's third medieval fairy tale, written during his courtship of Elsie Martindale. It is the story of Eldrida, Queen of the Narrowlands, who literally flies away from her royal responsibilities. Thanks to a talking bat dwelling in her garden, who reveals to her the secret of flight, she is able to start a marvellous journey flying from town to town. Defined as the best and most accomplished of Ford's fairy tales, *The Queen Who Flew* is also conceptually interwoven with the *Arabian Nights*, blending two and more Oriental stories. 'The Second Voyage of Sinbad the Sailor' and 'The Adventures of Hasan of Basrah' are the most prominent stories whose 'flying' and 'elixir of life' scripts are restructured in *The Queen Who Flew*. Of particular interest is the figure of the witch, Mrs Hexer, blending together the magical powers of Bahram and Queen Labe, the alchemist and the Circe-like sorceress in the *Arabian Nights*. The frontispiece by Burne-Jones, depicting a robed woman leaning over to pour water from a large jug on to some flowers, may be a visual reminder of the witch and her well containing the elixir of life. Linguistically speaking, Ford's use of litotes as a form of verbal irony, as well as the lexical priming aimed at evoking atmospheric fear, are stylistic features that help him to recreate the marvellous atmosphere of the *Arabian Nights*. *The Queen Who Flew* is a narrative blend that allows new understandings of the pervasive influence of the *Arabian Nights* on Pre-Raphaelite writers and associates.

Once upon a time a Queen sat in her garden. She was quite a young, young Queen; but that was a long while ago, so she would be older now. But, for all she was Queen over a great and powerful country, she led a very quiet life, and sat a great deal alone in her garden watching the roses grow, and talking to a bat that hung, head downwards, with its wings folded, for all the world like an umbrella, beneath the shade of a rose tree overhanging her favourite marble seat. She did not know much about the bat, not even that it could fly, for her servants and nurses would never allow her to be out at dusk, and the bat was a great deal too weak-eyed to fly about in the broad daylight.

But, one summer day, it happened that there was a revolution in the land, and the Queen's servants, not knowing who was likely to get the upper hand, left the Queen all alone, and went to look at the fight that was raging.

But you must understand that in those days a revolution was a thing very different from what it would be to-day.

Instead of trying to get rid of the Queen altogether, the great nobles of the kingdom merely fought violently with each other for possession of the Queen's person. Then they would proclaim themselves Regents of the kingdom and would issue bills of attainder against all their rivals, saying they were traitors against the Queen's Government.

In fact, a revolution in those days was like what is called a change of Ministry now, save for the fact that they were rather fond of indulging themselves by decapitating their rivals when they had the chance, which of course one would never think of doing nowadays.

The Queen and the bat had been talking a good deal that afternoon about the weather and about the revolution and the colour of cats and the like.

'The raven will have a good time of it for a day or two,' the bat said.

But the Queen shuddered. 'Don't be horrid,' she said.

'I wonder who'll get the upper hand?' the bat said.

'I'm sure I don't care a bit,' the Queen retorted. 'It doesn't make any difference to me. They all give me things to sign, and they all say I'm very beautiful.'

'That's because they want to marry you,' the bat said.

And the Queen answered, 'I suppose it is; but I shan't marry them. And I wish all my attendants weren't deaf and dumb; it makes it so awfully dull for me.'

[. . .]

Under the overhanging rose tree the Queen sat awaiting the bat's awakening.

'It never does to wake him up,' she said. 'It makes him so bad tempered.'

So she sat patiently and watched the rose-petals that every now and then fluttered down on the wind.

It was well on towards the afternoon, after the Queen had had her dinner, before he awoke.

'Oh, you're there?' he said. He had made the same remark every day for the last two years which made seven hundred and thirty-one times, one of the years having been leap-year.

The Queen said, 'Yes, here I am.'

The bat yawned. 'What's the weather like?' he asked.

The Queen answered, 'Oh, it's very nice, and you promised to tell me the flower that would make me fly.'

'I shan't,' the bat said. 'You'd eat up all the flies a great thing like you.'

The Queen's eyes filled with tears, it was so disappointing.'

'Oh, I promise I won't eat any flies,' she said; 'and I'll go right away and leave you in peace.'

The bat said, 'Um! there's something in that.'

'And look,' the Queen continued, 'I've brought you your meat and flannel, and some stuff that's good for rheumatism.'

The bat's eyes twinkled with delight. 'Well, I'll tell you,' he said. 'Only you must promise, first, that you won't tell any one the secret; and secondly, that you won't eat any flies.'

'Oh yes, I'll promise that willingly enough.'

'Well, put the things up here on the top of the seat and I'll tell you.'

The Queen did as she was bidden, and the bat continued –

'The flower you want is at this moment being trodden on by your foot.'

The Queen felt a little startled, but, looking down, saw a delicate white flower that had trailed from a border and was being crushed beneath her small green shoes.

'What! the wind-flower?' she said. 'I always thought it was only a weed.'

'You shouldn't think,' the bat said. 'It's as bad as supposing.'

'Well, and how am I to set about flying?' the Queen asked.

And the bat answered sharply, 'Why, fly. Put the flower somewhere about you, and then go off. Only be careful not to knock against things.'

The Queen thought for a moment, and then plucked a handful and a handful and yet a handful of the wind-flowers, and, having twined them into a carcanet, wound them into her soft gold-brown hair, beneath her small crown royal.

'Good-bye, dear bat,' she said. She had grown to like the bat, for all his strange appearance and surly speeches.

The bat remarked, 'Good riddance.' He was always a little irritable just after awakening.

So the Queen went out from under the arbour, and made a first essay at flying.

'I'll make just a short flight at first,' she said, and gave a little jump, and in a moment she flew right over a rose bush and came down softly on the turf on its further side, quite like a not too timid pigeon that has to make a little flight from before a horse's feet.

[. . .]

And there, in a hollow among the sand-dunes, stood a funny little black erection, such as you might see upon a beach.

So the Queen alighted and walked towards the house. In front of the door a cat was sitting – a black cat. But not a magnificent creature with a glossy coat that sits on the rug in front of the drawing-room fire and only drinks cream, deeming mice too vulgar. This was a long-limbed, little creature, that looked half-starved and seemed as if its proper occupation would be stealing along, very lanky and grim in the moonlight, over the dunes to catch rabbits.

So the Queen stopped and looked at the cat, and the cat sat and looked at the Queen.

The black pupils of its yellow eyes dilated and diminished in a most composed manner.

'Poor pussy!' the Queen said, and bent to scratch its neck.

[. . .]

The Queen sat herself down at the table, and the old woman and the cat were engaged in sitting on the hearth watching the fire.

They did not seem at all talkative, and so the Queen held her peace.

At last the old woman gave a grunt, for the goose was done, and so she got up and found a plate and knife and fork, and put them before the Queen, with the goose on a dish and a large hunk of bread.

'There,' she said, 'that's all I can give you.'

And so, although the food was by no means as dainty as what she would have had at home in the palace, the Queen was so remarkably hungry that she made a much larger meal than she ever remembered to have made.

And all the while the cat sat and stared at her, and seemed to grow positively bigger with staring so much, though when the Queen held out a piece of the goose to it, it merely sniffed contemptuously so that the Queen felt quite humiliated.

'Your cat doesn't seem to be very sociable,' she said to the old woman.

And the old woman answered, 'Why should he be?' and took up a large twig broom to sweep the hearth with.

That done, she leant upon it and regarded the Queen malevolently.

'Aren't you ever going to finish?' she said.

The Queen answered, 'Well, I was rather hungry, you see; but I've finished now. There's no great hurry, is there?'

'I want *my* dinner,' the old woman said, with such an emphasis on the "my" that the Queen was quite amused.

'Why, the goose is there; at least, there's some of it left.'

'But I don't like goose,' the old woman said.

Her manner was growing more and more peculiar.

'Any one would think you were going to eat me,' the Queen said; and the cat licked its jaws.

'So I am,' the old woman said, and her eyes gleamed.

But the Queen said, 'Nonsense!'

'But it's not nonsense,' the old woman said; and the cat began to grow visibly.

'Well, but you didn't say anything about it before,' the Queen said. 'I only agreed to herd your geese.'

'But you won't be able to,' the old woman said.

The Queen said, 'Why not?'

'Because they're wild ones.'

The cat was growing larger and larger, till the Queen grew positively afraid.

'Well, at any rate, I'll have a try,' she said.

And the old woman answered, 'You may as well save yourself the trouble.'

But the Queen insisted, and so they went outside, the old woman carrying her broom, for all the world like a crossing-sweeper.

The great cat rubbed against her skirt and licked its jaws. It was about the size of a lion now.

They came to the back of the house, and there the pen was – a cage covered completely over, and filled with a multitude of geese. The old woman undid the door and threw it wide, and immediately, with a mighty rustle of wings filling the air, the geese swept out of the pen away into the sky.

The old woman chuckled, and the cat crouched itself down as if preparing to spring, lashing its sides with its long tail But the Queen only smiled, and started off straight into the air, faster even than the geese had gone.

The old woman gave a shriek, and the cat a horrible yell, and then the Queen saw the one mounted upon her broom, and the other without any sort of steed at all, come flying after her.

Bibliography

Primary Sources

Aeschylus, 1824, *The Agamemnon*, trans. John Symmons, London: Taylor and Hessey.

Beardsley, Aubrey, 1921, *Under the Hill and Other Essays in Prose and Verse*, London: John Lane.

—, 1974, *The Story of Venus and Tannhäuser: Or, 'Under the Hill'*, ed. Robert Oresko, London: Academy Editions.

Burton, Sir Richard, ed., 1885, *The Book of the Thousand Nights and a Night*, London: Burton Club.

Dickens, Charles, 1850, 'Old Lamps for New Ones', *Household Words: A Weekly Journal*, 12 (15 June): 265–6.

—, 1855, 'The Story of the Talkative Barber', *Household Words: A Weekly Journal* 11 (May): 313–15.

—, 1998, *Hard Times*, Oxford: Oxford University Press.

—, 2009, *Martin Chuzzlewit*, ed. Margaret Cardwell, Oxford: Oxford University Press.

Flaubert, Gustave, 1913, *Les Tentations de Saint Antoine*, Paris: Georges Crès et Cie.

Ford, Ford Madox, 1892a, *The Brown Owl: A Fairy Story*, illustr. Ford Madox Brown, New York: Cassell Publishing Company.

—, 1892b, *The Feather*, illustr. Ford Madox Brown, London: T. Fisher Unwin.

—, 1894, *The Queen Who Flew*, illustr. Edward Burne-Jones, London: Bliss, Sands & Foster.

—, 1908, *Mr Apollo: A Just Possible Story*, London: Methuen.

—, 1911, *Ladies Whose Bright Eyes: A Romance*, London: Constable.

—, 1923, *Women and Men*, Paris: Three Mountains Press.

—, 1963, *Parade's End*, London: Bodley Head.

—, 1994, *The March of Literature: From Confucius' Day to Our Own* [1939], ed. Alexander Theroux, Normal, IL: Dalkey Archive Press.

—, 2002, *Critical Essays*, Max Saunders and Richard Stang, eds, Manchester: Carcanet Press.

—, 2003a, *Ford Madox Ford: Selected Poems*, ed. Max Saunders, Manchester: Carcanet Press.

—, 2003b, *The Good Soldier: A Tale of Passion*, ed. Kenneth Womack and William Baker, Peterborough: Broadview.

—, 2012, *Critical Essays*, ed. Max Saunders and Richard Stang, Manchester: Carcanet Press.

—, and Violet Hunt, 1916, *Zeppelin Nights: A London Entertainment*, London: John Lane, The Bodley Head.

Lane, Edward William, ed., 1853, *The Arabian Nights' Entertainments*, Boston: Little, Brown and Company.

Lang, Andrew, ed., 1898, *Arabian Nights' Entertainments*, London, New York and Bombay: Longmans, Green and Co.

Mack, Robert L., ed., 1995, *Arabian Nights' Entertainments*, Oxford: Oxford University Press.

Mardrus, J. C., ed., 2005, *The Book of the Thousand and One Nights*, trans. E. P. Mathers, vol. 3, London and New York: Routledge.

Marlowe, Christopher, 1998, *Doctor Faustus and Other Plays*, ed. David M. Bevington and Eric Rasmussen, Oxford: Oxford University Press.

Mondschein, Ken, ed., 2011, *The Arabian Nights*, trans. Sir Richard Burton, San Diego: Canterbury Classics.

Morris, William, 1890, *The Earthly Paradise*, London: Reeves and Turner.

—, 1910–15, *The Collected Works of William Morris*, ed. May Morris, London: Longmans, Green & Co.

—, 1913 [1890], *The House of the Wolfings*, London and New York: Longmans, Green & Co.

—, 1971 [1897], *The Water of the Wondrous Isles*, ed. Lin Carter, London: Ballantine.

—, 1994, *Hopes and Fears for Art and Signs of Change*, ed. Peter Faulkner, Bristol: Thoemmes.

—, 1996, *On Architecture*, ed. Chris Miele, Sheffield: Sheffield Academic.

—, 2001, *The Earthly Paradise*, ed. Florence S. Boos, New York: Routledge.

Rossetti, Christina, 2008, *Poems and Prose*, ed. Simon Humphries, Oxford: Oxford University Press.

Rossetti, D. G., ed., 1861, *The Early Italian Poets Together with Dante's Vita Nuova*, London: Dent.

—, 1999, *The Collected Writings of D. G. Rossetti*, ed. Jan Marsh, London: Dent.

—, 2008, *Aladdin, or The Wonderful Lamp*, http://www.rossettiarchive.org/docs/1-1835.safrica.rad.html #p24 (last accessed 19 July 2017).

Rossetti, W. M., ed., 1895, *Dante Gabriel Rossetti: His Family-Letters with a Memoir*, London: Ellis.

—, ed., 1903, *Rossetti Papers 1862–70*, New York: Charles Scribner's Sons.

—, ed., 1904, *The Poetical Works of Christina Georgina Rossetti with Memoir and Notes*, London and New York: Macmillan.

—, 1906, *Some Reminiscences*, New York: Charles Scribner's Sons.

—, 1908, *Family Letters of Christina Georgina Rossetti*, London: Brown & Langham.

Ruskin, John, 1851, *The Stones of Venice: The Foundations*, New York: John Wiley.

—, 1858, *The Stones of Venice*, London: Smith, Elder and Co.

—, 1860, *The King of the Golden River*, illustr. Richard Doyle, Boston: Mayhew and Baker.

—, 1867, *The Stones of Venice*, London: Smith, Elder and Co.

—, 1869, *The Two Paths: Being Lectures on Art, and Its Application to Decoration and Manufacture*, New York: John Wiley and Son.

—, 1900, *Sesame and Lilies*, ed. Agnes Spofford Cook, New York: Silver, Burdett and Co.

—, 1908a, *The Ethics of the Dust*, London: J. M. Dent and Co.

—, 1908b, *The Works of John Ruskin*, ed. E. T. Cook and Alexander Wedderburn, London: George Allen.

—, 1920, *Unto This Last and Other Writings*, ed. Susan Cunnington, London: Dent.

—, 2012, *Praeterita*, ed. Francis O'Gorman, Oxford: Oxford University Press.

Swinburne, Algernon Charles, 1894, *Studies in Prose and Poetry*, London: Chatto & Windus.

—, 1904, *The Poems of Algernon Charles Swinburne*, 6 vols, London: Chatto & Windus.

Secondary Sources

Ali, Muhsin Jassim, 1981, *Scheherazade in England: A Study of Nineteenth-century English Criticism of the Arabian Nights*, Washington, DC: Three Continents Press.

Allen, Susan, 1995, '"Finding the Walls of Troy": Frank Calvert, Excavator', *American Journal of Archaeology* 99(3): 379–407.

Antosa, Silvia, 2013, *Richard Francis Burton: Victorian Explorer and Translator*, Bern: Peter Lang.

Bachelard, Gaston, 1991, *L'Eau et les rêves: Essai sur l'imagination de la matière*, Paris: Corti.

Bade, Patrick, 2001, *Aubrey Beardsley*, Bournemouth: Parkstone.

Bedigian, Dorothea, 2010, *Sesame: The Genus Sesamum*, London and New York: CRC Press.

Benkovitz, Miriam J., 1981, *Aubrey Beardsley: An Account of His Life*, New York: G. P. Putnam's Sons.

Bhabha, Homi, 1994, *The Location of Culture*, London: Routledge.

Bloom, Harold, 2005, *Christina Rossetti*, Philadelphia: Chelsea House.

—, 2012, 'Gardens of Unearthly Delights', *The New York Times Book Review* CXVII.13 (23 March), http://www.nytimes.com/2012/03/25/books/review/stranger-magic-by-marina-warner.html (last accessed 18 September 2017).

Bolter, Jay David, and Richard Grusin, 1996, 'Remediation', *Configurations* 4(3): 311–58.

Boos, Florence S., 1991, *The Design of William Morris' The Earthly Paradise*, Lewiston, NY: Edwin Mellen Press.

Booth, Martin, 1996, *Opium: A History*, New York: St Martin's Griffin.

Borges, Jorge Louis, 1970, 'The Garden of the Forking Paths', in *Labyrinths*, London: Penguin.

—, 1981, 'The *Translators of the 1001 Nights*', in Emir Rodríguez Monegal and Alastair Reid, eds, *Borges: A Reader*, New York: Dutton, pp. 73–86.

Bradley, John Lewis, and Ian Ousby, eds, 1987, *The Correspondence of John Ruskin and Charles Eliot Norton*, Cambridge: Cambridge University Press.

Brantlinger, Patrick, 1996, 'A Postindustrial Prelude to Postcolonialism: John Ruskin, William Morris, and Gandhism', *Critical Inquiry* 22(3): 466–85.

Bronzini, Stefano, 2014, 'Narrare le amare illusioni. Una nota su "Great Expectations" di Charles Dickens', in Augusto Ponzio, ed., *Figure e forme del narrare. Incontro di prospettive*, Lecce: Milella, pp. 294–300.

Bullen, J. B., 1998, *The Pre-Raphaelite Body: Fear and Desire in Painting, Poetry, and Criticism*, Oxford: Clarendon Press.

—, 2006, *Byzantium Rediscovered*, London: Phaidon Press.

Burlinson, Kathryn, 1998, *Christina Rossetti*, Plymouth: Northcote House Publishers.

Byron, Baron George Gordon, 1829, *The Works of John Byron*, London: John Murray.

Caracciolo, Peter, ed., 1988, *The Arabian Nights in English Literature: Studies in the Reception of 'The Thousand and One Nights' into British Culture*, New York: St Martin's Press.

Cate, George Allan, ed., 1982, *The Correspondence of Thomas Carlyle and John Ruskin*, Stanford: Stanford University Press.

Christensen, Allen C., Francesco Marroni and David Paroissien, eds, 2015, *Dialogic Dickens: Invention and Transformation*, Chieti: Solfanelli.

Christian, John, 2011, *Edward Burne-Jones: The Hidden Humourist*, London: British Museum Press.

Clouston, W. A., 1884, *The Book of Sinbad*, Glasgow: J. Cameron.

Cook, Edward Tyas, 2009, *The Life of John Ruskin 1860–1900*, New York: Cambridge University Press.

Costantini, Mariaconcetta, 2000, *Poesia e sovversione: Christina Rossetti, Gerard Manley Hopkins*, Pescara: Edizioni Tracce.

Crane, Walter, 2014, *Of the Decorative Illustrations of Books Old and New*, Cambridge: Cambridge University Press.

Culler, Jonathan D., ed., 1983, *Roland Barthes*, New York: Oxford University Press.

Doughty, Charles Montagu, 2010, *Travels in Arabia Deserta*, Cambridge: Cambridge University Press.

Douthwaite, John, 2000, *Towards a Linguistic Theory of Foregrounding*, Alessandria: Edizioni dell'Orso.

Duchan, J. F., G. A. Bruder and L. E. Hewitt, eds, 1995, *Deixis in Narrative: A Cognitive Science Perspective*, Hillsdale, NJ: Lawrence Erlbaum.

Easton, Malcolm, 1972, *Aubrey and the Dying Lady: A Beardsley Riddle*, London: Martin Secker and Warburg.

Ebbatson, Roger, 2013, *Landscape and Literature 1830–1914: Nature, Text, Aura*, London: Palgrave.

Emerson, R. W., and H. D. Thoreau, 2012, *Nature and Walking*, Boston: Beacon Press.

Emmott, G., 1997, *Narrative Comprehension: A Discourse Perspective*, Oxford: Oxford University Press.

Evans, B. Ifor, 1933, 'The Sources of Christina Rossetti's "Goblin Market"', *The Modern Language Review* 28(2) (April): 156–65.

Fauconnier, G., 1997, *Mappings in Thought and Language*, Cambridge: Cambridge University Press.

Fauconnier, Gilles and Mark Turner, 1994, *Conceptual Projection and Middle Spaces*, San Diego: University of California Press.

Fillmore, Charles, 1982, 'Frame Semantics', in *Linguistics in the Morning Calm*, Seoul: Hanshin Publishing Company, pp. 111–37.

—, 1985, 'Frames and the Semantics of Understanding', *Quaderni di Semantica* 6: 222–54.

Foxcroft, Louise, 2007, *The Making of Addiction: The 'Use and Abuse' of Opium in Nineteenth-Century Britain*, Aldershot: Ashgate.

Gavins, Joanna, and Gerard Steen, eds, 2003, *Cognitive Poetics in Practice*, London: Routledge.

Gibbs, Raymond W., Jr, 2006, *Embodiment and Cognitive Science*, Cambridge: Cambridge University Press.

Gitter, Elisabeth, 1984, 'The Power of Women's Hair in the Victorian Imagination', *PMLA* 99(5) (October): 936–54.

Goatly, Andrew, 1997, *The Language of Metaphors*, London: Routledge.

Goldberg, Adele, ed., 1995, *New Essays in Deixis: Discourse, Narrative, Literature*, Amsterdam: Rodopi.

Goldring, Douglas, 1948, *The Last Pre-Raphaelite: A Record of the Life and Writings of Ford Madox Ford*, London: Macdonald and Co.

Golledge, Reginald G., 2010, *Wayfinding Behaviour: Cognitive Mapping and Other Spatial Processes*, Baltimore: Johns Hopkins University Press.

Gorlée, Dinda L., 1994, *Semiotics and the Problem of Translation with Special Reference to the Semiotics of Charles S. Pierce*, Amsterdam: Rodopi.

—, 2012, *Wittgenstein in Translation: Exploring Semiotic Signatures*, Berlin and Boston: De Gruyter Mouton.

Grabar, Oleg, 1973, *The Formation of Islamic Art*, New Haven, CT: Yale University Press.

Grady, J. E., 1999, 'A Typology of Motivation for Conceptual Metaphor: Correlation Vs. Resemblance', in R. W. Gibbs and G. J. Steen, eds, *Metaphor in Cognitive Linguistics*, Amsterdam: John Benjamins, pp. 79–100.

Grieve, Alastair, 1969, 'The Pre-Raphaelite Brotherhood and the Anglican High Church', *Burlington Magazine* 111: 294–5.

Haddad, Emily A., 2002, *Orientalist Poetics: The Islamic Middle East in Nineteenth-century English and French Poetry*, Aldershot: Ashgate.

Hamilton, Craig, 2003, 'A Cognitive Grammar of "Hospital Barge" by Wilfred Owen', in Joanna Gavins and Gerard Steen, eds, *Cognitive Poetics in Practice*, London and New York: Routledge.

Harris, Frank, 1963, *My Life and Loves*, New York: Grove Press.

Harrison, Antony H., 1988, *Christina Rossetti in Context*, Brighton: Harvester.

Harrison, Chloe, Louise Nuttall, Peter Stockwell and Wenjuan Yuan, eds, 2014, *Cognitive Grammar in Literature*, Amsterdam: John Benjamins.

Hart-Davis, Rupert, ed., 1962, *The Letters of Oscar Wilde*, London: Hart-Davis.

Harvey, Charles, and Jon Press, eds, 1991, *William Morris: Design and Enterprise in Victorian Britain*, Manchester: Manchester University Press.

Herodotus, 1992, *The Histories*, ed. Jennifer Tolbert Roberts, trans. Walter Blanco, New York and London: W. W. Norton & Company.

Hollander, Anne, 1993, *Seeing Through Clothes*, Berkeley, Los Angeles and London: University of California Press.

Howard, Deborah, 2000, *Venice and the East: The Impact of the Islamic World on Venetian Architecture 1100–1500*, New Haven, CT, and London: Yale University Press.

Hunt, William Holman, 1860, letter to William Bell Scott, February, London: Troxell Collection, Princeton University.

—, 1905, *Pre-Raphaelitism*, London: Macmillan.

Irwin, Robert, 2004, *The Arabian Nights: A Companion*, New York: Tauris Parke Paperback.

Johnson, M., 1987, *The Body in the Mind*, Chicago: Chicago University Press.

Keightley, Thomas, 1828, *The Fairy Mythology*, London: W. H. Ainsworth.

Kelvin, Norman, ed., 1996, *The Collected Letters of William Morris*, ed. Norman Kelvin, Princeton: Princeton University Press.

Kennedy, Dane, 2000, '"Captain Burton's Oriental Muck Heap": The Book of the *Thousand Nights* and the Uses of Orientalism', *Journal of British Studies* 39(3) (July): 317–39.

Knoepflmacher, U. C., 2016, 'John Ruskin', in Anne E. Duggan and Donald Haase, eds, *Folktales and Fairy Tales: Traditions and Texts from Around the World*, pp. 873–4.

Kooistra, Lorraine Janzen, 2002, *Christina Rossetti and Illustrations: A Publishing History*, Athens: Ohio University Press.

Kotoula, Dimitra, 2015, 'Arts and Crafts and the "Byzantine": The Greek Connection', in Roland Betancourt and Maria Taroutina, eds, *Byzantium/Modernism: The Byzantine as Method in Modernity*, Leiden and Boston: Brill.

Kövecses, Zoltán, 1986, *Metaphors of Anger, Pride, and Love: A Lexical Approach to the Structure of Concepts*, Amsterdam/Philadelphia: John Benjamins.

—, 1990, *Emotion Concepts*, New York: Springer.

—, 2000, *Metaphor and Emotion: Language, Culture and Body in Human Feeling*, Cambridge: Cambridge University Press.

Lakoff, George, 1993, 'The Contemporary Theory of Metaphor', in A. Ortony, ed., *Metaphor and Thought*, Cambridge: Cambridge University Press, pp. 202–51.

—, and Mark Johnson, 1980, *Metaphors We Live By*, Chicago: Chicago University Press.

—, and Mark Johnson, eds, 1999, *Philosophy in The Flesh: The Embodied Mind and Its Challenge to Western Thought*, New York: Basic Books.

Landow, George P., 1982, 'William Holman Hunt's "Oriental Mania" and his Uffizi Self-portrait', *Art Bulletin* 64: 646–55.

—, 2014, '"Life touching lips with immortality": Rossetti's Temporal Structures', in *Victorian Types, Victorian Shadows: Biblical Typology in Victorian Literature, Art, and Thought*, Abingdon and New York: Routledge, pp. 187–202.

Lang, Cecil Y., ed., 1959, *The Swinburne Letters*, New Haven, CT: Yale University Press.

—, 1975, *The Pre-Raphaelites and Their Circle*, Chicago: University of Chicago Press.

Lupack, Barbara Tepa, and Alan Lupack, eds, 2008, *Illustrating Camelot*, Cambridge: D. S. Brewer.

Lutz, Deborah, 2011, *Pleasure Bound: Victorian Sex Rebels and the New Eroticism*, New York: Norton and Company.

Maas, Henry, J. L. Duncan and W. G. Good, eds, 1970, *The Letters of Aubrey Beardsley*, Rutherford, NJ: Fairleigh Dickinson University Press.

McAlindon, T., 1967, 'The Idea of Byzantium in William Morris and W. B. Yeats', *Modern Philology* 64(4) (May): 307–19.

McGann, Jerome, 2000, *The Game That Must Be Lost*, New Haven, CT, and London: Yale University Press.

—, 2008, *The Complete Writings and Pictures of Dante Gabriel Rossetti. A Hypermedia Archive*, http://www.rossettiarchive.org/ (last accessed 18 September 2017).

Mackail, J. W., 1995, *The Life of William Morris*, New York: Dover Publications.

McMichael Nurse, Paul, 2010, *Eastern Dreams: How The Arabian Nights Came to the World*, Toronto: Viking.

Marillier, H. C., 1899, *Dante Gabriel Rossetti: An Illustrated Memorial of His Art and Life*, London: George Bell and Sons.

Marroni, Francesco, 2010, *Victorian Disharmonies: A Reconsideration of Nineteenth-century English Fiction*, Newark: University of Delaware Press.

—, 2012, 'Goblin Market: Christina Rossetti e i "frutti" della traduzione', in *Confluenze intertestuali. In onore di Angelo Righetti*, ed. Annalisa Pes and Susanna Zinato, Naples: Liguori, pp. 153–66.

Marroni, Michela, 2009–10, '"No understanding of any power of antiquity": Ruskin on Dickens's Idea of Progress', *Rivista di Studi Vittoriani* XIV/XV, 28–9 (July–January): 71–83.

Marx, Karl, 2007, *Capital: A Critique of Political Economy - The Process of Capitalist Production*, ed. Friedrich Engels, New York: Cosimo.

Marzolph, Ulrich, Richard van Leeuwen and Hassan Wassouf, eds, 2004, *The Arabian Nights Encyclopedia*, Santa Barbara and Oxford: ABC-Clio.

Melman, Billie, 1992, *Women's Orients: English Women and the Middle East, 1718–1918: Sexuality, Religion and Work*, London: Macmillan.

Muddiman, Bernard, 1921, *The Men of the Nineties*, New York: Putnam.

Novalis, Hardenberg Friedrich Leopold von, 1802, *Heinrich von Ofterdingen*, Berlin: Reimer.

Oatley, K. and Johnson-Laird, P. N., 1987, 'Towards a Cognitive Theory of Emotions', *Cognition and Emotion* 1: 29–50.

Palusci, Oriana, and Katherine Russo, eds, 2010, *Translating East and West*, Trento: Tangram.

Patey, Caroline, and Laura Scuriatti, eds, 2009, *The Exhibit in the Text: The Museological Practices of Literature*, Bern: Peter Lang.

Pease, Allison, 2000, *Modernism, Mass Culture, and the Aesthetics of Obscenity*, Cambridge: Cambridge University Press.

Psomiades, Kathy Alexis, 1997, *Beauty's Body: Femininity and Representation in British Aestheticism*, Stanford: Stanford University Press.

Reade, B., 1967, *Aubrey Beardsley*, New York: Bonanza Books.

Reeve, Henry, 1886, review of *The Book of a Thousand Nights and a Night*, trans. Richard Burton, *Edinburgh Review* 335 (July): 183–4.

Rice, Edward, 2001, *Captain Sir Richard Francis Burton: A Biography*, Cambridge, MA: Da Capo Press.

Riede, David G., 1978, *Swinburne: A Study of Romantic Mythmaking*, Charlottesville: University Press of Virginia.

—, 1992, *Dante Gabriel Rossetti Revisited*, New York: Twayne Publishers.

Rollins, Hyder Edward, ed., 1958, *Letters of John Keats*, Cambridge, MA: Harvard University Press.

Rooksby, Rikky, 1997, *A. C. Swinburne: A Poet's Life*, Aldershot: Scolar Press.

Rumelhart, David E., and Donald A. Norman, 1978, 'Accretion, Tuning, and Restructuring: Three Modes of Learning', in J. W. Cotton and R.

Klatzky, eds, *Semantic Factors in Cognition*, Hillsdale, NJ: Lawrence Erlbaum, pp. 37–53.

Said, Edward, 1977, *Orientalism*, London: Penguin.

Sanford, A. J., and S. C. Garrod, 1981, *Understanding Written Language: Explorations in Comprehension Beyond the Sentence*, Chichester: John Wiley and Sons.

Sasso, Eleonora, 2011, *How the Writings of William Morris Shaped the Literary Style of Tennyson, Swinburne, Gissing, and Yeats: Barthesian Rewritings Based on the Pleasure of Distorting Repetition*, New York and Lampeter: Edwin Mellen Press.

Saunders, Max, 2012, *Ford Madox Ford: A Dual Life*, Oxford: Oxford University Press.

Schank, Roger C., 1982, *Dynamic Memory*, New York: Cambridge University Press.

—, 1999, *Dynamic Memory Revisited*, Cambridge: Cambridge University Press.

Semino, Elena, and Jonathan Culpeper, eds, 2002, *Cognitive Stylistics: Language and Cognition in Text Analysis*, Amsterdam and Philadelphia: John Benjamins.

Shaw, Bernard, 1936, *William Morris as I Knew Him*, New York: Dodd, Mead.

Simon, Sherry, 1996, *Translation and Interlingual Creations in the Contact Zone*, Montreal: Concordia University.

Simpson, Marc A., 1982, 'The Dream of the Dragon: Ruskin's Serpent Imagery', in John Dixon Hunt and Faith M. Holland, eds, *The Ruskin Polygon: Essays on the Imagination of John Ruskin*, Manchester: Manchester University Press, pp. 137–58.

Smith, Grover, 1986, 'Ford Madox Ford and the Christina Rossetti Influence', *English Literature in Transition* 29(3): 287–96.

Snodgrass, Chris, 1995, *Aubrey Beardsley, Dandy of the Grotesque*, Oxford: Oxford University Press.

Stockwell, P., 2002, *Cognitive Poetics: An Introduction*, London: Routledge.

Sturgis, Matthew, 1998, *Aubrey Beardsley: A Biography*, London: HarperCollins.

Surtees, Virginia, 1971, *A Catalogue Raisonné*, Oxford: Clarendon Press.

Thudichum, J. L. W., 1861, 'The Turkish Bath', *British Medical Journal* 1 (January 1861): 291–2.

Todorov, Tzvetan, 1975, *The Fantastic: A Structural Approach to a Literary Genre*, New York: Cornell University Press.

Vallance, Aymer, 1898, 'The Invention of Aubrey Beardsley', *Magazine of Art* (21 May): 362–9.

Walker, R. A., 1948, *The Best of Beardsley*, London: The Bodley Head.

Warner, Marina, 2011, *Stranger Magic: Charmed States and the Arabian Nights*, London: Chatto.

Watts-Dunton, Theodore, 1883, 'The Truth about Rossetti', *The Nineteenth Century* 13 (March): 404–23.

Weintraub, Stanley, 1978, *Four Rossettis: A Victorian Biography*, London: W. H. Allen.

—, 2000, *Aubrey Beardsley: Imp of the Perverse*, University Park: Pennsylvania State University Press.

Weiss, Timothy, 1984, *Fairy Tale and Romance in Works of Ford Madox Ford*, New York: Lanham.

Weltman, Sharon Aronofsky, 2007, *Performing the Victorian: John Ruskin and Identity in Theater, Science, and Education*, Columbus: Ohio State University Press.

Wen-chin Ouyang, and Geert Jan van Gelder, eds, 2005, *New Perspectives on Arabian Nights*, London and New York: Routledge.

Willemen, Paul, ed., 1977, *Pier Paolo Pasolini*, London: British Film Institute.

Wright, Thomas, 1906, *The Life of Sir Richard Burton*, Alexandria: Library of Alexandria.

Yamanaka, Yuriko, and Tetsuo Nishio, eds, 2006, *The Arabian Nights and Orientalism: Perspectives from East and West*, New York: I. B. Tauris.

Yeats, W. B., 1919, *The Wild Swans at Coole*, London: Macmillan.

Zasempa, Marek, 2011, 'Mythological Evildoers in Dante Gabriel Rossetti's Poetry and Painting', in April Anson, ed., *The Evil Body*, Oxford: Inter-Disciplinary Press, pp. 27–36.

Zatlin, Linda Gerther, 1990, *Aubrey Beardsley and Victorian Sexual Politics*, Oxford: Clarendon Press.

Index

Printed and bound by CPI Group (UK) Ltd, Croydon, CR0 4YY

18/03/2025

01834138-0007